WEIMAR GERMANY

BLANDFORD HISTORY SERIES
(General Editor R. W. Harris)

THE HISTORY OF EUROPE

RENAISSANCE, REFORMATION AND THE OUTER WORLD 1450–1660	M. L. Bush
ABSOLUTISM AND ENLIGHTENMENT 1660–1789	R. W. Harris
THE AGE OF TRANSFORMATION 1789–1871	R. F. Leslie
THE END OF EUROPEAN PRIMACY 1871–1945	J. R. Western
RUIN AND RESURGENCE 1939–1965	R. C. Mowat

THE HISTORY OF ENGLAND

REFORMATION AND RESURGENCE 1485–1603 England in the Sixteenth Century	G. W. O. Woodward
THE STRUGGLE FOR THE CONSTITUTION 1603–1689 England in the Seventeenth Century	G. E. Aylmer
ENGLAND IN THE EIGHTEENTH CENTURY 1689–1793 A Balanced Constitution and New Horizons	R. W. Harris
REACTION AND REFORM 1793–1868 England in the Early Nineteenth Century	J. W. Derry
DEMOCRACY AND WORLD CONFLICT 1868–1970 A History of Modern Britain	T. L. Jarman

PROBLEMS OF HISTORY

THE REIGN OF HENRY VII	R. L. Storey
THE DISSOLUTION OF THE MONASTERIES	G. W. O. Woodward
PAPISTS AND PURITANS UNDER ELIZABETH I	P. McGrath
COLONIES INTO COMMONWEALTH	W. D. McIntyre
THE EXPANSION OF EUROPE IN THE EIGHTEENTH CENTURY	G. Williams
FRANCE AND THE DREYFUS AFFAIR	D. Johnson
THE CHURCH AND MAN'S STRUGGLE FOR UNITY	H. Waddams
ROYAL MYSTERIES AND PRETENDERS	S. B.-R. Poole
MONARCHY AND REVOLUTION	J. R. Western

HISTORY AND LITERATURE

THE TRIUMPH OF ENGLISH 1350–1400	B. Cottle
THE CHORUS OF HISTORY Literary–Historical Relations in Renaissance Britain 1485–1558	A. M. Kinghorn
SHAKESPEARE'S EDEN The Commonwealth of England 1558–1629	B. L. Joseph
REASON AND NATURE IN EIGHTEENTH-CENTURY THOUGHT 1714–1780	R. W. Harris
ROMANTICISM AND THE SOCIAL ORDER 1780–1830	R. W. Harris
DOCUMENTARY AND IMAGINATIVE LITERATURE 1880–1920	J. A. V. Chapple

Weimar Germany
1918–1933

JOHN R. P. McKENZIE

ROWMAN AND LITTLEFIELD
TOTOWA, N. J.

FIRST PUBLISHED IN THE UNITED STATES 1971
by Rowman and Littlefield, Totowa, New Jersey
© 1971 Blandford Press Ltd

ISBN–0–87471–067–7

Printed in Great Britain by
Richard Clay (The Chaucer Press), Ltd.,
Bungay, Suffolk

Contents

	Acknowledgments	vi
	List of Illustrations	vii
	Preface	ix
	Maps	x
Chapter 1	The German Empire and the First World War	1
2	The Revolution	25
3	Versailles, Weimar Constitution and Domestic Insurrection	45
4	Continuing Instability 1920–23	97
5	The 'Golden Years' of the Republic 1924–29	153
6	The End of the Republic	207
7	Conclusions	253
	Abbreviations	259
	Bibliography	261
	Selective Index	265

Acknowledgments

Acknowledgment is due to the following for their kind permission to reproduce illustrations:

Langewiesche-Brandt Verlag (illustrations from *Anschläge: deutsche Plakate als Dokuments der Zeit 1900–60*, ed. F. Arnold) 15, 16, 18, 34, 35, 36, 42, 43, 46, 47, 48, 54

Radio Times Hulton Picture Library 1, 4, 5, 6, 8, 9, 10, 11, 13, 14, 19, 21, 22, 23, 24, 29, 38, 40, 45, 49, 50, 52, 53

Staatsbibliothek, Berlin 7, 17, 20

Ullstein GmbH/Bilderdienst 25, 26, 27, 28, 30, 32, 33, 37, 41, 44, 51

List of Illustrations

(between pages 116 *and* 117)

1 Kaiser Wilhelm II
2 Paul von Hindenburg
3 Erich von Ludendorff
4 Hindenburg, the Kaiser and Ludendorff
5 Karl Liebknecht
6 Rosa Luxemburg
7 Matthias Erzberger
8 Friedrich Ebert
9 Wilhelm Groener
10 Philipp Scheidemann
11 Scheidemann proclaiming the Republic
12 Gustav Noske and Freikorps troops
13 Sailors in revolt in Berlin
14 Spartacist guards during the Berlin Rising
15 DDP election poster, 1920
16 Spartakus election poster, 1920
17 Kurt Eisner
18 BVP election poster, 1919
19 Clemenceau, Wilson and Lloyd George
20 Captain Ehrhardt during the Kapp Putsch
21 Wolfgang Kapp
22 General Hans von Seeckt
23 Walther Rathenau
24 Adolf Hitler
25 Ernst Röhm
26 French Occupation troops in the Ruhr

27 Fifty million Mark bank note, 1923
28 One billion Mark bank note, 1923
29 Gustav Stresemann
30 Men and women searching for fuel, 1922
31 Wilhelm Marx
32 Hjalmar Schacht
33 SA troops arriving in Munich
34 NSDAP election poster, 1924
35 NSDAP election poster, 1924
36 SDP election poster, 1924
37 Hermann Müller
38 Alfred Hugenberg
39 Chamberlain, Stresemann and Briand in Lugano
40 Kurt von Schleicher
41 Heinrich Brüning
42 DVP election poster, 1930
43 DNVP election poster, 1932
44 Papen and Schleicher
45 Franz von Papen
46 SPD election poster, 1932
47 Zentrum election poster, 1932
48 NSDAP election poster, 1932
49 Hitler shaking hands with Hindenburg
50 Marius van der Lubbe
51 The Reichstag on fire
52 Hermann Goering
53 Joseph Goebbels
54 One People, one Reich, one Leader

Preface

In November 1918 the Weimar Republic was proclaimed successor to the bankrupt Wilhelminian Empire. To many the establishment of republican government under the guidance of the Social Democrats heralded the end of the old order and the creation of a truly democratic state, but the subsequent development of the Republic was to disappoint them deeply. The aim of this short work is twofold: to present a factual account of the political history of Germany between 1918 and 1933, and to suggest reasons for the failure of parliamentary democracy and the success of National Socialism.

While not aiming to present radically new material to the reader, the work attempts to provide a synthesis of several leading studies of the period. The scope of the work has been determined to a considerable degree by the needs of university students of German whose main interests were literary and who were required to pursue a course in German history with little prior knowledge of the subject. It is hoped, however, that this text-book may prove valuable to a wider audience such as sixth-form scholars, first-year university and college students of history and interested laymen.

Thanks are due to the many friends and colleagues who have assisted in the preparation of this work.

J. R. P. McK.

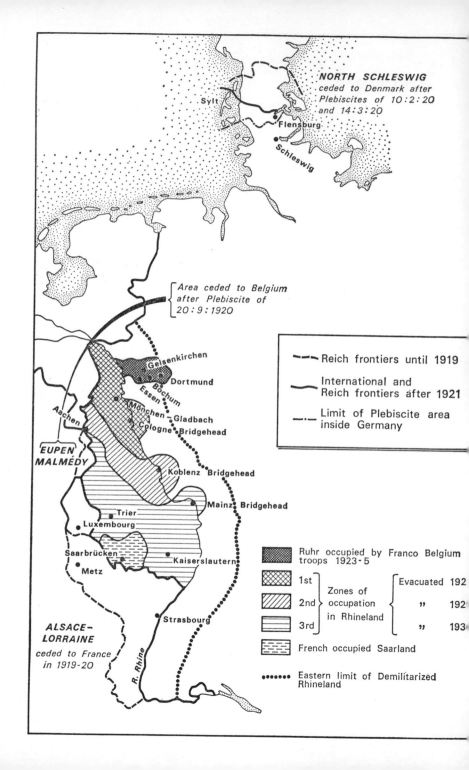

NORTH SCHLESWIG
ceded to Denmark after
Plebiscites of 10:2:20
and 14:3:20

Sylt

Flensburg

Schleswig

Area ceded to Belgium
after Plebiscite of
20:9:1920

Gelsenkirchen

Dortmund

Bochum

Essen

Mönchen-Gladbach

Cologne Bridgehead

Aachen

EUPEN
MALMÉDY

Koblenz Bridgehead

Mainz Bridgehead

Trier

Luxembourg

Saarbrücken

Kaiserslautern

Metz

Strasbourg

ALSACE-
LORRAINE
ceded to France
in 1919-20

R. Rhine

- - - Reich frontiers until 1919

—— International and
Reich frontiers after 1921

-·-· Limit of Plebiscite area
inside Germany

▓ Ruhr occupied by Franco Belgium
troops 1923-5

▨ 1st ⎫ Zones of
▧ 2nd ⎬ occupation
▤ 3rd ⎭ in Rhineland

⎱ Evacuated 192
⎰ "   192
  "   193

▤ French occupied Saarland

•••••• Eastern limit of Demilitarized
Rhineland

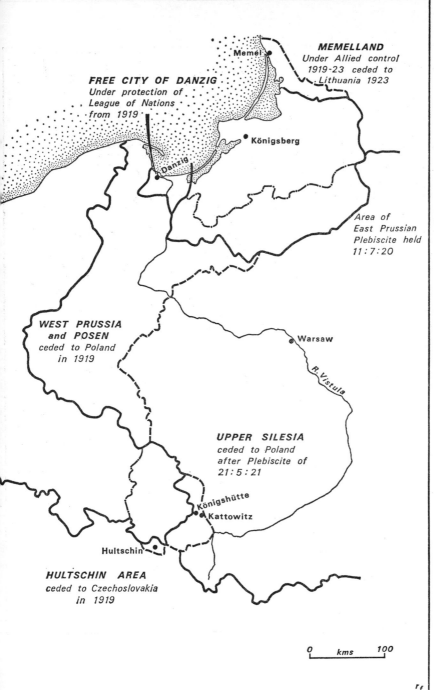

FREE CITY OF DANZIG
Under protection of
League of Nations
from 1919

MEMELLAND
Under Allied control
1919-23 ceded to
Lithuania 1923

Memel

Königsberg

Danzig

Area of
East Prussian
Plebiscite held
11:7:20

WEST PRUSSIA
and POSEN
ceded to Poland
in 1919

Warsaw

R. Vistula

UPPER SILESIA
ceded to Poland
after Plebiscite of
21:5:21

Königshütte

Kattowitz

Hultschin

HULTSCHIN AREA
ceded to Czechoslovakia
in 1919

0   kms   100

r_f

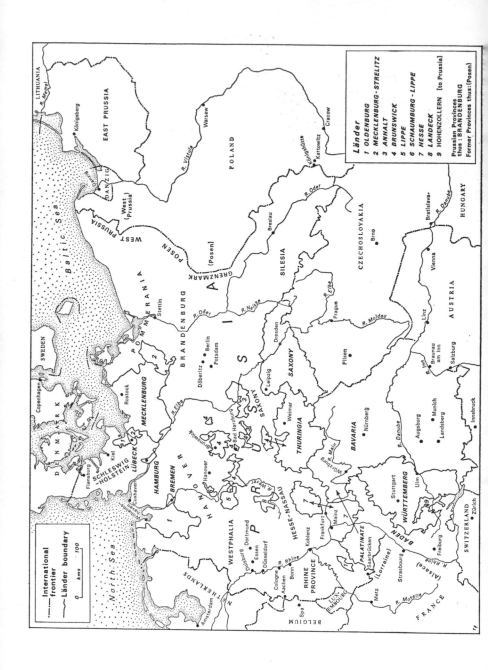

Länder

1 OLDENBURG
2 MECKLENBURG-STRELITZ
3 ANHALT
4 BRUNSWICK
5 LIPPE
6 SCHAUMBURG-LIPPE
7 HESSE
8 LANDECK
9 HOHENZOLLERN   [to Prussia]

Prussian Provinces
thus : BRANDENBURG
Former Provinces thus:(Posen)

International
frontier
Länder boundary

0   kms.   100

1

The German Empire and the First World War

The Establishment of the German Empire

THE HISTORY of the Republic and its eventual dissolution were due in no small measure to the social and political legacy of the German Empire. The German Empire, *Deutsches Reich*, was proclaimed in January 1871 in the Hall of Mirrors in the Palace of Versailles after the victory in the Franco-Prussian war of the combined military forces of the German states over the French army. The newly created Empire failed, however, to achieve the unification of German-speaking states: it deliberately excluded German-speaking Austria. More accurately, it consummated the aggrandizement of Prussia at the expense of the lesser German states, twenty-two monarchies and three free cities. The Prussian Prime Minister, Otto von Bismarck, had achieved his objective. Prussia now accounted for two-thirds of both the geographical area and the total population of the Reich.

The enlargement of Prussia under the guise of German unification was confirmed in Bismarck's Imperial Constitution. The King of Prussia, Wilhelm I, assumed the title of German Emperor, *Deutscher Kaiser*, while Bismarck's position of political preeminence was assured by the union of the office of the Prussian Premier with that of Imperial Chancellor, *Reichskanzler*; this formula accurately reflected the peculiar relationship that existed between Wilhelm and Bismarck. The Constitution provided for a monarchy which was virtually absolute in practice, although a popularly elected but ineffectual national parliament, *Reichstag*, existed. The powers of the Reichstag were severely limited. It had no direct

1

control over the decisions of the government, though it was empowered to reject its annual budget. It was permitted to propose legislation to the competent body, the Federal Diet of the constituent German states, the *Bundesrat*. Bismarck assured Prussia's continuing predominance by decreeing that any measure introduced before the Bundesrat could be rejected by fourteen votes out of a total representation of fifty-eight votes, of which Prussia possessed seventeen. As a result of this clause the politics of Imperial Germany remained to all intents and purposes identical with those of Prussia.

The Kaiser together with the *Kanzler*, the sole responsible member of the cabinet, constituted the government. Other members of the cabinet, called, significantly, secretaries of state, not ministers, fulfilled a purely advisory rôle. To prevent the Reichstag from fortuitously acquiring a measure of influence over the cabinet, it was expressly forbidden by the Constitution for any secretary of state to function simultaneously as a parliamentary delegate. The Kaiser enjoyed further absolute powers: he nominated the members of the judiciary who, although they were independent of governmental control and enjoyed secure tenure of their office for life, were naturally carefully chosen for their proven loyalty to the régime; moreover the Kaiser appointed army and naval officers and retained supreme command of the armed forces.

Within Prussia the interests of the established ruling clique, the feudal landed gentry, *Junkers*, of north-eastern Prussia, were artificially preserved by the existence of an iniquitous franchise which had been laid down in the Prussian Constitution of 1849. The three-class voting system, as it was called, decreed that the representation of each social class in the Prussian state parliament, the *Landtag*, was related directly to the amount it contributed in taxes to the state treasury. The few voters in the first, wealthy, class were accorded the same number of representatives in parliament as those in the larger second class and those in the enormous third class which included the broad mass of the electorate, workers and peasants, who were poorly paid and who therefore contributed little or nothing to the tax revenue of the state. Thus the same number of deputies represented the first eight per cent, the second twenty per cent and the remaining seventy-two per cent of the population. This system effectively prevented the left-wing parties, the Social Democrats and the Progressive Liberals, from gaining influence in the Landtag. The system in fact forced the left-wing parties into permanent opposition – in 1875 the socialist parties were banned – and deprived them of the opportunity of experiencing for themselves the realities of political power.

As long as Bismarck succeeded in maintaining his position of power within the government of Prussia and the Reich – which he did by making himself indispensable to the Kaiser – the Constitution appeared to function smoothly. In 1890, however, when Wilhelm II, within three months of his accession to the throne, dismissed Bismarck and became prey to the machinations of palace *camarillas* the inherent weakness of the Constitution became obvious. It had appeared efficient while the conditions for which it was designed persisted, namely the maintenance of a semi-feudal, authoritarian society based on the principle of privilege and dominated by a ruthless, able Reichskanzler in collaboration with a weak, amenable Kaiser. Now it showed itself incapable of the adaptation necessary to accommodate the changing circumstances in the social, political and economic life of the country.

Social, Political and Economic Developments under the Empire

The belated industrialization of Germany in the second half of the nineteenth century produced new social tensions. Society was composed not as before of aristocracy and bourgeoisie and peasants but of capitalists and workers, employers and employees. The structure of society altered radically in the late nineteenth century with the creation of a large urban proletariat, attracted to the centres of industrial activity and high employment from the economically depressed agrarian provinces. The population increased in the second half of the century by over seventy-five per cent, from thirty-five millions to sixty millions. The affluent bourgeoisie naturally felt their position of privilege threatened by the emergent proletariat and, consequently, sought common cause with the aristocracy in keeping the workers in subjugation. Their attitude found expression in Wilhelm's rejection of socialist demands in January 1890 for the introduction of an eight-hour working day. It would, he maintained, encourage immoral behaviour, drunkenness and political unrest among workers in their extended leisure time. Working wives would be encouraged to remain at home and the youth would run wild. Worse, German industry would lose its competitiveness over foreign firms.

The quality of life of the proletariat was wretched: they existed on low wages, lived in appalling conditions in inhuman tenement blocks and suffered the debilitating effects of an inadequate diet, hunger and disease. Exhausted by lack of food and hard work they had neither the physical strength nor sufficient money with which to enjoy what little free time they were granted. Women and children were also obliged to work long hours to supplement the family income.

The arrival of unprecedented economic prosperity was widely believed to be the consequence of the establishment of the Empire; in fact it was simply coincidental with it. This erroneous belief, together with a growing respect abroad for the achievements of the new German state, encouraged exaggerated national pride and a desire to express the newly found self-awareness by undertaking prestige projects. Berlin was to become the glittering, brash capital of the second most powerful state in Europe, truly representative of the country's military and economic might. New-rich industrialists with pretensions to the aristocratic way of life erected ludicrously over-ornate stately mansions. Towns spawned acres of new, would-be gracious suburbs in which the affluent middle classes could build their monstrous, Wilhelminian villas. Pompous memorials of dubious aesthetic merit commemorating Germany's glorious recent past littered the broad, tree-lined avenues which fanned out from the city centres. Imperial designs on a grander scale included the belated acquisition of colonies and an accompanying assertion of military and naval strength in direct competition with other industrially developed countries. 'Our future,' Admiral Tirpitz, Commander-in-Chief of the German navy, predicted with considerable inaccuracy, 'lies on the water.' Nationalistic sentiments pervaded society: the jingoistic cult of the fatherland and the belief in the superiority of German institutions and culture accompanied a growing chauvinism which manifested itself in anti-semitism, anti-catholicism and anti-marxism and in xenophobia in general.

To the credit of the new state, it introduced the most progressive system of social welfare in the world in an attempt to forestall the demands of the Social Democrats. Germany's newly established industry was efficient and produced well-made goods which were

readily exported abroad. The economic, social and political importance of the representative bodies of industry, the trade unions and
the industrialists' organizations was, however, characteristically
ignored by successive cabinets who refused them the participation
in government which was their right and which the state needed.

The government of both the Empire and the constituent states
was greatly assisted by the established bureaucracy which, in contrast
with that of many other European states, was both efficient and
apparently uncorrupt. On the other hand, the existence of such an
administration tended to arrest the political development of the
state. There was little popular demand in Germany for the introduction of parliamentary democracy when the existing system,
albeit paternalistic, functioned smoothly and, within its terms of
reference, fairly. 'The best constitution,' according to a proverb of
the time, 'is a good administration.' Political parties and professional
politicians did not enjoy high public esteem; why, it was asked, should
the delegates in the 'gossip shop', as the Reichstag was often called,
be allowed to interfere with the practice of government? The man
in the street cannot be blamed for failing to notice the extent to which
the efficiency of the civil service, largely the product of years of
routine, masked serious shortcomings and deficiencies in the
government. When the republican parties came to power in 1918
the supposed excellence of the civil service continued to mesmerize
them and they neglected to purge it of its anti-democratic members.

The five major political parties represented in the Reichstag –
Conservatives, National Liberals, Progressives, Centrists and
Social Democrats – shared, surprisingly, a uniformly negative
attitude towards the introduction of parliamentary democracy.
The Conservative Party, predictably, was pledged to uphold the
existing order. The National Liberal Party had long since abandoned
their original liberal cause, parliamentary democracy, for fear of
thereby opening the way for a socialist government, which they
abhorred. The same fear was to be found in members of the Left
Liberal (or Progressive) Party, while the Centre Party, as champions
of the interests of Roman Catholics, was naturally opposed to the
danger to the church which they considered implicit in socialist
doctrine. Ironically, the Social Democrats themselves had abandoned
revolution in favour of gradualism. They showed little enthusiasm
for constitutional reform and although they paid lip-service to the

cause it was relegated to a low position on their list of priorities, becoming a long-term aim. Their immediate goal was social reform and they preferred to work within the existing system rather than jeopardize their slowly improving standard of living for it could no longer be maintained that the workers, as the *Communist Manifesto* proclaimed, had nothing to lose but their chains.

The Outbreak of the First World War

In 1890 Wilhelm II became King of Prussia and Emperor of Germany; he was the last Hohenzollern monarch. He proved to be headstrong, indiscreet and wholly inexperienced in knowledge of men. One of his first blunders was to dismiss Bismarck from office – an action depicted in a contemporary *Punch* cartoon as a ship's captain dropping the pilot – before he had allowed himself sufficient opportunity to accustom himself to the realities of political life and before he had found an adequate successor for the Chancellorship. It is doubtful whether Wilhelm had the ability to come to terms with the responsibility which his position forced upon him. His belief in his divinely bestowed mission to govern the Empire single-handed as an anachronistic benevolent despot with little to guide him except the unreliable advice of his palace camarilla provoked many unfortunate incidents. The tensions in international relations, which culminated ultimately in the outbreak of the war, were increased in no small measure by Wilhelm's frequent diplomatic indiscretions. Most infamous among these was his disclosure in October 1908 to a reporter on the London *Daily Telegraph* that Germany had supported Britain in the Boer War. The age of autocratic government based on the principle of command and obedience had long since passed, but such was the inflexibility of the German Constitution and the intense conservatism of the German *élite* that essential and long overdue political reform was simply not contemplated.

A discussion of the origins of the First World War lies beyond the scope of this work. Suffice it to say that Germany, as the other nations involved in hostilities, was neither without blame nor solely responsible for its outbreak. It is, however, relevant to note that the majority of Germans truly believed that they were engaged in fighting a purely defensive battle for the integrity – political and economic – of the Empire. Even the Social Democrats in the Reichstag responded to the Kaiser's plea that they forget inter-party disagreement for the sake of national unity, and he could affirm with some justification, 'I no longer recognize parties, I recognize only Germans now.' With the exception of left-wing dissenters they voted in favour of granting the war credits required by the government in order to finance the country's military and naval operations, thereby denying their avowed faith in international socialism. The Socialist deputy, Hugo Haase, joint party chairman with Friedrich Ebert and representative of the left wing of the party, spoke on behalf of his party, 'We are threatened by enemy invasion. We have not to decide in favour of or against war today but to discuss the question of providing the necessary measures for the defence of our country.' The Socialists would not leave the Reich in the lurch. After being outlawed for years as 'enemies of the Reich' (Wilhelm II) they now felt themselves integrated into the life of the nation and found a desire to come to its aid against the common enemy, the anti-socialist, anti-German Czar of Russia. It was a far cry from the hard-line international pacifism which they had written into their party programme twenty-four years earlier.

The Reichstag also accepted the government's assurances that Germany's territorial integrity could be assured only by extending her frontiers both eastwards through Russian-occupied Poland and westwards to include Belgium. The policy was underwritten by all parties except the Social Democrats who alone registered their open opposition to annexations. For the practical purposes of waging war, however, the government could rely on an inter-party truce in the Reichstag.

Throughout the war the German people were led to believe both in Germany's military supremacy over Russia and the *Entente* powers, Britain and France, and, equally important, in her moral rectitude in waging a defensive war. Germany's efficient censorship and propaganda machine prevented all opposing views from achieving popular currency. In fact, the root cause of Germany's ultimate military defeat lay in the failure in 1914 of the Schlieffen Plan, for according to its strategy a swift victory was to be won in the west by launching a strong attack through Belgian territory into north-western France while a defensive front was maintained in the east. The failure of this plan, due largely to the inadequacy of Germany's Army High Command, involved the Central Powers,

Germany and Austro-Hungary, in conducting a war simultaneously on two and, later, on three fronts when Italy entered the war on the side of the Entente. In turn this resulted in protracted trench warfare which imposed intolerable strains on the German economy.

The effects of waging a major war were felt by all sections of the community. All men between seventeen and seventy years of age were liable to national service either at the front or in the enormous armaments industry.

Though the troops were well disciplined, conscientious and courageous the army leadership proved to be incapable of organizing modern warfare. Moreover the equipment of the army was patently less efficient than that of the enemy. Germany's strategic position became even more acute after the imposition by the Entente forces of a shipping blockade which not only paralysed the German navy for the duration of the war but, worse, deprived the country of her essential supplies of food and raw materials from overseas.

The Appointment of Hindenburg and Ludendorff

As the war progressed it became increasingly clear that the quick victory in the west, which Germany had confidently expected, would not be achieved. With the failure of the Schlieffen Plan, the opposing forces had resigned themselves to a protracted war of attrition waged from the trenches. The existing Chief of the German High Command, Erich von Falkenhayn, showed himself incompetent to deal with an unfamiliar military situation. The Chancellor, Theobald von Beth-mann Hollweg, urged the Kaiser to replace Falkenhayn with two military leaders, Field-Marshal Paul von Hindenburg and General Erich Ludendorff, men who enjoyed the confidence of the public and considerable (albeit undeserved) military fame since their now mythical victory over Russian troops at Tannenberg in 1914. The Kaiser agreed to the Chancellor's request and on 29 August 1916 Hindenburg was appointed Chief of Staff and Ludendorff First Quartermaster-General – a title devised after Ludendorff had refused what he considered the belittling rank of Second Chief of General Staff. Ludendorff soon became the supreme war lord in Germany, in effect if not in name. He dominated Hindenburg's passive nature and lack of political awareness and consistently imposed his will on his superior, while carefully allowing Hindenburg to retain all responsibility for the actions and decisions of the

Supreme Command. He basked in the reflected glory of Hindenburg's immense popularity, a measure of which was the fantastic spectacle enacted in Berlin in 1915, when an enormous wooden statue of Hindenburg was unveiled as the main attraction of a fund-raising campaign. Those who lent money for the war effort were permitted in return to hammer nails into the wooden titan.

The Establishment of the Military Dictatorship

With Ludendorff's assumption of power Germany became virtually a military dictatorship. His decisions prevailed over those of the Chancellor, whose indecisive attitude failed to check the increasing power of the military. The Reichstag and the Bundesrat likewise showed themselves to be helpless in the face of Ludendorff's ascendancy. Only the Kaiser as supremo of the armed forces was constitutionally empowered to challenge Ludendorff but he showed no desire to interfere with Ludendorff's interpretation of his position, which the latter saw as that of a military regent rather than that of an army leader.

Ludendorff militarized Germany's whole political life within a short time of his appointment. He increased his military power by bringing the air force under the Supreme Army Command. He asserted his authority in foreign affairs by setting up a permanent liaison office with the Foreign Office – which he characteristically nicknamed the *Idiotenhaus*, the lunatic asylum. His control over home affairs was assured by the establishment of the General War Office, *Allgemeines Kriegsamt*, which controlled the movement and deployment of labour, the production of munitions and the supplies of food and raw materials within the Reich. Such an office was necessary as the German bureaucracy was becoming daily less able to cope with the increasing volume of work forced upon it by the rapidly altering situation of the war, but it also further increased Ludendorff's personal control as he maintained strict supervision over the dealings of the office.

The First Abortive Attempt to Conclude Peace

In December 1916 Bethmann Hollweg, aware that a German victory in the war was becoming less likely, contacted Woodrow Wilson, President of the United States, with a tentative proposal that the U.S. government might negotiate between the Allies and the Central Powers. Ludendorff was outraged when he discovered Bethmann Hollweg's action, which had been undertaken behind his back, and refused to allow the Chancellor to formulate definite peace terms, thus effectively thwarting the initiative. Convinced of his superior judgement, he was certain that military victory could be achieved. The reintroduction of unrestricted submarine warfare would, he argued, cut off U.S. supplies to the Allies. Bethmann Hollweg pointed out that a resumption of submarine warfare would provoke the U.S.A. into entering the war on the Allied side, which would produce a combined military force vastly superior to that of the Central Powers. Hindenburg and Ludendorff countered the Chancellor's objection by threatening to resign if their demands were not met. Faced with such barefaced blackmail (which incidentally violated the oath of allegiance to the Kaiser sworn by all members of the armed forces) Wilhelm had little option but to accede to their demands.

Bethmann Hollweg had correctly assessed the situation for, within two months of the resumption of submarine warfare, the United States declared war on Germany thereby ending any German hopes of inflicting defeat on the British navy and, indeed, of winning the war.

The Divisions among Social Democracy

Since the outbreak of the war, the task of governing the country has been facilitated by an inter-party truce in parliament. As the war progressed, however, the Social Democrats had become increasingly aware of their bargaining power in the Reichstag and the opportunity of achieving several long-standing aims. They made their continued support of the government's handling of the war dependent on an undertaking that internal parliamentary reforms would be implemented at the end of the war. These included the abolition of the Prussian three-class voting system and the introduction of the principle of ministerial responsibility before parliament. The Socialists were tasting real political power for the first time. They could demand with greater conviction full rights of citizenship for their members now that the outcome of the war was seen to depend heavily on the efforts of the whole nation and the effects of war fell on the whole community and not as in previous campaigns only on the troops and those caught in the theatre of war.

Not all members of the SPD were content to let matters rest with the promise of post-war parliamentary reform. Several deputies were deeply concerned with the course of the war for the swift victory they had been promised in 1914 had not materialized. What had been described in 1914 as a defensive war had been transformed by the dictatorial Supreme Command into an offensive exercise. Indeed the presence alone of a military dictatorship provided an overwhelming cause for disquiet.

The longer the war continued, the worse conditions became both for the army who were suffering from the deprivations of trench warfare, and at home where food supplies were becoming increasingly scarce. The left-wing parties were also alarmed by the quality of the military command. The loyalty of the inter-party truce was being tried to the utmost and began to break. It broke completely in March 1916 when the Reichstag was asked to approve an emergency budget to finance rising military expenditure. Ebert, the Social Democratic leader, voted in favour of the budget, which he considered to be essential for the defence of the country against Allied invasion, but eighteen members of his party withheld their approval, thus destroying the seventeen-months-old truce.

The eighteen deputies who disagreed with the party leadership formally recognized their dissension a year later in April 1917 at a conference of left-wing Social Democrats held at Gotha. Under their leader, Hugo Haase, they broke away from the SPD and formed the Independent Social Democratic Party, *Unabhängige Sozialdemokratische Partei Deutschlands*, USPD. Their basic difference of opinion with the Majority Socialists, *Mehrheitssozialdemokratische Partei Deutschlands*, MSPD, as the parent party came to be known, was that they opposed the prolongation of the war. They held that an offensive war, for they did not subscribe to the view that it was a defensive operation, was immoral as such and that Germany could not sustain hostilities for much longer. They advocated a peace without victors and vanquished, but they were unable to impose their views, partly because they were numerically weak and partly because the military dictatorship had established an efficient censorship machine. They were also more insistent than the Majority Socialists on the question of the introduction of parliamentary democracy, rejecting the moderates' gradualist policy and calling for revolutionary tactics.

The Spartacist League

A second left-wing group, even more radical than the Independent Socialists, was the Spartacist League, *Spartakusbund*, led by Karl Liebknecht and Rosa Luxemburg, two prominent marxists. Liebknecht, born in 1871, was the son of Wilhelm Liebknecht, a friend of Marx and Engels. By profession a lawyer, he entered the Reichstag as a Socialist deputy in 1912. In August 1914 though he opposed the war he voted with his party in favour of war credits, but by December 1914 he had decided to oppose all further government requests for military finance. He was expelled from the party and conscripted into the army in May 1916. Deprived of parliamentary immunity, he was sentenced to four years' hard labour for publicly denouncing Germany's participation in the war. During his imprisonment he wrote letters under the pseudonym Spartakus, which when published provoked the formation of the Spartakusbund. Rosa Luxemburg was born in 1870 in Poland, the daughter of a middle-class Jewish family. A woman of considerable strength and determination, she was highly intelligent and became an outstanding Marxist theoretician while reading for a doctorate in Political Economy at the University of Zürich. After settling in Germany she rejected the evolutionary policies of the German Social Democrats and espoused the revolutionary cause, taking part in the Russian revolution of 1905. Like Liebknecht she indulged in constant agitation against the war and between 1914 and 1918 frequently found herself in gaol.

Both Liebknecht and Luxemburg were pledged to bring about the overthrow of capitalism in a world-wide socialist revolution. For them the war marked the beginning of the breakdown of the capitalist system. As early as May 1915 Liebknecht had issued a pamphlet in which he claimed that the true enemy of the German people was to be found within Germany herself, i.e. the capitalists and war lords. On Labour Day, 1 May 1916, Liebknecht continued his anti-war propaganda in a speech in Potsdamer Platz in Berlin in which he condemned the war and encouraged mass strikes. It was this act of political agitation which resulted in his imprisonment until October 1918. At this stage the Spartacists worked closely with the Independent Socialists, becoming members of the party, for they found it a convenient organization through which they could disseminate their revolutionary views. They formed small workers' councils, *Räte*, on the model of Russian soviets. These provided the necessary foundation for the establishment in 1918 of councils throughout Germany.

Erzberger's Peace Resolution

The inter-party truce finally disintegrated in the summer of 1917. On 19 July Matthias Erzberger, leader of the Catholic Centre Party – so called because it occupied central seats in the Reichstag – introduced a peace resolution in parliament. Erzberger, born in Württemberg in 1875, was one of the Centre Party's most gifted politicians. He entered the Reichstag at the age of twenty-eight and became the party's spokesman on financial matters. Though a left-winger he had supported his colleagues in voting in favour of war credits in 1914 but now he insisted that the Kaiser's assurance of 4 August 1914 that Germany was not embarking on a war of conquest must remain valid. As Germany was simply defending her freedom, her independence and the integrity of her territory, the Reichstag sought only to achieve a peace of understanding and lasting reconciliation between nations. Consequently, the resolution argued, there was no question of Germany's demanding an annexationist peace. Until the enemy declared itself willing to negotiate on the basis of such a peace, however, Germany would continue to fight for her rights. The resolution was based on sound information: its supporters correctly surmised that Germany would be hard pressed to endure a further winter of austerity in food and fuel. They were also convinced that submarine warfare would not be decisive and that the war, if continued for any length of time, would ultimately lead Germany to ruin. Though the resolution was based on a sound appraisal of the situation it was a tactical error in as much as it aroused perplexed anxiety among the population, who until this time had been led to believe that the German forces were doing well. They were, after all, occupying large areas of France and the whole of Belgium.

Erzberger's speech expressed the feelings not only of the Centre Party but also of the Social Democrats and the Progressives (left-wing Liberals). The resolution was accepted by the Reichstag by two hundred and twelve votes to one hundred and twenty-six: the opponents came from the Conservative and National Liberal deputies. The three parties which supported the resolution, and which later formed the Weimar Coalition, joined forces to provide a permanent majority in the Reichstag. They formed an inter-party committee which determined a common policy and formed a third political force in Germany alongside the emasculated Reich government and the dictatorial Supreme Army Command. The elected representatives in the Reichstag had belatedly come to realize their power and for the first time in the history of the Empire they had seized the initiative. Unannounced, the germ of parliamentary democracy began spontaneously to develop. The three parties now subscribed to a programme of moderate constitutional reform, demanding the introduction of equal franchise in Prussia and of the principle of ministerial responsibility.

The National Liberals occupied an ambivalent position in the re-alignment of party political forces in the Reichstag. They opposed the peace resolution since the big-business interests which they represented were in favour of the economic expansion following annexations by Germany. On the other hand, they supported the new coalition in its demand for constitutional reform.

The Kaiser faced with such overwhelming support for reform and with a wary eye to the consequences of rigid authoritarianism recently evident in Russia, agreed to the democratization of the Prussian electoral system, which was to take effect at the next election. He did not, however, accede to the demand for ministerial responsibility.

The Conservatives, supporters of the wealthy, reactionary middle classes and of the nobility, naturally supported the maintenance of the *status quo* and underwrote Ludendorff's military rule, believing, as he did, that Germany could emerge from the war richer and greater.

Germany's fortunes on the western front did not improve and throughout the country morale began to sag. Ludendorff characteristically attributed this phenomenon to the ineffectualness of the Chancellor's policies and in May 1917 blackmailed the Kaiser into dismissing Bethmann Hollweg. That he had assumed most of the Chancellor's powers himself was a fact he chose to ignore. As if to offer the Reichstag a further insult Hindenburg chose as successor to Bethmann Hollweg an unknown, pedestrian bureaucrat, Dr Georg Michaelis, who possessed all the qualities likely to make him a tool of the Supreme Command. Popular mistrust of Michaelis – he refused to implement the Peace Resolution – forced the Kaiser to dismiss him within five months of his having taken up his office. Again an unsuitable successor was chosen, Count Georg von Hertling, a Centrist deputy, in the hope that his appointment would placate the parliamentary coalition. Hertling proved, however, no more successful than his predecessor in opposing the will of the Supreme Command and showed little sympathy for the proposed constitutional reforms. Within eleven months he had followed Michaelis into retirement from an office which had virtually ceased to have any function beyond that of providing a useful façade behind which Hindenburg and Ludendorff if necessary could hide.

The Bolshevik Revolution and the Treaty of Brest-Litovsk

After Lenin and Trotsky had established the Bolshevik régime in Russia in October 1917, they set about concluding a peace treaty with the Central Powers. Negotiations between the two sides were opened at Brest-Litovsk at the beginning of 1918. The Supreme Army Command took it upon itself to dictate peace terms to the politicians who represented Germany at the conference and despite assurances made by the Foreign Minister to the Reichstag that Germany would demand no annexations, Ludendorff insisted that territorial expansion was strategically necessary on military grounds and again threatened to resign if his demands were not accepted by the politicians. Parliament had once more proved unable to resist the military dictators. The Soviet régime was obliged on military grounds to accede to Germany's terms and a treaty was signed on 3 March 1918. Under the terms of the treaty Germany, by acquiring the Ukraine, deprived Russia of one-third of her population and agricultural land, half of her heavy industry and nine-tenths of her coal mines. Its severity was not forgotten when a year later peace terms were drawn up by the Allies at Versailles, nor did it facilitate the efforts of those politicians who were actively seeking possibilities of negotiating with the Allies.

In the Reichstag debate on Brest-Litovsk, the Centre Party and the Progressives voted in favour of the treaty, together with the National Liberals and the Conservatives who were committed to annexations. Only the Independent Socialists voted against – the Majority Socialists abstained on the dubious grounds that they could not vote against the peace as this would prolong the war.

The revolution in Russia provoked an even wider split between the two Socialist parties. The Majority Socialists, the avowed enemies of bloodshed, denounced the revolution for its violence and because they held it to be undemocratic: their resolve to oppose any such movement in the Reich was strengthened. The Independent Socialists, however, were inspired by events in Russia and moved politically even further to the left.

The Bolshevik revolutionary cry was eagerly taken up by the Spartacists who were determined to derive maximal political advantage from the situation. Pointing to the failure of the Peace Resolution and the severity of the peace terms which Germany was about to force on the Soviet régime, they incited in January 1918 over one million workers in munition factories vital to the war effort to strike in an attempt to force the military's hand.

The appalling conditions of life in the winter of 1917–18 strengthened the strikers' resolve. There was an almost complete lack of fuel for domestic heating and a severe shortage of food. Housewives were forced to apply their ingenuity to the utmost and produce *ersatz* dishes from turnips, the sole indigenous food-stuff in plentiful supply. (Not surprisingly, the period became known as the turnip winter, *Steckrübenwinter*.)

The strike was organized by a committee of shop stewards, *Obleute*, extreme left-wing Independent Socialists who formed a ginger group within the trade unions. The Majority Socialist trade unionists were characteristically lukewarm towards the strike: Ebert, the Majority Socialist leader and a life-long trade unionist, who was drawn into the strike against his will, did his utmost to bring it to a swift end. This strange decision not to give absolute support to the strikers was motivated partly by a misguided wish not to make difficulties for the government and partly by a real fear of being forced into a position whereby they would be obliged to underwrite the revolutionary aims of the Independents and Spartacists.

The Spring Offensive and the Fourteen Points

Brest-Litovsk presented Ludendorff and Hindenburg with a totally unexpected military advantage: troops could be withdrawn from the east and deployed on the western front as much-needed reinforcements.

Ludendorff decided to launch an all-out offensive on the western front in the spring in a final attempt to restore Germany's military position before the expected arrival of the U.S. troops in the summer, and to force the Allies to sue for peace. In February 1918 Ludendorff admitted to Max von Baden, shortly to become Chancellor, that if the spring offensive were to fail, Germany would be ruined. He was prepared to gamble the future of the country in a bid to restore the honour of the *Reichswehr* at a time when there was a favourable opportunity to end the war by diplomatic means. A few weeks earlier, on 8 January 1918, Woodrow Wilson, President of the United States, had in an address to the U.S. Congress presented a programme, to become known as the Fourteen Points, which he hoped would provide a basis for negotiating a permanent peace in Europe.

The programme provided for an end to secret diplomacy, multilateral disarmament, 'a free, open-minded and absolutely impartial adjustment of colonial claims', the evacuation by Germany of occupied Russia and Belgium, the restoration of Alsace-Lorraine to France, and the establishment of a 'general association of nations' to act as a peace-keeping body. The Fourteen Points were confirmed and amplified in three subsequent pronouncements* in which Wilson stressed the importance of the principle of popular self-determination in the settlement of territorial claims and the necessity that the negotiating bodies should observe strict impartiality in their dealings with one another.

Copies of the text of Wilson's Fourteen Points were distributed to the German people by Allied aeroplanes. The Reichstag debated them but the Chancellor, Hertling, failed to take any positive action to initiate negotiations. The imposition of the Peace of Brest-Litovsk on the Russians, which was in direct opposition to the spirit of the Fourteen Points, revived and increased Allied suspicion of Germany's aims, and Ludendorff's decision to carry out the spring offensive, offers of peace notwithstanding, further reduced the chances of an early settlement.

Despite several tactical successes the German forces failed to improve on their strategic position. The loss of life was enormous on both sides but human suffering and wholesale slaughter were considerations which came low in Ludendorff's order of priorities

* The Four Principles of 11 February, the Four Points of 4 July and the Five Particulars of 27 September 1918.

(the same was true of Haig, the British Commander-in-Chief). Whereas the Allies could rely upon American reinforcements, fresh to the battlefields, the German forces could not afford to sustain the heavy losses – half a million in 1918 alone – inflicted on them, and were consequently unable to supply replacements for the dead, the injured and the exhausted front-line troops.

On 8 August Allied forces united for the first time under the Supreme Command of Maréchal Foch made a decisive break through the German lines near Amiens with a massive force of tanks. Ludendorff openly admitted that after this 'black day of the German Army', as he called it, Germany's military position could no longer be maintained. Only a month earlier Ludendorff had dismissed the Foreign Minister, Richard von Kühlmann, after he had voiced the opinion in the Reichstag that diplomatic negotiations with the Allies should begin at once since Germany was no longer in a position to enforce a military solution.

The German army's reversal of fortune was by no means due solely to their lack of reserves. Years of inadequate diet and the privations of life in the trenches had lowered both their spirit and their resistance to disease. An epidemic of Spanish influenza which broke out at the front in the last few months of the war proved to be more debilitating for them than for the Allies. In the early days of the spring offensive German troops had been disillusioned by their discovery that British and French troops had been enjoying vastly superior food and material comforts – something which German propaganda had successfully concealed from them. Undoubtedly this contributed to a rising cynicism among the German rank and file along with a growing consciousness of the futility of the war effort. The Spartacists naturally took full advantage of this growing unrest among the ranks; troops and left-wingers who had been drafted to the front line as punishment for civil disobedience found themselves in an unrivalled position to spread dissent. Troops going on leave were urged not to return to the front, while replacements for retiring troops were accused of black-legging by their comrades and of prolonging hostilities.

Ludendorff's Call for Armistice Negotiations

On 14 August at a meeting of the Privy Council at Spa, the head-quarters of the Supreme Command, Ludendorff, in a complete *volte-face*, described the continuation of the war as an 'irresponsible gamble'. Showing signs of considerable mental strain Ludendorff lost his former optimism and succumbed to a mood of unrelieved depression. Clearly Germany could not seek an Armistice from a position of overt military weakness. Hostilities would therefore have to continue until negotiations with the Allies were begun.

Despite Ludendorff's expressed anxiety about the military position, the following month was spent in unproductive delay. It was not until reports of the capitulation of Germany's ally Bulgaria reached Berlin on 26 September, together with rumours of the imminent collapse of Austria, that the Reichstag was informed of the severity of the military crisis, and constructive political decisions were made.

On 29 September Ludendorff and Hindenburg ordered the Foreign Minister, von Hintze, to initiate negotiations with Woodrow Wilson for an Armistice based on the Fourteen Points. Ludendorff's decision was prompted primarily by his fear of a humiliating military defeat. Characteristically he regarded an Armistice not as an end to the war but as a necessary condition for the resumption of hostilities, for it would bring a period of cease-fire in which Germany could rearm and rebuild her military forces. Hindenburg, long since hopelessly out of touch with the political situation, continued to demand the annexation of mining areas in north-eastern France as a condition for peace!

The Advent of Parliamentary Democracy

Von Hintze's reply to the Supreme Command spelled out the implications of their demand for Armistice negotiations on the basis of the Fourteen Points. He made it clear that he considered it essential to introduce constitutional reforms, in particular parliamentary democracy, if lenient terms were to be obtained from Wilson, and, equally important, if they were to avoid the outbreak of revolution at home which would probably occur when the general public learned that the promised victory was soon to turn into defeat. After protracted discussion Ludendorff reluctantly agreed to von Hintze's demands. Parliamentary democracy was thus to be introduced not on account of widespread popular demand but as a result of Ludendorff's decision to appease Wilson and to anticipate revolution from below by revolution from above. The constitutional change held a further, personal appeal for Ludendorff. He foresaw with the customary astuteness which he employed whenever his own interests were at stake that the introduction of a parliamentary system of government would conveniently shift the responsibility for the fate of the country from himself to the professional politicians.

Count von Hertling, who as Chancellor had consistently opposed the champions of constitutional reform, was obliged to resign his post. On 1 October the Kaiser chose a successor, Prince Max of Baden, cousin and heir of the reigning Duke of Baden, to head a new government which would enjoy the confidence of parliament. He was a compromise figure. As a man of liberal views and an advocate of a negotiated peace he was sure of support from the Centre, the Progressives and the Majority Socialists. A member of the aristocracy who was considered likely to safeguard the monarchy from far-reaching constitutional amendments, he was also acceptable to the right wing.

The First Popular Government

As a first step towards the introduction of democratic government Prince Max decided to form a popular cabinet composed of Reichstag deputies. Implicit in this decision was an important amendment of Bismarck's Constitution which barred parliamentary deputies from membership of the cabinet. The cabinet contained members of the Centre, the Progressive Party and, after certain assurances had been secured, the Majority Socialists. Their conditions, to which Prince Max readily agreed, included an assurance that after the cessation of hostilities Belgium would be restored to her former status (there was still a powerful lobby in the Reichstag that sought to annex Belgian territory permanently). They further demanded the reform of Prussia's electoral system, and the introduction of full parliamentary democracy in the Reich. The Conservatives and National Liberals were forced into the rôle of opposition parties. The foundation of parliamentary democracy had been laid, for the government was now to all intents and purposes dependent on the confidence of parliament and open to its censure and questioning. Other reforms were enacted. The Prussian electoral system was given a broader democratic basis in accordance with the pledge secured by the Socialists. Equally progressive was the decision to limit the powers of the Kaiser. He was deprived of the supreme command of the armed forces (he had in fact not exercised this right since Ludendorff's assumption of power). His decisions now needed the countersignature of a government minister. Thus the monarchy was transformed in effect into a representative institution while real power was transferred to the cabinet ministers and parliament.

Apart from constitutional reforms, the programme of the new government, announced on 5 October 1918, contained a radical revision of Germany's foreign policy. The government accepted unconditionally the terms of the Peace Resolution and formerly disclaimed the annexationist aims of the Conservatives, the National Liberals and the Army Supreme Command. The independence and integrity of those countries occupied by German troops were guaranteed and a revision of the peace treaties imposed by Germany on Rumania and Russia was promised.

The Attitude of the Independents and the Spartacists to the Constitutional Changes

While the advent of parliamentary democracy and the limitation of the monarch's power largely contented the MSPD, the Independent Socialists remained sceptical to the 'revolution from above'. They maintained that the MSPD would simply be discredited in the eyes of the public by agreeing to join the government when Germany's fortunes were at their nadir; participation in government at this stage in the war was tantamount to collaboration with the old order. They adopted different tactics, hoping to exploit the situation by encouraging popular demand for a truly socialist republic while retaining the parliamentary system.

The left wing of the Independent Socialist Party, composed largely of radical shop stewards, Obleute, and their supporters among the workers in heavy industry, under their leader, Emil Barth, came out in favour of a popular rising which, they hoped, would produce a more radical solution than that advocated by their less extreme colleagues.

The Spartacists were likewise dissatisfied. On 7 October they met to draw up their plan of action. They demanded the establishment of a dictatorship of the proletariat to be operated at the grass roots. Parliament was to be dissolved since they considered it to be no more than a bourgeois confidence trick, 'the fig-leaf of democracy' (Wilhelm Liebknecht), established to encourage in the workers the illusion of participation in government while ensuring that real power remained vested in the middle classes. The reorganization of society was also necessary. Citadels of the Establishment in the judiciary, the army leadership and the bureaucracy would have to suffer radical transformation if anti-proletarian forces were to be eliminated. The expropriation of capitalists and land owners would follow. The Spartacists experienced the same difficulties as the Independents: they were numerically too weak to be able to disseminate their views effectively, and suffered from their ideological dislike of running an efficient administration.

In fact many of the constitutional changes which were enacted were lost on the population at large which for the most part was politically unaware. The replacement in the chancellorship of a count by a prince admittedly lacked the appearance of a revolutionary development. The MSPD, traditionally the mouthpiece for popular discontent, now often found itself in an uncomfortable position. As members of the government they now had to justify their actions and to contain public unrest, a rôle which demanded considerable skill and tact.

Continued Armistice Negotiations

On 3 October Prince Max at the request of Hindenburg and Ludendorff and after receiving their written confirmation that there was no reasonable prospect of Germany's being able to force peace on the Allies, sent a diplomatic note to Woodrow Wilson requesting the opening of peace negotiations on the basis of his Fourteen Points. The Allies remained sceptical about Germany's motives: the revolution from above smacked of political panic and had the appearance of a ruse to avert harsh peace terms.

Prince Max's message to Wilson was followed by an exchange of diplomatic notes between Germany and the U.S.A. which lasted for nearly a month. Wilson stated his conditions in successive communications. These included the immediate evacuation of all occupied territory and the suspension of submarine warfare. He further announced that the U.S. government would deal only with a fully democratic German government. 'If it must deal', he stated, voicing Allied doubts, 'with the military masters and the monarchial autocrats of Germany now or if it is likely to have to deal with them later in regard to the international obligations of the German Empire it must demand, not peace negotiations, but surrender.' This ultimatum eventually provoked the desired reaction: within three days Ludendorff resigned from his post and parliamentary democracy received statutory recognition. The abdication of the Kaiser, which the note demanded by implication, followed shortly afterwards. Before these changes occurred, there was a further period of confusion in Germany while the military dictators stubbornly clung to power.

Ludendorff's Resignation

As if to exemplify Wilson's doubts about the German leadership, Ludendorff and Hindenburg chose to continue war rather than accept the humiliation of unconditional surrender. On 24 October they brought matters to a head by issuing a manifesto to the troops in which they stated that the Allies intended to force Germany to capitulate and that Wilson's former assurances about a just peace were worthless. Germany, they announced, would therefore continue hostilities with the enemy. This manifesto, needless to say, had not been seen by the government and was issued without their knowledge. The unconstitutional action of the army leadership presented Prince Max with a suitable opportunity to press the Kaiser for Ludendorff's dismissal. Ludendorff, hearing of the Chancellor's request, anticipated matters by submitting his resignation to the Kaiser on 26 October. This action was not prompted by any courteous desire to avoid embarrassing the Kaiser for Ludendorff's motives were as ever purely selfish. Conscious that defeat could not be staved off for much longer, he was eager to avoid blame for the disaster when it came. The fate of the country occupied his thoughts less than the preservation of his 'honour'. Ludendorff's strategem, which was successful from his own point of view, exerted a destructive influence on the republican régime of post-war Germany. Having successfully relieved himself of the responsibility of agreeing to Armistice terms, Ludendorff, like so many others, blamed the politicians for the plight of Germany in the 1920s, a situation to which he had contributed so much himself.

The Kaiser, displeased by Ludendorff's actions, readily accepted his resignation. Hindenburg's resignation, offered at the same time, was, however, rejected. Prince Max argued that Hindenburg's presence was necessary as a symbol of continuity in the Army Command. This well-intentioned decision was widely interpreted as exonerating Hindenburg from all blame. Ludendorff was succeeded by General Wilhelm Groener, one of the few army leaders who had opposed the war aims of the Supreme Command and who was later to offer active support to the Republic as soldier and politician.

Parliamentary Ratification of the Constitutional Amendments

On the same day, 26 October, the Reichstag met for the last time under the monarchy. It gave legal authorization to the *de facto* system of parliamentary democracy and to the limitation of the Kaiser's prerogative. The legislation came into force two days later. The decision of parliament to dissolve itself at this time clearly demonstrates its unwillingness to play its full rôle in the critical weeks which lay ahead, and as such was an act of utter frivolity.

The general public was unmoved by the events of 26 October. Thanks to the efficient censorship practised by the Supreme Army Command they failed to appreciate the implications of Ludendorff's resignation. The statutory recognition of the constitutional amendments, ratification of the revolution from above, held little appeal for a population preoccupied by the miseries of war-time existence: a chronic shortage of fuel, near starvation and widespread disease.

On the following day the government informed Wilson that they agreed to all his conditions. Prince Max had even tried to persuade the Kaiser to abdicate, which he felt Wilson had implied on 23 October in his last note. The Kaiser ignored the Chancellor's hint and decided on 29 October to seek refuge in Spa from the political upheaval of Berlin.

The death blow to the monarchy was dealt not by the Kaiser himself, as many had expected, but ironically by his favourite branch of the forces, the navy, whose Commander-in-Chief chose this moment to launch one of the most impolitic and unlikely adventures of the war.

2

The Revolution

The November Revolution

THE REVOLUTION broke out at the end of October 1918. Five factors determined its course: first, the revolt of the fleet at Kiel and the setting up of revolutionary sailors' and workers' councils; second, the reaction to this of the Imperial government under Max von Baden; third, the dilatoriness and indecision of the Kaiser and his entourage at Spa; fourth, the need to choose as a constitutional alternative to the defunct monarchy, either proletarian dictatorship or a parliamentary democracy, which engaged the three Socialist groups, the Majority Socialists, the Independent Socialists and the Spartacists in rivalry; and fifth, the fateful pact between Ebert, the leader of the provisional government, and Groener, the Chief of the Supreme Army Command, which assured the government of military support and which led to the suppression of the extreme left. There followed a period of confusion and intense political activity which lasted until March 1919.

The Revolt of the Fleet

On 30 September Admiral Scheer, Chief of Naval Staff, had ordered the German fleet, which had been immobilized by the Allied blockade for most of the war, to assemble in the North Sea off Wilhelmshaven at the end of October. They were to engage in a final operation against the British fleet, thereby relieving the military on the western front. Scheer was eager to demonstrate the power of the navy, to show that it was still capable of fighting, even if he doubted its ability to win a battle. Earlier in 1918 he had launched the *Scheer Programm* which had provided for a massive construction of submarines and he was outraged to discover in October that the cessation of submarine warfare was a precondition for Armistice, to which Ludendorff had agreed without consulting his naval colleague. Humiliated to the utmost, Scheer resolved to take the last opportunity of proving the honour and restoring the prestige of the navy in a last-ditch offensive against the British fleet, which he knew to be destined to failure. The Chancellor was left ignorant of Scheer's tactically senseless decision to sacrifice the navy in the doubtful cause of honour.

The naval ratings grasped the reality of the situation. They refused to obey the orders of their officers in Wilhelmshaven on 29 October, orders which would have engaged them in a suicidal battle. They had been shabbily treated for most of the war, had seen little active service, had little respect for their commanding officers and even less for the romantic notion of death with honour. They were for the most part supporters of Social Democracy and had no wish to see efforts to achieve an Armistice sabotaged by the whims of Admiral Scheer.

From Wilhelmshaven the mutiny spread rapidly through German ports. On 4 November the newly formed sailors' council took over the town of Kiel which became the centre of the revolt: every ship flew the red flag at its mast. This did not imply a popular demand for Bolshevik revolution; it was an attempt, by claiming the end of the old order, to avoid the severe legal penalties to which mutineers were subject. Councils, originally the product of a belief in an extreme form of democracy aiming at both legislative and executive power, were in Germany more an expression of dislike for authoritarian bureaucracy and militarism. In the ports they sprang from a determination specifically to alleviate the poor conditions of service which the naval ratings had to endure.

It fell to Gustav Noske, a right-wing Social Democratic delegate, to bring the revolt under control by a personal appeal to the troops in Kiel. On 5 November they elected him chairman of the sailors' council. The council's demands for reform went little further than those already accepted by the government as just and necessary, with one exception: they insisted on the abdication of the Kaiser.

The revolt spread quickly through north and west Germany and by 6 November all the North Sea ports and several major industrial cities were in the hands of the councils as workers joined the sailors. There was little the government could do to check the spread of the revolt for troops sent to quell the revolutionaries, not wishing to maintain the fiction that Germany was still at war, joined their comrades in the revolt.

The End of the Imperial Government and the Monarchy. The Conflicting Attitudes of the Socialist Parties

By 7 November the leaders of the Majority Socialists realized that they would have to take the initiative if they were to remain at the head of the revolutionary movement and avoid losing the sympathy of their rank and file to the Independents. Now that Socialist members had entered the cabinet, the danger that the soldiers and workers in revolt would turn against the party increased daily. They therefore presented the Chancellor, Max von Baden, with an ultimatum: unless the Kaiser abdicated and the Crown Prince renounced his right of succession by noon the following day, they would withdraw from the government.

Max had already tried unsuccessfully to persuade Wilhelm that his voluntary abdication was essential if the German monarchy was to survive. In their invincible ignorance of the true state of affairs in the Reich, the Kaiser's military entourage at Spa disagreed. It was only on the evening of 8 November, when troops guarding the Imperial Headquarters against possible rebel attack from the east laid down their arms and deserted, that the generals admitted to themselves that the Kaiser's position was hopeless. They refused to disturb Wilhelm's sleep, however, though they had been assured by Max that every hour's delay would further aggravate the crisis in Germany. The privacy of the Kaiser – even if he were to remain Kaiser for only one more day – took precedence over mere political considerations. By the time their decision had been made it was already too late. With the expiry of their dead-line, the Socialist ministers had withdrawn from the last Imperial government.

The left-wing Independents were also embarrassed by the course of the revolution. It had taken the form that they had so often advocated, that of a spontaneous uprising, but it was the sailors who had made the running, not the revolutionary Obleute, the shop stewards in heavy industry, who considered themselves leaders of the workers. Emil Barth, spokesman for the Obleute, planned to regain leadership of the revolution by staging a popular uprising on Saturday, 9 November, led, of course, by his followers.

When news of Barth's revolutionary plans became known on the morning of 8 November the government had still received no announcement from the Kaiser. The Majority Socialists decided they would have to take a positive lead if they were to prevent a Bolshevik *Putsch*, to which they were passionately opposed, or, equally undesirable, the outbreak of anarchy. Accordingly they ordered the staging of a general strike in Berlin to demand the Kaiser's abdication. From mid-morning the streets of the city were thronged with workers who had answered the call. Max, still determined if possible to preserve the monarchy, decided to anticipate the official message from Spa and announced the Kaiser's abdication at noon. He also decided to resign his own post. The Socialist leadership visited Max at midday and agreed to his suggestion that they should form a provisional government under the chancellorship of Friedrich Ebert until they could hold nation-wide elections to a Constituent National Assembly, which would decide the future constitution of the German state. He believed that if the whole electorate were allowed to express its will in free elections, there would be little chance that a workers' state *à la Russe* would be set up in Germany. Max's choice of successor in the chancellorship was based on his conviction that Ebert was the Socialist politician most likely to preserve the monarchy and most unlikely to tolerate a proletarian dictatorship. Legally Max had no competence to bequeath the chancellorship, for according to the Constitution this required the ratification by the Reichstag. From a practical stand-point however the recall of parliament was out of the question for communications and transport had been badly disrupted. Moreover the opinion of the old Reichstag was now irrelevant.

The Proclamation of the Republic

While eating a meagre lunch in the Reichstag building, Ebert and Scheidemann learned that Liebknecht planned to proclaim a soviet republic that afternoon. Scheidemann, who shared his colleagues' total opposition to Bolshevism, decided to forestall Liebknecht and announce the decision to convene a Constituent National Assembly. At 2 p.m. from a Reichstag balcony he addressed the crowd assembled below and announced, 'The Kaiser has abdi-cated. He and his friends have disappeared. The people have scored a sweeping victory over them. Prince Max of Baden has handed over his office of Reich Chancellor to the parliamentary deputy, Ebert. The old, rotten monarchy has collapsed. Long live the new German Republic!' Ebert, who had been determined to adhere to constitutional methods and to abjure revolution, was deeply distressed by Scheidemann's announcement. Ebert had been given no cause to expect that his colleague would proclaim a republic and he maintained that no one individual had the right to make the decision. The future political system of the country was a matter for an elected Constituent National Assembly to decide. It is difficult to determine Scheidemann's motives: whether he had previously intended to declare the overthrow of the monarchy or whether he had acted on impulse. The question is largely academic for Scheidemann's proclamation was irrevocable and even though Ebert 'hated the republic like sin' he had no option but to make the best of it.

The lesser German monarchs with the exception of the exiled Wittelsbach, Ludwig III of Bavaria, followed Wilhelm's abdication and renounced their thrones. Though the rule of the Hohenzollerns, the most concrete symbol of the old order, had ended, the competence of the Republic which had 'come into the world almost by accident, and covered with apologies' (Gay) remained unproven.

At 4 o'clock that same afternoon from the balcony of the Royal Palace, Liebknecht announced the establishment of a 'rival' free socialist republic, a proletarian dictatorship under the control of workers' and soldiers' councils. The tension in the streets of Berlin increased hourly and it was by no means clear which proclamation the masses would endorse. Two days earlier a separatist republic had been proclaimed in Bavaria. Ebert, therefore, despite his misgivings about the Independents' policies, decided that he needed the combined support of both the MSPD and the USPD if he were to keep the revolution in check and to preserve national unity. The mistrust was mutual, for the Independents suspected the Majority Socialists of coming into power on the coat tails of the revolutionaries. They doubted the sincerity of Ebert's belief in socialism for in their eyes he had compromised himself by his attitude to the bourgeois parties. Influenced by Liebknecht, the left wing of the USPD advocated collaboration with Ebert for three days only so that an Armistice could be concluded with the Allies, after which power was to be relinquished to the councils. This suggestion was naturally unacceptable to the Majority Socialists. A compromise was eventually agreed upon between the MSPD and the right-wing Independents, while the leftists dissociated themselves from the decisions of their colleagues. They adopted a formula which was sufficiently imprecise to accommodate the interests of the councils and of both parties, namely: elections to a Constituent National Assembly would not be held until the gains of the revolution, i.e. the advancement of the working class, had been consolidated.

The new government – officially named the Council of People's Representatives, *Rat der Volksbeauftragten*, in deference to the Independents' dislike of the bourgeois term 'cabinet' – was composed of three Majority Socialists, Ebert, Scheidemann and Otto Landsberg, and three Independents, Hugo Haase, Wilhelm Dittmann and Emil Barth. Liebknecht rejected Ebert's invitation to participate in the Council. All six shared responsibility for the offices of President and Chancellor. The former secretaries of state in the Imperial government remained at their ministries and continued to function in an advisory and administrative capacity, though they were not admitted to the deliberations of the inner Council which determined government policy. In practice their influence on government affairs remained considerable.

As the only real authority in the country lay with the workers' and soldiers' councils, it was from them that the new government would have to require legitimization, and since the majority of Berlin soldiers and workers stood firmly behind the MSPD, authorization of Ebert's provisional government was certain. In the afternoon of 10 November the representatives of the Berlin soldiers' and workers' councils met under the big top of the Busch Circus. Acting on behalf of the councils throughout the country they approved the composition of the new cabinet which was to be under Ebert's chairmanship. Control over the government was to be exercised by an executive committee elected from among the delegates at the assembly. Fortunately the relationship between the government and executive committee remained vague and this prevented major disagreements between the two. The members of the councils had for the most part few definite political aims, being content to entrust the functions of government to the two socialist parties.

The meeting in the Busch Circus ended the first stage of the revolution. It had been, as Heiber has pointed out, essentially constitutional in its course. There was no question of sovereignty having been usurped: parliamentary democracy had been imposed from above in October and approved from below a few weeks later. A large majority of the members of the councils was opposed to the establishment of proletarian dictatorship. They favoured the maintenance of parliamentary democracy, advocated by the MSPD to which most of them belonged. In so doing they subconsciously confirmed the inherently bourgeois outlook of the MSPD.

The working agreement between the two socialist parties, ratified by the meeting in the Busch Circus, was, for the most part, a marriage of convenience. The Majority Socialists needed the support of the Independents to guarantee the stability of the provisional government. For their part the Independents saw participation in the cabinet as a means towards achieving further socialization of the state and, accordingly, the three Independent members of the cabinet now lent their support to the activities of the councils. They were, however, divided among themselves. Dittmann and Haase agreed to the convening of a Constituent National Assembly but wished the elections to be delayed until a programme of democratization and socialization was achieved. Barth maintained his demand for the preservation of government by popular councils, a system which would, of course, disfranchise the bourgeois classes. Again, despite Barth's dissension a compromise was reached: the question of the date of the elections, which the Majority Socialists wished to hold in February, was to be referred to the National Congress of Workers' and Soldiers' Councils, due to be held in Berlin in December.

The Conclusion of the Armistice

Meanwhile a German delegation had concluded an Armistice with the military leaders of the Allied powers. On 6 November Wilson had notified the German government that the Allies were willing to sign an Armistice with Germany on the basis of the Fourteen Points. Negotiations on behalf of the Allies would be conducted not by himself, as had been expected in Germany and abroad, but by the Allied Supreme Commander, Maréchal Foch, a man who did not share Wilson's idealistic philosophy.

On the advice of the German Supreme Command Prince Max decided to include Matthias Erzberger in the German delegation. On 7 November Erzberger arrived in Spa to meet the military and naval representatives, only to discover that – with Hindenburg's approval – he had been appointed head of the delegation. This decision by the High Command was again an attempt to impress the Allies with Germany's new democratic face, and, more sinister, it was a strategem which transferred to the civilian government the odium which would cling to those formally responsible for accepting the Armistice terms. In so doing, it concealed from the general public those who were historically responsible for Germany's defeat.

On the morning of 8 November the special train bringing the German delegation arrived in the forest of Compiègne, the meeting place for the talks. The two delegations met in a railway carriage at ten o'clock. The Allied delegation was headed by Maréchal Foch, the Allied military leader, and contained no U.S. representative. There were no negotiations. Foch simply presented the German delegation with an ultimatum: they had seventy-two hours to decide whether to accept the Allied terms *in toto* or whether to reject them and abandon discussions. Hostilities would continue until the German government had made its decision.

The conditions, laid down in some thirty-four articles, were severe: the Allies were determined to prevent Germany from resuming hostilities at a later date. Germany was to evacuate occupied Belgium and French territory and also the *Reichsland* of Alsace-Lorraine within fourteen days, an operation which would be extremely difficult to execute. An Allied Military Control Authority was to occupy the left bank of the Rhine and the bridgeheads of Cologne, Koblenz and Mainz to a depth of thirty kilometres on the right bank. Further, a strip of territory ten kilometres deep on the right bank of the Rhine was to be demilitarized. In the east, Germany was to renounce the peace treaties of Brest-Litovsk with Russia and of Bucharest with Rumania, and to retire within her 1914 frontiers. Germany's colonies in East Africa were to be surrendered. The unilateral repatriation of Allied prisoners of war in Germany was to be executed immediately (the document made no mention of German prisoners in Allied hands). The German authorities were to surrender substantial booty to the Allies, including weapons, warships, submarines, aircraft, locomotives and rolling stock. The Allies would meanwhile maintain their blockade on German shipping, which prevented food supplies from abroad from reaching Germany by sea, an action which was bound to aggravate the already widespread famine in the Reich.

The delegation contacted Hindenburg to seek his advice on the military situation. They asked whether Germany could afford to reject the Allied terms and continue the war. On 10 November Hindenburg telegraphed his reply: the delegation should attempt to secure concessions on the length of time allowed for the evacuation of the occupied areas and on the date of the lifting of the blockade, but if no progress could be made on either of these two points, then nevertheless the Armistice should be accepted on the Allies' terms as further military opposition on Germany's part was out of the question. The Imperial cabinet, meeting for the last time, concurred though apprehensive that the attitude of the Allies at Compiègne foreshadowed the imposition of an unjust, even ruinous peace treaty.

The Allies were not willing to make concessions and the German delegation was left with no option but to accept the imposed conditions. The Armistice was signed at 5 o'clock on the morning of 11 November by Erzberger, and came into force six hours later. At a subsequent meeting between the Allies and Germany on 13 December, arranged to ratify an extension of the Armistice pending the conclusion of a peace treaty, one minor concession was granted. A clause was added to the treaty, which promised provision of food supplies by the Allies. These proved to be so inadequate that the fears of widespread death from malnutrition in the winter of 1918–19 were realized in all their horror. This concession had been achieved at a high price, for in return Germany had to agree to put the greater part of her merchant fleet at the disposal of the Allies for the duration of the Armistice.

There is convincing logic in the argument that the Allies committed a grave tactical error in not occupying the whole of Germany, for the conclusion of an Armistice with limited rights of occupation led easily to the myth that the German army had not been defeated in the field. It was likewise foolish to impose such primitive and inhuman terms as the continued blockade and the non-repatriation of German prisoners of war. The consequences of the Allies' wish to negotiate with a civilian plenipotentiary and a member of a liberal political party proved subsequently to have sinister consequences for the Republic. It relieved the military of the odious task of accepting Armistice terms in person. If the generals, especially Hindenburg, responsible for Germany's defeat had been seen to accede to Allied demands, the legend that Germany had been stabbed in the back by its politicians, which right-wing politicians were soon to foster, could never have thrived.

The Ebert–Groener Pact

The leader of the provisional government, Friedrich Ebert, was born in Heidelberg in 1871, the son of a master-tailor. Unable for lack of funds to attend university as he had wished, Ebert became an apprentice in a saddler's shop. He developed an interest in social democracy and in 1889 became a member of the party, one who worked conscientiously to improve workers' conditions. In 1912 he was elected party leader and supervised the SPD's development into an evolutionary party, a process which accorded with his trade-unionist brand of social democracy.

Ebert's policy during his first two months in power was dictated by two principles. First, he was determined to maintain law and order, not out of any mistaken respect for traditional Prussian authoritarianism, but in the conviction that peaceful conditions were essential for the survival of democracy. Secondly, he was determined that parliamentary democracy, which he interpreted as a partnership between all social classes and in particular between employer and employee, should emerge as the future political system of the country.

On the evening of 10 November Ebert received a telephone call from the Chief of Army Command, General Groener, who offered to place the army at Ebert's disposal in return for an undertaking that the government would oppose any outbreak of Bolshevism in Germany and refrain from revolutionary reorganization of the army. Ebert felt obliged to accept Groener's offer of an alliance since the government possessed no other means of defence and because he had good reason to believe that the Allies would invade the country if a Bolshevik revolt were staged. The decision was, however, to have serious consequences not only for the image of the MSPD but also for the future of the Republic.

Groener and his fellow officers in Army Headquarters appreciated that their best chance of preventing a proletarian revolution and of preserving the power of the officer corps in the new régime lay in supporting Ebert, even though the majority despised the man for his background and for the progressive ideals which he symbolized.

Hindenburg wrote to Ebert assuring him of his full support, and each evening Ebert and Groener discussed by telephone the measures necessary to deal with the ever-changing situation inside Germany.

The alliance between Ebert and Groener, between the new and the old orders, met its first real test of strength within a few weeks at the end of December. Evidence of the MSPD's hard line towards left-wing threats had already been provided by their reaction to the unrest which flared up in Berlin early in December. A group of counter-revolutionary conspirators, opposing the existence of soldiers' and workers' councils, attacked the Berlin Executive Committee, the supreme organ of the Berlin councils, which supervised the actions of the cabinet. Fearing a successful counter-revolution, unarmed Spartacist demonstrators marched on the centre of Berlin. Armed troops under the command of the MSPD member Otto Wels, Army Commandant of Berlin, engaged with the Spartacists and, on their own initiative, opened fire, killing sixteen and injuring many more. The Spartacist leadership launched a violent verbal attack on the government, accusing Ebert of being in the pay of the counter-revolutionaries. This accusation, though without foundation, was all the more forceful since it had been independently revealed that Ebert had been offered the post of head of state by the right-wing conspirators.

The Programme of the Council of People's Representatives
On 12 November the Council of People's Representatives issued a proclamation which carried the force of law and which was to come into effect at once. The liberty of the individual was restored: the state of siege ended, censorship abolished and freedom of speech and assembly guaranteed. Workers' rights suspended during the war were reinstated. Further social measures, the limitation of the working day and social insurance, were to be introduced at the earliest opportunity. The Council undertook to alleviate the material plight of the population which with the return of winter was suffering extreme hardship because of the scarcity of fuel, food and housing. The Council further stated its determination to defend private property and to hold elections to a Constituent National Assembly, a clear indication at the beginning of its period of office that it intended to prevent Bolshevism. Their revisionist programme, as it was pejoratively labelled by left-wing opponents, found an

immediate echo in the unexpected agreement reached between the two sides of industry.

Agreement between Employers and Trade Unions

While the power struggle between the socialist parties raged in the councils and on the streets, representatives of the two sides of industry met in Berlin to negotiate an agreement which was to influence considerably the course of the revolution. On 15 November employers' representatives and trade union leaders formed, with the connivance and support of the government, a Central Community of Labour, *Zentralarbeitsgemeinschaft*, which was to ensure that the interests of both sides were looked after. The employers undertook to improve working conditions, to adopt a programme of social insurance and to recognize the trade unions as equal partners in industry. In return the trade unions agreed to increase industrial productivity and, tacitly, not to insist on wholesale nationalization. The workers demanded the introduction of an eight-hour day, the legal enforcement of collective wage agreements and legislation to provide retirement pensions and health, disablement and unemployment insurance.

On 23 November the government issued a decree enforcing the eight-hour day. Its introduction was hailed by gradualist trade unionists as the achievement of the main revolutionary aim, a reception which betrayed the limitation of their vision. Their words were prophetic for it indeed remained the sole major reform of the revolution, other demands being either abandoned or postponed.

Ebert hoped that the agreement in industry would ensure the success of his vision of a national state, one in which all sections of the community would work and live together harmoniously. It was a naïve if noble faith which failed to take into account human failings: greed and stupidity at home and calculated opposition from abroad.

The outcome of the agreement fell far short of the trade unions' expectations. Many Independent Socialists who had agreed as an expedient not to insist on nationalization in 1918–19 nevertheless intended to return to their demands once the confusion of the immediate post-war period had been resolved. The employers were equally devious. The partnership between employer and employee, eagerly promoted by the employers while they remained vulnerable to the revolution, was rejected summarily as soon as they were able to regain their impregnable status. Trade union leaders were subsequently accused of short-sighted opportunism and of betraying the workers' interests. Leaving aside the limitations of the workers' spokesmen at the time of the revolution, it is pertinent to ask what other path they could usefully have followed, given the government's determination to prevent social upheaval. The winter of 1918–19 was hardly a time for trade unions to advocate far-reaching social and industrial experiments. Food was in short supply, unemployment, owing to the return home of demobilized troops, was high and industry had come to a virtual standstill. Only the most extreme revolutionary who put long-term political aims before immediate humanitarian demands could have contemplated a radically different course of action.

The National Congress of Workers' and Soldiers' Councils

The government's bloody and brutal suppression of the Spartacists early in December threatened to overshadow the deliberations of the National Congress of Workers' and Soldiers' Councils shortly to be held in Berlin. The Congress, which opened on 16 December in the Prussian *Land* Parliament Building in Berlin, was charged with determining whether Germany's future political system was to be founded on the principle of parliamentary democracy as advocated by Ebert's government or on that of government by workers' councils which the Obleute and Spartacus League demanded. The Spartacists had badly miscalculated: they had pressed for the Congress to be held, but neither Rosa Luxemburg nor Karl Liebknecht was elected delegate by the cautious council members. In fact, in spite of the bloody clash ten days earlier between Spartacist demonstrators and government troops, the Majority Socialists won most support. The extreme leftists did all within their power to disrupt the Congress in an attempt to gain recognition for government by councils. They demanded the dismissal of Ebert and an end to the collaboration of the government with the Reichswehr which was to be replaced by a people's militia. While rejecting their more revolutionary ideas the Congress passed a motion condemning Ebert's deployment of former Imperial troops in suppressing the Spartacists. Ebert, however, ignored their decision: he remained determined to suppress left-wing extremism and left

Groener and Hindenburg with their powers undiminished. The opportunity to put an end to Imperial German militarism had been lost.

On 19 December Scheidemann put the view of the Majority Socialists before the Congress. The councils, he maintained, had achieved much for the working classes during and since the revolution, but their task, he argued, was now complete and they should no longer retain their supreme position in the state. The outraged protests of the Spartacists and the left-wing Independents were of no avail. The Congress endorsed Scheidemann's views by three hundred and forty-four votes to ninety-eight and thus effectively put an end to their function within the system of government. The Congress then elected a permanent Central Committee, *Zentralrat*, to replace the Berlin Executive Committee as the steering group for the government. It proved to be as ineffectual as its predecessor. The Independent Socialists despaired: they had hoped at least to postpone the date of the forthcoming general election to allow the councils to consolidate their power and influence. Now that the councils had voluntarily abdicated their powers, the Independents refused to participate further in the affairs of the Congress and abstained from voting for the Central Committee which they – rightly – considered to be little more than decorative. The three Independent Socialist members of the cabinet decided for the present to remain in office, but as private individuals, not as representatives of their party.

A further motion, calling for the advancement of the general election for the National Constituent Assembly to 19 January 1919, the earliest practicable date, was put to the Congress and accepted by an overwhelming majority of four hundred to fifty votes – a clear indication that the delegates rejected revolution and stood firmly behind the MSPD's advocacy of parliamentary democracy and that despite their dislike of Ebert's methods they endorsed his determination to restore law and order at the earliest opportunity. Having completed its work with this historic anti-revolutionary decision, the Congress adjourned.

The Sailors' Revolt and the Split between the Majority and the Independent Socialists

The position of the Independent members in the cabinet, now deprived of party political support, grew daily more difficult and finally became wholly untenable, when for the second time within four weeks Ebert ordered the armed suppression of left-wing insurrection, organized on this occasion by frustrated naval ratings. At the beginning of November three thousand sailors from Cuxhaven, members of the self-styled People's Naval Division, had travelled to Berlin ostensibly to protect the Republic. They were housed in the former Royal Palace. In December they were accused of disorderly behaviour – including robbery – and ordered to leave the Palace by Otto Wels, the Majority Socialist Commandant of Berlin. The sailors promptly claimed payment of eighty thousand marks salary in arrears; in return they undertook to evacuate the building. The opposing sides reached deadlock; the sailors refused to hand over possession of the Palace to Wels, who in turn, refused to distribute the cash. Fearing the prospect of being penniless at Christmas, the sailors took matters into their own hands and on the morning of 23 December marched on the Chancellery, the office of the former Reich Chancellor. They placed all government officials including Ebert, whom they found inside the building, under house arrest, severing telephone communications with the outside world. Wels was also taken prisoner and incarcerated in the *Marstall*, the royal stables.

That the government of the country could be almost totally paralysed by a few thousand sailors was clearly intolerable to Ebert and his colleagues. The revolt had to be put down at once. Fortunately for the government, the sailors were unaware of the private telephone line between the Chancellery and Army Headquarters in use since 10 November. Ebert contracted Groener and requested the help of the army in suppressing the revolt. The Reichswehr leaders were delighted to be given a further opportunity of attacking left-wing extremists with impunity and sent in the horse-guards from Potsdam.

Although the sailors immediately released Wels on hearing of the impending intervention by the Reichswehr, Ebert could not be contacted in time to withdraw his request to the army. Early on the morning of 24 December, troops under the command of the former Imperial general, von Lequis, opened fire on the Palace and the Marstall killing several sailors. After an engagement lasting two hours, the two sides agreed to hold negotiations – an agreement facilitated by the distinct lack of enthusiasm of Lequis' troops for their assignment. Their leaders may have harboured counter-revolutionary sympathies but they themselves had little desire to become involved in a prolonged attack on their comrades. In return for the evacuation of the Palace the sailors were granted a full amnesty and were given the promise that the pay they claimed would be distributed in full. In addition they were assured that Wels, a suitable scapegoat for both parties, would be removed from his post.

The adventure resulted in a double defeat for the government. Not only had it shown itself vulnerable to paralysis by a small force of rebellious sailors, but it was also severely condemned for its consequent handling of the situation: republican sailors had been shot dead by troops under the command of a counter-revolutionary Imperial general and opponents of the Majority Socialists were able to label them *Matrosenmörder*, assassins of the sailors, and class traitors.

The December revolt finally brought about the complete rupture between the two socialist parties. As a result of their own committed opposition to militarism and to Ebert's collaboration with the Reichswehr, the Independents felt obliged to bring to an end the precariously united socialist front. On 28 December Barth, Haase and Dittmann, encouraged by party-political considerations, withdrew from the government, realizing that the left wing and in particular the Obleute would not tolerate their continuing participation in a cabinet dominated by the socially ambitious, renegade Majority Socialists. The posts they vacated were filled by other Majority Socialists. The renewed government crisis further increased the danger of an outbreak of civil war. Gustav Noske, the trouble-shooter who had pacified the naval mutineers in Kiel some seven weeks previously, accepted ministerial responsibility for dealing with any further unrest with philosophic resignation: someone had to be the 'bloodhound' and maintain law and order within the country. Since most regular army units had disbanded he could muster less than two hundred troops, and therefore he set about forming a temporary armed force, *Freikorps*, composed of a small number of workers loyal to the government and many rootless, who, for the most part were anti-republican adventurers. In return for a prolongation of their military career the newly repatriated troops agreed to support the government. In practice their support was unreliable, for, although committed to assisting the government in the maintenance of law and order, their sympathies lay unmistakably with the right wing. In subsequent engagements they suppressed left-wing revolts with vigour while all but ignored the, admittedly few, counter-revolutionary disturbances. The formation of the Freikorps had provoked few objections from government supporters for this was held to be politically necessary. The composition of the force, however, gave real cause for concern, all the more so since within a few weeks of its formation many of the workers left the corps and an unhappy situation arose in which anti-republican troops became the sole guardians of the republican government.

The Spartacist Conference and Putsch

On 30 December a national conference of the Spartacist League opened in Berlin under the presidency of Wilhelm Pieck who after the Second World War was to become the first president of the German Democratic Republic. The conference, to determine the future policy of the League towards Germany's political development, began by formally dissociating themselves from the USPD and founding the Communist Party, KPD. On Lenin's advice they deliberately avoided calling themselves Social Democrats since the term had become tainted by revisionists.

Rosa Luxemburg presented the conference with a draft programme which was enthusiastically, though uncritically, received. She rejected co-operation with the MSPD which, she alleged, had already betrayed Social Democracy and strengthened the hand of the counter-revolutionaries. A Spartacist *coup d'état* was out of the question – power was to be assumed only if a large majority of the proletariat desired it. The achievement of true socialism would take many years for it could not be imposed on a dissenting population if its success was to be assured, and, as she insisted, something more than a hollow victory was to be won.

Despite the delegates' acceptance of Rosa Luxemburg's essentially realistic programme, the subsequent discussion about the forthcoming elections to the National Assembly was dominated by Utopian factions. Luxemburg and Liebknecht advocated participation in the election, as the first step towards eventual success, but were heavily outvoted by the idealists, who demanded a total boycott of the elections. In this they were not simply recording their opposition to bourgeois government, but also tacitly encouraging their members to launch a putsch against the régime, even though this contradicted the principle of gradualism and persuasion contained in the newly accepted party programme. Notwithstanding their conviction that a Spartacist Putsch at this time was doomed to failure, Luxemburg and Liebknecht accepted the decision of the majority, a fateful political miscalculation on their part.

The departure of the Independents from the cabinet had led to a purge by the MSPD of many officials who were known to be sympathetic to the left wing. On 4 January the government ordered the dismissal of Emil Eichhorn, the Independent Socialist Chief of Police in Berlin. He refused to accept the government's decision since he was reluctant to relinquish an office which provided a potentially effective centre of proletarian agitation against the government. The Independents, with support from the Spartacists, instructed Eichhorn to remain in office. On 5 January they issued a joint manifesto accusing Ebert's government of attempting to crush the proletariat with military power and of fostering the cause of bourgeois capitalism. They urged the workers to take part in mass demonstrations to destroy the government and reawaken the revolutionary spirit of the previous November.

The manifesto produced quick results. On the same day a large crowd of workers moved through the streets of Berlin towards the offices of the chief of police, who had now assumed an aura of martyrdom. Spartacist troops occupied several press offices including those of the Majority Socialist Party's newspaper, *Vorwärts*, an act motivated more by defiance than by strategic considerations. The demobilized troops remained neutral, as did the majority of Berlin workers, who were largely out of sympathy with the aims of the extremists, and it became clear by the evening of 6 January that through lack of widespread support the revolt had failed. As Rosenberg has pointed out, not only were the Independents wholly unprepared for a full-scale revolution, they were for the most part opposed to it. This was also true of many Obleute. Despite Luxemburg's advice not to proceed with the putsch, the fanatical elements who had occupied the press offices refused to leave, blinded by their Utopian fervour to the hopelessness of their struggle. Acting out of misplaced comradeship Luxemburg and Liebknecht stood by their besieged colleagues.

Dittmann attempted to mediate between the two sides but found Ebert more intransigent than the Spartacists. Ebert had decided to demonstrate once and for all that the government was in control, and he called upon Noske, who had been made Commander-in-Chief of the government forces, to order military intervention against the Bolshevik threat. On 11 January Noske ordered a regular army unit from Potsdam and a detachment of Freikorps to shell the besieged *Vorwärts* building. Several Spartacists, who soon surrendered, were shot while emerging from the building. Rosa Luxemburg and Karl Liebknecht were clubbed to death in cold blood by cavalry officers while on their way to prison in Moabit on 15 January, several days after order had been restored. Their murder was followed by many more atrocities as right-wing troops wrought their vengeance on the left-wing Putschists, and indulged their anti-Bolshevik *ressentiments* and their dislike of the régime. The assassination deprived the German left of its two most independently minded figures. Their successors were pale imitations who soon fell under the control of Moscow.

The assassins of Liebknecht and Luxemburg were tried by court martial – a court of justice which could not at the time be relied upon for impartiality, and whose continuing existence after the revolution was incompatible with the democratic ideals of the Republic. Several accomplices were discharged and those who were condemned were subsequently helped to escape from detention. A double standard of justice had become the order of the day: it was to continue throughout the fourteen years of the Republic.

Further revolutionary outbreaks which occurred during the following weeks were swiftly contained by the Freikorps and as the socialist workers in the ranks were replaced by recruits from the demobilized Reichswehr divisions, their anti-revolutionary vigour increased. A rear-guard action was fought in March by the Berlin Workers' Councils who had realized too late that the revolution had misfired. They called for a general strike in a last attempt to restore the power of the councils. Noske ordered that anyone found with a weapon in his possession was to be shot summarily. This order gave in effect, if not in its intention, *carte blanche* to the Freikorps, and led to the murder of over a thousand workers. The effect of the Freikorps intervention was twofold. It decided the fate of the councils for all time; from this point they survived only in the form of works councils, *Betriebsräte*, which possessed little effective power. It also alienated many workers who had previously supported the Ebert régime. This decline in support for the government was the direct result of the conflict between the opposing socialist groups: between the continuing revolution demanded by the Spartacists and other extremists and the policy of cautious evolution of the Majority Socialists.

In one sense the Majority Socialists had become a conservative political force identifying themselves increasingly with the state and the tradition of the Empire, and avoiding introducing radical innovations. On the other hand it is essential to ask whether they could have considered following an alternative, revolutionary, policy. The supply of food and work was considered more important than the achievement of doctrinaire socialist aims. The broad mass of the population wished for nothing more than the restoration of law and order and return to peace-time conditions. Nevertheless, the civil war between the parties of the left, the most tragic event in the revolution, produced a permanent split in German Social Democracy, which constantly prevented the Republic from establishing itself. 'The enemy on the right,' had, as Gay remarks, 'only to wait.'

3

Versailles, Weimar Constitution and Domestic Insurrection

Survey of the Period 1919–20

THE DECISION of the Council of People's Representatives to hold elections to a National Constituent Assembly formally brought the revolutionary period to an end. The National Assembly would have two main functions. It was to formulate a Constitution for the Republic which would provide basic legislation for the political, social and economic structure of the state and it was to be responsible for the formidable task of negotiating a peace treaty with the Allies.

Apart from fulfilling these two formal duties the government would have to deal with the many urgent domestic problems which faced the Republic. Most serious were the threats posed to its integrity by Bolshevik revolutionaries in Bavaria and by the counter-revolutionary Freikorps in Berlin. The attitude of the army leadership to the two Putsches aroused grave misgivings for while it eagerly suppressed the Bavarian revolt, it remained benevolently neutral towards the right-wing Putschists, by not intervening against them on the side of the legal government. Despite the army's questionable behaviour it was allowed to develop into an autonomous body, free from close parliamentary control.

The progress of the Republic was thus hindered both by strong internal opposition and by difficulties owing to the severity of the Allied peace terms. Germany was presented with an ultimatum: non-acceptance of the treaty would provoke a resumption of hostilities. The government, a coalition of Majority Socialists and Centrists, had no option but to sign. For this they incurred the eternal hatred of the right wing who subscribed to the stab-in-the-back legend which maintained that the Reich had not suffered military defeat but had been betrayed by left-wing politicians with ulterior motives – a legend which won widespread credence. One of the major failings of the Constitution was that it made no provision for dealing with anti-democratic threats. A model 'free' Constitution, it failed to realize that democracy can only flourish in a society which wishes to be democratic. By granting extremists the right to undermine democratic government, the Constitution formally contributed to the downfall of the Republic.

The Political Parties Competing in 1919

The parties competing for the electors' votes in 1919 were, from a political and sociological standpoint, largely unchanged, despite the appearance of many new faces and the adoption of new political labels. Social Democracy, Liberalism and Conservatism still constituted the three main socio-political groups. Within these groups, however, there occurred a considerable realignment of political factions.

Liberal Germany had been split into two parties since the unification of the nation in 1871. The parent National Liberal Party, more national than liberal, underwrote with the Conservatives Bismarck's policies. It was abandoned by its left-wingers who formed the new Progressive Party, *Fortschrittspartei*. The Progressives, concerned by the erosion of liberalism, joined with the Socialists in opposing Bismarck. In November 1918 several of the country's most able and intelligent politicians, including many members of the Progressive Party, who had forecast the impending disaster of 1918 and had formerly dissociated themselves from the jingoism of the National Liberals, decided to found the German Democratic Party, *Deutsche Demokratische Partei*, DDP, in which they hoped to unite truly radical liberals. Their main support came from the progressive middle classes: industrialists, financiers, professional men and academics. Their membership included many of Germany's most gifted men: Friedrich Naumann, the political theorist and social reformer; Hugo Preuss, the constitutional lawyer; Max Weber, the Heidelberg professor, historian and founder of sociology as an academic discipline; Theodor Wolff, editor of the *Berliner Tageblatt*, a newspaper that had maintained its progressive liberal identity through the darkest days of the war; Hjalmar Schacht, the Berlin bank director; Walther Rathenau, the managing director of Germany's great industrial concern AEG, *Allgemeine Elektrizitätsgesellschaft*, and Carl von Siemens, head of the electrical firm. It was a truly impressive list of men, all leaders in their particular fields, who joined together to promote a progressive policy of radical economic and social reform within the framework of parliamentary democracy.

The founders of the DDP excluded from the leadership, though not from party membership, those whom they regarded to be political liabilities. One such potentially compromising figure was Gustav Stresemann, leader of the National Liberal Party. Stresemann, born in 1878, was the son of a Berlin beer merchant. In 1905 he entered the Reichstag as a National Liberal deputy at the age of twenty-eight, already a successful businessman. Despite his youth he became leader of the parliamentary party within twelve years, chosen for his remarkable energy, intelligence and political flair. Throughout the war, together with the majority of his party colleagues, he remained a staunch annexationist and supporter of unrestricted submarine warfare. Politically tainted with the reputation of being a 'Ludendorff man', Stresemann found that he had backed the wrong horse and would have to pay for his mistakes. He had hoped to participate in reuniting the liberal parties but, denied a leading rôle in the DDP, he decided to form his own German People's Party, *Deutsche Volkspartei*, DVP, which was formally constituted on 15 December 1918.

Ironically, Stresemann stood further left than many Democrats, but he was forced to seek support from the moderate right-wing politicians, drawn mainly from the right wing of the National Liberals and the former Free Conservatives, a splinter group which had broken away from the main Conservative Party. He thus found himself in the company of many with whom he disagreed violently. Among the party's staunchest members were business magnates, such as Hugo Stinnes and Fritz Thyssen, who had grave misgivings about the régime believing that it would introduce widespread nationalization. Further support came from the professions, the civil service and the financial world. The DVP remained in open opposition to the Republic until the early 1920s, its programme encumbered with outdated shibboleths about the virtues and lofty ideals of the Hohenzollern Empire. Campaigning for the election presented the DVP with a major problem, for in most constituencies the party organization of the National Liberal Party had been taken over by the Democrats, and they had little time to construct a new machine. A desperate attempt to attract middle-class voters was made by professing support for equality and personal liberty, while raising the spectre of Bolshevik socialism, to which they declared themselves to be wholly opposed. Despite any verbal concessions to Liberalism, however, they remained essentially a conservative party.

In the middle of November 1918 a number of Conservatives, racialist members of the Free Conservatives, members of the super-patriotic Fatherland Party, *Vaterlandspartei*, and sundry right-wingers, combined to form a party of the far right, the German National People's Party, *Deutschnationale Volkspartei*, DNVP. Paradoxically, as Heiber points out, the more removed a party was from the people, the greater it felt the need to pay lip-service to popular rule by including the word *Volk* in its title. While recognizing the existence of parliamentary democracy – it could hardly do otherwise if it wished to have a voice in the Reichstag – it pledged its support for the restoration of the monarchy, and for the maintenance of the privileged classes. It further undertook to suppress left-wing associations – in particular the trade unions – and to oppose all social reform. It championed the continuation of Prussian predominance in the Reich, for it was in Prussia that it enjoyed most support. Its adherents came predictably from capitalist groups: the land-owning Junkers of the north east, industrialists and the upper middle classes. Other right-wing sectors of the community provided further members, among whom were to be found many army officers and academics, monarchists and a large number of Protestant North Germans. They were united in their determination to rally behind the black, white and red flag of the Empire, symbol of their former position of privilege.

Apart from the three socialist parties, whose genesis, membership and aims have already been discussed, there was a further large political party, the Centre Party, *Zentrumspartei*, Z. Its composition did not conform to the politico-sociological principles which determined that of other parties, for it was essentially confessional. Its prime function was to safeguard the interests of the Roman Catholic Church. It had been founded in 1871 specifically to defend Catholicism against Bismarck's systematic attack on the Church –

the *Kulturkampf*. Its followers, united by a common faith, not by political or economic interest, represented a broad cross-section of society. It was, therefore, less committed than other parties to political dogma and could afford to tolerate a wide spectrum of opinion among its politicians. This flexibility facilitated its transition into a republican party and its participation in succeeding governments until 1932. Indeed, its leader, Matthias Erzberger, had introduced the peace resolution into the Reichstag in 1917. The only reservation about the Republic voiced by delegates at a party conference at the end of December 1918 was that it should be democratic, not socialist, by which they meant that they supported government by parliamentary democracy, not government by popular councils, for only democracy would, they believed, guarantee them freedom to practise their faith without interference. On 12 November 1918 two Bavarian members of the Centre Party announced their decision to form a splinter party, the Bavarian People's Party, *Bayrische Volkspartei*, BVP, in the newly proclaimed Free State of Bavaria. They continued to work in collaboration with the parent party in the Reichstag until January 1920 when, in reaction against Erzberger's attack on the financial independence of the *Länder*, they formally broke off relations. Dyed-in-the-wool particularists, they refused to tolerate the dominance of Prussian North Germany over the remainder of the country. Their separatist slogan, Bavaria for the Bavarians, *Bayern für die Bayern*, indicates that particularism took precedence in their minds over the claims of a united Catholic party. The unreliability of the BVP in questions affecting the stability of the Reich was to become all too evident in the attitude of their member, Gustav von Kahr, who as Bavarian Prime Minister maintained a relentless opposition to the Reich. Only when Hitler attempted to seize power in Munich in 1923 did the BVP moderate its hostility.

The Reich Election of January 1919

With law and order restored in the streets of Berlin, the elections for the National Assembly took place as planned on 19 January 1919, only four days after the murder of Liebknecht and Luxemburg. The elections were conducted according to a provisional electoral law, which had been drafted by Hugo Preuss, Secretary of State for Internal Affairs in the Provisional Government, and which had been accepted by the popular representatives on 30 November 1918. In contrast to the electoral law introduced in Bismarck's period of office, it provided for universal suffrage for all over the age of twenty (formerly only men over twenty-five years of age had enjoyed the franchise). Majority voting was rejected in favour of proportional representation.

THE ELECTION OF 19 JANUARY 1919

The results of the election were as follows:

		Votes cast (to nearest thousand)	Number of seats	Percentage of total vote
USPD	Independent Social Democratic	2,317,000	22	7·6
MSPD	Majority Social Democratic	11,509,000	163	37·9
DDP	Democratic	5,642,000	75	18·6
Z	Centre	5,980,000	91	19·7
DVP	People's	1,346,000	19	4·4
DNVP	Nationalist	3,121,000	44	10·3
Others		484,000	7	1·7
Total (to nearest hundred thousand)		30,500,000	421	

83 per cent of the electorate voted.

Statistics taken from *Die Zerstörung der deutschen Politik* ed. H. Pross.

The result was a great success for the three parties who had pledged their unqualified support for the régime, the MSPD, the DDP and the *Zentrum*. Contrary to expectations, the combined vote of the two socialist parties failed to command a majority in the country. Many of their former supporters appear to have transferred their allegiance to the Democrats and Centrists. The extremist parties of the left and right, USPD, DVP and DNVP, came off badly. Their hostility to the Republic was clearly not shared by many voters at this time. In fact quite a large majority of the electorate, seventy-six per cent, had declared itself in favour of the Republic and parliamentary democracy, rejecting both proletarian dictatorship and a return to authoritarian monarchy. The MSPD leadership, though they had hoped for a greater share of the vote, accepted the implications of the poll and initiated negotiations with other parties with the aim of forming a coalition government.

On 3 February 1919 Ebert formally relinquished the sovereignty which had been vested in him by Max of Baden and the workers' and soldiers' councils and handed control of the country's government to the National Assembly. The three months' rule of the Provisional Government had come to an end.

The First Session of the National Assembly and the Election of the President

The National Assembly decided to convene in the Thuringian town, Weimar. The choice was not fortuitous. It was feared that undue pressures might be exerted on parliament if it met in Berlin for it could not be guaranteed that there would be no further *coups d'état* mounted in the capital. Indeed, the outcome of the attempted Putsch in March 1919 might well have been different if the government had been within striking distance, rather than some eighty-five miles away. Weimar also commended itself for its symbolic value. It was Germany's cultural shrine, the dwelling place of Goethe and Schiller, the town which lent its name to Weimar Classicism, the period of German literature dedicated to the humane ideal. The choice of Weimar, however, could not, as Gay observes, guarantee the nature or even the survival of the régime.

Ebert opened the first session of parliament on 6 February with a speech in which he extolled the virtues of republican government and parliamentary democracy. He reminded the deputies that the country's present misery had been caused not by those who had assumed power during the revolution but by the deposed monarchs and their henchmen, a fact which many already conveniently overlooked. Ebert went on to warn the Allies against imposing a revanchist peace treaty on Germany. Now that Imperial Germany had been destroyed – the Allies' alleged war aim – the democratic régime should be treated fairly, in accordance with Wilson's Fourteen Points. He concluded by exhorting the Assembly to create an egalitarian society, an aim which every citizen should strive to achieve.

The Assembly's first task was to elect a president of the Reich, and on 11 February under a provisional constitutional law Ebert was chosen as first President of the Republic. He accepted the formidable appointment in the conviction that at that critical time it was essential that every citizen should fulfil whatever duties the state imposed. He assured the Assembly that he would perform his duties to the best of his abilities and without conscious political bias, acting in accordance with the Constitution as a representative of the whole population. He was realistic and honest enough to remind the Assembly that as a product of the working class and one who had embraced the ideals of Social Democracy at an early age, he could not and did not wish to deny his origins and beliefs. He realized that although his election to the presidency did not imply that the Assembly endorsed an exclusively socialist policy, it nevertheless thereby recognized the important rôle to be played by the working class in the future of the country. He pledged himself to uphold maximum personal freedom in so far as this was consistent with the maintenance of the rule of law; accordingly, he would oppose tyranny from whatever source. His immediate aim was the conclusion of a peace treaty which, he believed, would restore the right of Germans to self-determination. He further intended to see the introduction of a new constitution which would safeguard economic and social equality. His political belief, if one analyses this speech together with that delivered five days earlier, can be characterized as an amalgam of right-wing Socialism and progressive liberalism, a creed which he believed would foster the partnership between employer and employee and unite the two sides of industry and, ultimately, society.

The Formation of the Weimar Coalition

Ebert's first task as President was to nominate a Prime Minister. He chose his old colleague, Philipp Scheidemann, and asked him to form a government. As the MSPD controlled only one hundred and sixty-five seats out of four hundred and twenty-one, a coalition would have to be created. The Majority Socialists were willing to collaborate in a government with the Independents on condition that the wishes of the electorate were respected and that no further internal unrest was contemplated. The Independents refused to accept the MSPD's offer; they did not wish to compromise themselves by joining forces once again with a 'bourgeois, militarist' party. Scheidemann had no option, therefore, but to turn to the bourgeois parties and to resurrect the coalition which had opposed the Imperial Government before the revolution, a coalition of the Majority Socialists, the Centre Party and the Democrats, successors to the Progressive Party. The MSPD stipulated that their coalition partners should pledge their support to the Republic, accept a programme of social reform, including, possibly, nationalization, and agree to a financial and taxation policy which would ensure that the burdens imposed by the war were placed on the shoulders of those who could most afford to bear them. The Centrists under pressure from the Christian trade unions, who had no wish to protect capital interests, and the Democrats accepted the conditions and the coalition, known henceforth as the Weimar Coalition, came into being. The collaboration of three parties of differing shades of opinion, atheist Socialists, anti-clerical, liberal Democrats and Catholic Centrists, naturally obliged the cabinet to adopt a policy of compromise, of government by common consent, as a condition for its continuing existence. This fundamental principle of compromise, so often overlooked or condemned by opponents and often even by party members, determined to a large extent the frequent apparent inconsistencies of policy of successive coalitions.

The cabinet was composed of seven Socialists and an equal number of ministers drawn from the bourgeois parties. As well as the premiership, the Socialists were given all but two of the most influential portfolios: Noske remained Minister of Defence, *Reichswehrminister*, Landsberg continued as Minister of Justice and Wissell as Minister of Economics; Bauer joined the government as Minister of Labour. Preuss, a Democrat, remained Minister of the Interior, while Erzberger, the Centrist leader, became Minister without Portfolio. Count Brockdorff-Rantzau, who had been Secretary of State at the Foreign Office since December 1918, was retained as Foreign Minister; though an aristocrat and party-politically independent, he was progressive and liberal in outlook. It was considered that he would be an asset at the subsequent peace negotiations with the Allies. The remaining cabinet posts were filled by two Socialists, two Democrats and two Centrists.

The Programme of the National Assembly and the Bavarian Crisis

The newly-elected National Assembly had three main tasks to accomplish. It had to conclude a peace treaty with the Allied powers since the government's ability to tackle the many domestic problems with which it was faced depended to a considerable degree on the restoration of 'normal' international relations. It had also to adopt a new constitution to provide the legal basis for the Republic. In addition to these formal duties the government was faced with the immediate necessity of dealing with further internal insurrection, for the authority and integrity of the Reich was being seriously challenged by Bavarian separatists.

On 7 November 1918, before the announcement of the Kaiser's abdication, a separatist Bavarian Republic was proclaimed by the leader of the Bavarian Independent Social Democratic Party, Kurt Eisner. The same night the Bavarian King, Ludwig III, fled the state. Eisner, a fifty-year-old Schwabing bohemian intellectual, and former editor of the SPD newspaper, *Vorwärts*, headed the provisional government of Independent and Majority Socialists, which relied for its authority on the numerous workers', soldiers' and peasants' councils which had sprouted in Bavaria as elsewhere in the Reich. A passionate pacifist and violent opponent of 'Prussian militarism', he had been jailed for his views during the war. He refused to countenance using the methods of the Bolsheviks, holding that the electorate had to be convinced by rational argument of the validity of his political system. An opportunity to express their views was to be given them in a general election planned for the New Year.

The elections to the Bavarian Landtag, held on 12 January 1919, resulted in a severe defeat for Eisner's party which received only three mandates out of a total of one hundred and eighty. Even though the Centrists, now renamed Bavarian People's Party, remained the strongest party, they had lost their overall majority, while the Majority Socialists with only sixty-four mandates were in no position to form a coalition with Eisner. When he realized that all attempts to reach a compromise with other parties would prove fruitless Eisner decided on 21 February to tender his resignation. On his way to the Landtag he was shot dead by Count Anton von Arco-Valley, a twenty-one-year-old army lieutenant who resented Eisner's politics and Jewish faith. On learning of the assassination one of Eisner's more ardent supporters entered the parliamentary chamber armed. He shot and wounded Erhard Auer, the leader of the Majority Socialists, killing an officer who came to his aid, and attempted to hit other deputies. Gunfire burst forth from all sides of the chamber, another deputy was killed and several others wounded. Violence broke out throughout Bavaria. The soldiers' and workers' councils called a general strike and formed a Central Committee to supervise government policy. Intimidated by the gravity of the situation, the Landtag granted full powers to a Socialist government headed by Johannes Hoffmann which could count on the support of their colleagues in the Central Committee of Councils.

Several Independent Socialists, a majority of the members of the Central Committee and many Utopian intellectuals, such as the anarchist, Gustav Landauer, and the dramatist, Ernst Toller, were inspired to follow the lead of Béla Kun, who in March 1919 seized power in Hungary and established a Bolshevik régime, and on 7 April they proclaimed a Soviet Republic in Munich. The 'legal' government fled north to Bamberg and begged Scheidemann's government for military assistance. Noske sent a detachment of Freikorps who, together with local volunteers, marched on Munich. The Toller régime crumbled at the prospect of armed intervention. The resulting power vacuum was filled on 13 April by the establishment of a second Soviet régime under the leadership of two Marxist extremists, Eugen Leviné and Max Levien, acting on the recommendations of the Third International which had been set up a month previously in Moscow with the aim of spreading Bolshevism throughout central Europe. Their hurriedly formed 'red' army managed to hold out against the resistance of the civilian population and the Freikorps until 3 May. In the last bloody encounters between government and rebel forces hundreds of people, supporters and opponents of the Soviet government, were summarily shot.

The Bavarian Social Democrats had demonstrated a determination to prevent a proletariat dictatorship equal to that of the Reich party. It was not, however, the Republic which emerged victorious from the encounter but Bavarian particularism and the extreme right-wing Freikorps. Nor did their suppression of the Soviet régime safeguard the future of parliamentary democracy in Bavaria. The councils were disbanded, the legal government returned to Munich and was widened to include Democrats and members of the Bavarian People's Party. From this time on Bavaria and, in particular, Munich became the acknowledged haven for extreme right-wing adventurers whose presence was not desired in other parts of the Reich. This situation was tolerated by the population which had had its fill of left-wing rule in the preceding six months and which from this time tarred the Social Democrats with the same brush as the Bolsheviks. The political fervour engendered in Bavaria in 1919 spawned many reactionary organizations, in particular the Nazi party.

The Attitude of the National Assembly to the Forthcoming Peace Treaty

The conclusion of a fair, even lenient, peace treaty was held by the government to be essential if the Republic was to get off to a good start. This wish was by no means unreasonable or even un-realistic at this stage. Germany had, after all, made a decisive break with her Imperial past and had introduced, albeit belatedly, a system of parliamentary democracy. The Armistice had been signed on the basis of Wilson's Fourteen Points and it could be confidently expected that the peace treaty would conform to their spirit. It would be in the Allied interest to ensure that German democracy flourished. In fact, the treaty proved to be anything but lenient and opponents of the new régime were presented with the, for them welcome, opportunity of discrediting the Republic from the outset. Democracy, they argued, had been introduced as a panic measure to appease the Allies but had not produced the expected results from the Allies. This trojan horse (Eschenburg) had introduced much that was undesirable into the country and should be destroyed immediately. The politicians, in particular the Socialists, were either fools or traitors to have allowed Germany to fall prey to the mercy of the revanchist Allies. That their argument was purely destructive – not to mention inaccurate – and that they had no alternative to offer, was an objection which did not occur to the politically unaware.

The Allied Negotiations

Negotiations to draft a peace treaty between Germany and the Allied and Associated Powers opened on 18 January 1919 in Paris. There were seventy delegates, representing thirty-two nations. The main protagonist, Germany, was not invited to send a delegation, a decision which may have helped to satisfy Allied sentiments of revenge but which did not accord with normal diplomatic procedure and which made the task of the German government immeasurably more difficult.

The four main Allied powers sent their leading statesmen to

Paris: Lloyd George, the British Prime Minister, Woodrow Wilson President of the United States, and Vittorio Emanuele Orlando, Prime Minister of Italy. The discussions were held under the chairmanship of the French Premier, Clemenceau. Their brief was to conclude separate peace treaties with each of the five Central Powers, to construct a new European order with frontiers drawn according to the principle of self-determination and to establish a League of Nations whose function would be the maintenance of world peace. They were charged also with two more immediate tasks: the alleviation of widespread famine and the prevention of a Bolshevik seizure of power in central Europe. The threat of a Bolshevik revolution's engulfing Germany became all the more probable in the early months of 1919 which saw in March the establishment by Béla Kun of a communist state in Hungary followed by the proclamation of a soviet régime in Bavaria, and the formation of Comintern, the Communist Third International. The committees working on various sections of the treaty were consequently placed under considerable pressure to produce their drafts in the shortest possible time. Harold Nicholson, a member of the British delegation, likened the atmosphere in Paris to a 'riot in a parrot house'. It was little wonder that they made many regrettable, anomalous decisions.

The Aims of the Allies

The nature of the final draft was, of course, largely determined by the varying interests – both domestic and international – of the individual Allied countries. Wilson was inclined to view the situation with his idealistic, hyper-liberal vision, convinced of the moral validity of his Fourteen Points. The U.S.A. was naturally concerned to prevent the restoration of a European order which had so patently outlived its usefulness and to replace the out-worn concept of balance of power by a system of collective security. This was also partly true of the British view for Great Britain was preoccupied with her world-wide Empire rather than the restricted European sphere. The British delegates, however, were also obliged to follow popular opinion at home. The general election of 1919 had been fought successfully by Lloyd George under the slogans of 'hang the Kaiser' and of forcing Germany to pay reparations 'to the limit of her ability'. In the famous words of Sir Eric Geddes, Germany was to be squeezed like a lemon 'until the pips squeak'. These remarks were made in the belief that the electorate demanded revenge: for years they had been fed a diet of anti-German jingoism and, it was argued, they did not appreciate the need to modify their feelings after the Armistice had been signed.

The French adopted a far more overtly hostile attitude to Germany. The shame of 1870, the devastation of the country and the death of a million and a half young Frenchmen between 1914 and 1918 produced a lust for revenge and a desire for *sécurité*, security, that is, against the possibility of future invasion of French territory.

Wilson was no match for his European colleagues in debate. They soon saw through his unrealistic idealism and his inability to come to terms with the problems of practical politics. Only when Clemenceau persuaded him against his wishes to visit the devastated French war zone was he convinced of the validity of the French desire for *sécurité*. He was able to modify French insistence on the creation of an independent Rhineland state by guaranteeing U.S. military support for France in the event of a future Franco-German dispute. Otherwise he was largely unsuccessful in attacking the entrenched position of the French delegates. They were not convinced by the argument that, in extorting every last penny from Germany in reparations, France was merely sowing the seeds of a future conflict. Reparations were regarded by the French as the means of inflicting permanent damage on the German economy. Lloyd George made an equally vain attempt to point out the illogicality of expecting Germany to surrender large sums in reparations when, at the same time, the utmost was being done to cripple the German economy. The French remained intransigent.

The German Delegation Receives the Draft Treaty

On 24 April 1919 a German parliamentary delegation, headed by the Foreign Minister and Plenipotentiary, Count Brockdorff-Rantzau, arrived by train in Paris after a journey which had been deliberately routed through the devastated wastes of north-eastern France, an action designed to humiliate the Germans. The delegates had been charged with the government brief of ensuring that the terms of the treaty corresponded with the principles contained in the Fourteen Points. Intentional press leaks had led the German government to suspect – accurately, as they were soon to discover – that the Allied terms would be severe.

The two sides met on 7 May in an atmosphere of mutual mistrust and *froideur* in the Trianon at Versailles. Clemenceau, as chairman of the conference, delivered a short, bitter speech and handed over a single copy of the Allied draft to Brockdorff-Rantzau. No discussion between the two sides was permitted. The Allies maintained, unreasonably, that the terms were non-negotiable. Germany had the alternatives of accepting or rejecting the treaty *in toto*. As a concession the German government was allowed three weeks to submit in writing its observations on the draft. Brockdorff-Rantzau was outraged. Remaining seated, an act regarded by the Allies as a calculated insult, he replied to Clemenceau in equally uncompromising terms. The publication of the peace terms was received with incredulity by the German population. Irrespective of their political views, they condemned the treaty outright as a vindictive, retributive *Diktat*. An examination of its terms will show the grounds for their rancour.

The Terms of the Treaty: Germany's War Guilt

The treaty which both sides finally adopted was a lengthy, verbose document consisting of no less than 440 articles. The justification for the severity of the Allied demands rests in the assertion that Germany bore sole responsibility for the war: 'The Allied and Associated Governments affirm and Germany accepts the responsibility of Germany and her allies for causing all the loss and damage to which the Allies and Associated Governments and their nationals have been subjected as a consequence of the war imposed on them by the aggression of Germany and her allies' (article 231). The hyper-sensitive German delegation and the German press assumed this to mean that Germany was to admit *sole* responsibility for the war, an assumption which the Allies did not refute. The anti-republicans in Germany were able by citing article 231 to discredit both the Allies and the German signatories for it flagrantly contradicted the conciliatory tenor of the Fourteen Points. Its inclusion was a colossal diplomatic blunder. The argument of sole guilt was implicit in preceding articles: the Kaiser was indicted 'for a supreme offence against international morality and the sanctities of treaties' (article 227) and a request was made for his extradition from the

Netherlands to stand trial. Similarly the German government was required to 'hand over to the Allies and Associated Powers . . . all persons accused of having committed an act in violation of the laws or customs of war' (article 228). They were to be tried by an Allied tribunal. It was widely believed both in Germany and abroad that these demands had been motivated by considerations of political expedience rather than by any real belief on the part of the Allies in the moral rectitude of their case. The Dutch government wisely refused to comply with the request to extradite Wilhelm, which would almost certainly have resulted in his being sentenced to death.

Reparations

The War Guilt Clause provided the justification for the demand that Germany should pay full reparation 'for all damage done to the civilian population' (article 232). Since the Allies could not agree among themselves how much Germany should pay, the details of the bill including the total sum were to be calculated by an Inter-Allied Reparation Commission which was given until May 1921 to report. The Commission was to 'consider the claims and give the German Government a just opportunity to be heard' (article 233), but Germany was, unwisely, not granted permanent representation on the Commission. An interim instalment of 20,000 million gold marks (about one thousand million pounds sterling or about five thousand million dollars) was to be paid immediately, pending the decision of the Commission (article 235). The demand was regarded by the German government as a gross violation of the terms of the Armistice whereby Germany had agreed to pay compensation for damage caused in the war. While it was traditional practice for a conquered nation (though, technically, Germany had not been defeated) to be required to pay a tribute to the conquerors as, for example, France had paid Germany in 1871, to expect Germany to sign a blank cheque was an outrageous demand on the part of the Allies. The question of reparations was to bedevil European relations for the next twelve years.

Immediate compensation was to be made in kind to France and Belgium. This could be offset against the payments in cash. A bizarre collection of farm animals was to be transported to France, including 500 stallions, 30,000 fillies, 90,000 milch cows, 2,000 bulls, 100,000 sheep and 1,000 rams, and a proportionately smaller number was to be delivered to Belgium (articles 236–44). Germany was, moreover, to cede to France the Saar Basin 'in full and absolute possession, with exclusive rights of exploitation, unencumbered and free from all debts and charges of any kind' (article 45), as compensation for the coal mines destroyed in north-east France. The territory was to be placed under the control of the League of Nations; after fifteen years a plebiscite was to be held to determine the future of the region (annex § 34). An example of the grotesque triviality with which the Allies busied themselves is contained in article 246 which demanded that the skull of the Sultan Mkwawa which had been removed from the Protectorate of German East Africa be surrendered to the British government.

Guarantees

Guarantees were imposed on Germany to ensure that the reparations demanded were paid and that the other provisions of the treaty were fulfilled. All territory west of the Rhine together with the strategically vital bridgeheads of Cologne, Koblenz and Mainz were to be occupied by Allied troops for a period of fifteen years (article 248). Earlier, piecemeal evacuation of the area would be considered 'if the conditions of the present treaty are faithfully carried out by Germany' (article 429). It could also be delayed 'if at that date the guarantees against unprovoked aggression by Germany are not considered sufficient' (ibid.). The total cost of maintaining Allied armies of occupation in Germany was to be met by the German economy. To assuage French fears further it was decreed that the whole Rhineland to a depth of fifty kilometres from the east bank was to remain a demilitarized zone in perpetuity (articles 42–3). Violation of this demand would constitute a 'hostile act against the Powers signatory of this present Treaty and as calculated to disturb the peace of the world' (article 44). This decision was the minimum guarantee acceptable to France in return for her abandoning Clemenceau's previous demand for the creation of an independent Rhineland buffer state between France and Germany. In March 1936 when Hitler called the bluff of the Allies and ordered the Reichswehr into the Rhineland, a violation of both the Versailles Treaty and the Locarno Treaty of 1925, the Allies merely issued verbal protests.

Disarmament

Disarmament 'to the lowest point consistent with domestic safety' as Wilson had demanded (Point 4), was enshrined in article 8 of the treaty. There was, however, one important modification of Wilson's provision: multilateral disarmament was to be delayed until Germany had disarmed unilaterally. The terms for German disarmament demanded root and branch surgery for her armed forces. The air force was wholly banned (article 198), conscription was to be abolished (article 173), and the army general staff was to be disbanded immediately (article 160). The army, limited to a force of a hundred thousand men was to be recruited on a voluntary basis with a minimum period of service of twelve years, a stipulation designed to prevent the accumulation of a large reserve of trained soldiers (article 174). The army's duties were to be limited to 'the maintenance of order within the territory and to the control of the frontiers' (article 160) and, accordingly, all heavy artillery and tanks were forbidden. The fleet was to be reduced to a tenth of its pre-war strength and limited to ships under ten thousand tons. Submarines and Dreadnought-class battleships were specifically forbidden (articles 190–1). The remainder of the German fleet, interned in Scapa Flow in the Orkneys, was to be surrendered to the Allies (article 185).

To alleviate the effects of these restrictions the German Defence Ministry decided to create an army and navy in which quality compensated for quantity. Both services were manned by specialists and men of proven ability. These had perforce to be drawn largely from the élite which had enjoyed high position in the Imperial armed forces. This allowed them to preserve and maintain their position of privilege and to exclude from their ranks anyone of an 'unsatisfactory political persuasion', that is, left-wing. By allowing the army and navy the right to select their own officers they remained a 'monarchistic island' (Eschenburg) within the Republic.

Territorial Adjustments

These territorial arrangements which adhered approximately to the Fourteen Points and to Wilson's principle of self-determination (one of the Four Points of 4 July 1918) constitute the most reasonable section of the treaty, and aroused little comment in Germany. These included the restoration of Alsace-Lorraine to French rule

(Point 8, article 57), the decision to hold a plebiscite in Schleswig to enable the population to decide whether it wished to remain German or become Danish (articles 109–14), and the guarantee of Belgian independence and territorial integrity (Point 7, article 31). Less palatable to Germany was the decision to hold plebiscites in the areas around Eupen, Malmédy and Moresnet, situated on the German–Belgian frontier (articles 32–9) but at least there was the assurance that a decision would be reached by the self-determination of the population (the plebiscite, when it was held, proved to be a travesty of justice, an event which the German government could hardly be expected to foresee at that time).

The creation of a Polish state with access to the sea (Point 13), had also been accepted as a precondition for the Armistice. This involved carving a corridor through German territory to link the landlocked Polish state to the Baltic. The loss of the province of Posen was more readily acceptable since it was largely Polish-speaking, but the confiscation of West Prussia produced considerable resentment in Germany for it involved the loss of a considerable German-speaking minority and, worse, it severed East Prussia from the rest of the Reich, a partition which in 1919 was unique (articles 27 and 87). Wholly unacceptable was the decision to detach the exclusively German-speaking port of Danzig and establish it as a free city under the protection of the League of Nations (articles 100–102). The port, at the mouth of the Vistula, Poland's main waterway, was essential to Poland's commerce and, as such, could not be left under German sovereignty. In an attempt not to betray wholly the crusade of self-determination the Allies had hit upon this uneasy compromise. The inhabitants of the city were to be given the choice between becoming nationals of the Free City of Danzig and retaining German citizenship; all those who opted for German citizenship were required 'during the ensuing twelve months (to) transfer their place of residence to Germany' (articles 105–6), a wholly unreasonable demand which proved to be another useful weapon for those who later accused the Weimar Coalition of agreeing to the break-up of the Reich.

Memelland, the strip of territory which lay on the German side of the frontier between East Prussia and the newly created Baltic state of Lithuania, was also detached from the Reich and put under the control of the League of Nations for it was similarly held to be essential to the commerce of Lithuania to have access to the port at the mouth of the river Memel (articles 28 and 99). This decision had been mentioned neither in Wilson's programme nor in the Armistice agreement and flatly contradicted self-determination. The Allies, however, wished to promote the interests of Lithuania, one of the states forming the so-called *cordon sanitaire* which continued southwards through Poland, Czechoslovakia, Hungary, Rumania and Bulgaria between Bolshevik Russia and the west, and when in 1923 the Memelland was illegally annexed by Lithuania, the action was tacitly condoned by the League.

In the draft treaty which was handed to Brockdorff-Rantzau it was decreed that Upper Silesia, one of Germany's richest sources of raw materials and a thriving industrial centre, was to be surrendered to Poland. This clause was condemned as wholly unacceptable by Germans of all political creeds. It was the only provision which the Allies agreed to modify at the insistence of the German government, an indication of their own uncertainty about the wisdom of the decision.

In determining Germany's frontier with the newly formed Czechoslovak Republic, a successor state of the former Austro-Hungarian Empire, it was decided to adopt the pre-war frontier between Germany and Austria-Hungary (article 82). This decision was geopolitically and economically sound but offended against the principle of self-determination for it resulted in the inclusion within Czechoslovakia of more than a million German-speaking people. This indicates more clearly than any other territorial adjustment the impracticability of determining frontiers solely on the basis of self-determination, a slogan that in practice was more often than not equated with membership of a linguistic group. In the late 1930s the German minority in Czechoslovakia, the Sudeten Germans, were encouraged by the Nazis to demand 'freedom from Slav rule', which led ultimately to the dismemberment of the Czechoslovak state after the Munich agreement of 1938.

Germany was further denied the right to self-determination over the question of German-speaking Austria's desire to join the German Republic. Article 80 stated that 'Germany acknowledges and will respect strictly the independence of Austria, . . . she agrees that this independence shall be inalienable, except with the consent of the Council of the League of Nations.' Politically, the Allies' decision was sound: after waging total war against the Central Powers for four years, they had no intention of allowing the union of the two principal enemies. France, already preoccupied with the presence of 'ten million too many Germans' was determined to prevent six million Austrians from joining the Reich. Nevertheless, their action could not be reconciled with Wilson's former determination that the enemy should be accorded impartial justice and lack of discrimination (Five Particulars of 27 September 1918). Opponents of the treaty were given further justification for levelling a charge of hypocrisy against the Allies.

German Colonies

A similar charge could be applied to the decision to deprive Germany of her colonies. Whereas Wilson's Fifth Point had demanded 'a free, open-minded and absolutely impartial adjustment of all colonial claims', Germany was in fact required in article 119 to 'renounce in favour of the Principal Allied and Associated Powers all her rights and titles over her oversea possession.' Surrendered to the control of the League, they were placed under the mandatory administration of France and Great Britain, 'advanced nations who by reasons of their resources, their experience or their geographical position can best undertake . . . the tutelage of such people'. This was, of course, pure humbug.

Economic Clauses and Consequences

The territorial readjustments imposed further strains on the economy. Over a third of the country's coal supplies and three-quarters of her iron ore deposits were transferred to foreign countries, as well as much valuable agricultural land. In all, over fourteen per cent of the former area of the Reich and ten per cent of her population were lost. Despite these severe deprivations Germany's industry, after riding out the inflation crisis of the early 1920s, managed to recover remarkably quickly. Arguably the confiscation of her colonies, though intended as an insult and a means of impoverishing Germany, saved her from having to squander scarce economic resources abroad, thus indirectly assisting her economic recovery.

That the Allies intended to delay – even prevent – the reconstruction of German industry is not in doubt. The enforced reduction of the fleet applied also to the merchant navy, and thereby was intended to benefit the export trade of the Allied nations. Further commercial clauses ensured that the importation of Allied goods into Germany would enjoy preference over those of other countries (article 264), while Germany was forbidden to export goods to any other foreign country at a price less than that quoted to an Allied state (articles 265–6),

The League of Nations

The opening articles of the treaty deal with the establishment of a League of Nations which had been an essential part in Wilson's vision of a peaceful world. The aims of the League were likewise noble: it was to 'promote international co-operation and to achieve international peace and security by the obligations not to resort to war, by the preservation of open, just and honourable relations between nations, by the firm establishment of the understanding of international law as the actual rule of conduct among Governments and by maintenance of justice and a scrupulous respect for all treaty obligations in the dealings of organized people with one another.' The lofty ideal of creating an international body whose authority was believed to exceed that of its individual members was seen as a means of preventing a recurrence of the international anarchy which had been largely responsible for the outbreak of war in 1914. It purported also to offer collective security for the member states against the imperialist strivings, whether Bolshevik or otherwise, of their stronger neighbours. Irrespective of the nature of the régimes they were to pledge themselves to live in friendly co-existence. However, the influence of the League was to remain purely moral. It had no means of imposing its will on recalcitrant sovereign member states.

The exclusion of Germany from the League was possibly the most shortsighted of the Allies' retributive peace terms. Germany's application for membership could not be considered, they sanctimoniously decreed, until she had mended her militaristic ways, one of the very dangers which the League intended to prevent. It seems clear that the exclusion of Germany, in defiance of Wilson's stated intention of founding 'a general association of nations', was motivated by an odious desire to teach Germany a lesson. The Allies' feelings of moral superiority and feelings of revenge towards

Germany blinded them to the harmful effect which their policy of deliberate obstruction would have on the struggling democratic Republic. It is a bitter irony that their ostracism of the Republic played into the hands of the opponents of democracy, those very sections of the population which had filled leading rôles in the war. Harold Nicholson wrote of his colleagues in Paris, 'The historian with every justification will come to the conclusion that we were very stupid men. I think we were. Yet I also think that the factor of stupidity is inseparable from all human affairs. It is too often disregarded as an inevitable concomitant of human behaviour; it is too often employed merely as a term of personal affront.'

The National Assembly's Debate on the Treaty

The President and the Reich government issued a proclamation on 8 May condemning the peace terms. It read: 'An act of boundless and immeasurable force is to be perpetrated on the German people. Such a dictated peace will provoke new hatred between peoples and in the course of history new murders. The world will lose all hope in a League of Nations which was intended to free peoples and secure peace. The aim of this forced peace is the fragmentation of the German people, the condemnation of German workers to wage slavery in the hands of foreign capitalism, the eternal bondage of the new German Republic by the imperialism of the Entente.' Despite the rhetoric the proclamation contained a fair and accurate assessment of Versailles and its consequences.

On 12 May the National Assembly debated the terms of the draft treaty. All delegates, with the exception of the Independent Socialists who acknowledged the futility of opposing the Allies and who confidently awaited the outbreak of world revolution, declared the terms to be unacceptable. Scheidemann, the Prime Minister (as the government leader was then known) predicted that the hand that fettered Germany by accepting the Diktat would surely perish. What even moderate politicians forgot, however, when attacking the immorality of the treaty was the severity of the terms which their predecessors had imposed on Russia at Brest-Litovsk a year previously. Would a victorious Germany have imposed less severe penalties on a defeated France?

Brockdorff-Rantzau submitted his government's observations on the draft to the Allies. In these exception was taken to numerous articles, in particular to the War Guilt Clause, thereby unwittingly ensuring, as Heiber points out, that it continued to be the subject of acrimonious debate throughout the life of the Republic and one which was used successfully by the Nazis to discredit the régime and those who signed the treaty.

The Allied Ultimatum and the Fall of the Scheidemann Cabinet

Reaction to the outrage which the terms had aroused in Germany was mixed. The British belatedly attempted to alleviate the severity of the terms, conscious of fostering German resentment. The French refused to modify their demands with the single exception of Upper Silesia, where a plebiscite would be held to determine whether the territory was to remain within Germany or be surrendered to Poland (article 88). On 16 June the Allies handed an ultimatum to the German delegation: the treaty was to be ratified by Germany within five days (later extended to seven), otherwise Germany would be invaded by Allied troops.

The members of the government were undecided whether to accept. Three leading members, Scheidemann, Brockdorff-Rantzau and Hugo Preuss, the Minister of the Interior, opposed acceptance, while Matthias Erzberger, Minister without Portfolio – though equally critical of the severity of the Allies' demands – argued that refusal to comply with the ultimatum would merely prolong the misery of the people and might encourage separatism in the Rhineland and Bavaria. Their dissent led to the dissolution of the cabinet on 20 June.

The Bauer Cabinet Accepts the Treaty

Ebert, whose task it was as President to choose a successor to Scheidemann, invited Gustav Bauer, Social Democratic Minister of Labour in the previous government, to head a new coalition. Since the Democrats refused to participate in a cabinet which would forever be remembered for having acceded to the Allied Diktat, it comprised only Social Democrats and Centrists. (The Democrats rejoined the coalition on 2 November when the danger was past.) Erzberger was created Vice-Chancellor and Minister of Finance and the Social Democrat, Hermann Müller, took over the Foreign Ministry from Brockdorff-Rantzau.

On 22 June, the day before the Allied ultimatum was due to expire, the National Assembly met to make their decision. Conscious of the odium they would certainly incur, the majority of the Social Democrats and the Centrists, under the threat of Allied invasion, reluctantly authorized acceptance of the treaty, while the Democrats, Populists and Nationalists voted against signing (two hundred and thirty-one votes for, one hundred and thirty-eight against). Acceptance was to be conditional on the deletion from the text of article 231, the War Guilt Clause, and article 228 which demanded the extradition of war criminals.

It was doubtful whether the Allies would have been willing to consider the exemption of the two clauses but news of two German acts of defiance, as Heiber remarks, decided the issue once and for all. On 21 June the commanders of the German fleet, which was interned in Scapa Flow and due to be surrendered to the British navy, decided to preserve their self-respect and ordered the scuttling of their ships. On the same day French standards which had been captured in the Franco-Prussian war and which under the terms of the treaty were to be returned to France were ceremoniously burned publicly in Berlin.

The Allies rejected both German provisos out of hand and insisted on their stated dead-line, 7 p.m. on 23 June. The German government was placed in a serious quandary, for they feared the reaction of the army if the treaty were accepted with the two 'humiliation clauses'. Hindenburg, while rejecting the possibility of military resistance, voiced his preference for a Wagnerian *Heldentod* to the acceptance of a dictated peace. Groener was hardly more helpful: as a private citizen he advised acceptance, but as First General Quartermaster he felt obliged to reject the treaty with its slur on the army. Thus the Hindenburg Myth and the honour of the Reichswehr were maintained.

On 23 June the Reichstag decided that the vote of the previous day should be deemed to cover acceptance of the whole treaty, a device intended to avoid any politician's incurring the blame for submitting to the Diktat – the opposition parties went as far as to recognize formally the patriotic motives of the government. Within a few days, however, an attempt was made on the life of Erzberger, the arch 'November Criminal', and the delegates, in particular the Foreign Minister, Hermann Müller, and Hans Bell, the Centrist

Minister of Transport, who signed the treaty were subjected to continuous criticism for their 'treacherous act'.

The treaty was signed on 28 June 1919 in the Hall of Mirrors at Versailles, the scene half a century earlier of the proclamation of the German Empire, a coincidence which was hardly fortuitous. Woodrow Wilson was not present for the U.S. Senate had refused to ratify the treaty and the establishment of the League: America's retreat into isolationism had begun. Wilson, his vision of a new world order shattered, collapsed in September 1919 and spent the last three years of his life as an invalid.

The Republic thus incurred the odium of accepting peace terms which concluded a war launched and waged by the defunct Empire. The army, whose Supreme Command had been largely responsible for the costly delay in concluding an armistice, emerged with an untarnished image. Shortly after the acceptance of the treaty Ludendorff and Hindenburg resigned their commissions, Groener resigned to take up a political career, and the Supreme Army Command, in accordance with Allied demands, was dissolved forthwith.

The Stab-in-the-Back Legend

Versailles presented the Nationalists with a persuasive pretext for heaping blame for Germany's plight on the Republic and its supporters. Scheidemann's remark about the 'fettering of Germany' was quoted as proof of an international conspiracy to destroy the Reich. Large sections of the middle class, who had been prepared to tolerate the Republic in the hope that it would succeed in obtaining favourable peace terms from the Allies, were easily wooed in their mood of despair to espouse the DNVP's anti-republican cause. The Allies, in failing to realize that the democratically elected government with which they were dealing could not be equated with the former Imperial régime, thus added fuel to the Nationalist fire.

Since the conclusion of the Armistice, there had arisen an acrimonious, heated debate: who was responsible for Germany's collapse? As early as November 1918 army spokesmen had bruited abroad the fallacious suggestion that the army had been betrayed by the civilian population: politicians, pacifists and war-profiteers. The myth grew throughout 1919, was incorporated into Ludendorff's memoirs in his attempt to exculpate himself from Germany's defeat, and found expression in Hindenburg's report to the committee set up by the National Assembly to enquire into the conduct of the war and the reasons for Germany's collapse. At Ludendorff's insistence his former comrade – they had both been obliged to resign from the High Command after the signing of the treaty – accompanied him to testify before the committee in November 1919. Hindenburg refrained from answering the committee's questions and read aloud a prepared statement about Germany's defeat. Purporting to quote the words of an English general, whose name unfortunately escaped him, he maintained that the army had been stabbed in the back by persons whom he need not point out. Hindenburg's statement, probably manufactured, Heiber suggests, by either Ludendorff or the Nationalist leader, Helfferich, occasioned wide publicity, and, though partly untrue, quickly won adherents, especially among those whose national pride had been severely shaken by the events of 1918 and 1919. After all, they argued, the German army had defeated the Russians in the east, had been able to concentrate its forces on the western front and at the time of the Armistice had been deep in enemy territory. On 11 November even Ebert had greeted the army on its return to Berlin with the words, 'You return unbeaten on the field, I salute you.' The Republic had been created as an act of treason, they deduced. In attacking the 'November Criminals' who had formed the Provisional Government – Socialists and Jews – these opponents of the régime could maintain that they were acting from patriotic motives. The simplistic doctrine was propagated by the Nationalist press, which launched a virulent campaign against the Republic and its advocates. The campaign, clothed in a mantle of moral superiority, led to a reign of terror which culminated in several political assassinations and the Kapp Putsch of 1920. Hitler later used the persuasive theory of the stab in the back as the basis of much of his political argument in *Mein Kampf* and learned much from the success of the 'big lie': as Bullock points out, the lie for all its enormity was eagerly accepted by many simply because they wanted to accept it.

The National Assembly Adopts the Weimar Constitution

Having concluded peace terms with the Allies the National Assembly could now turn its attention to its formal duty: the formulation and adoption of a constitution for the Republic.

Professor Hugo Preuss, a Berlin lawyer and founder member of the

Democratic Party, had been given the task of drafting a new constitution as early as 12 November 1918 by the Provisional Government in which he served in an advisory capacity as Secretary of State for the Interior. After the elections of February 1919 Preuss, now Reich Minister for the Interior, continued his work as chairman of a Constitutional Committee which was composed of delegates to the National Assembly drawn from each major political party. The draft Constitution formulated by the committee was submitted to the Assembly on 31 July 1919 and accepted by a majority of two hundred and sixty-two votes to seventy-five. Opposition to the Constitution came from the German National People's Party, the German People's Party and the Independent Social Democratic Party. The extreme right and left thus formally recorded their hostility to the régime. On 11 August the Constitution was signed and promulgated by the President.

The Drafting of the Constitution

The Preuss Committee was faced with a daunting task: that of drafting a constitution for a new republic with a modern industrial society. Those features of Bismarck's Constitution of 1871 which they considered valuable were retained or modified to provide a basis for the new document. To this foundation they added elements from the French, Swiss and U.S. Constitutions, a few socialist principles and many of the National Liberal ideals of the 1848 revolution. The final document was necessarily somewhat of a hotchpotch compromise, since it had to satisfy the wishes of the three coalition parties. On one vital topic in particular the Constitution was silent: as Eschenburg points out, it should have been considered more important in 1919 to initiate a programme of political and economic education for the electorate than to try to achieve a change of heart by means of constitutional innovation. Without the consent of the population and its appreciation of the political and economic situation no constitution, however ideal in theory, can function efficiently. It was surely an act of self-delusion to believe that the population was now markedly more politically aware than it had been before the war. The essentially legalistic approach to the introduction of democratic government testifies to the political inexperience of the Constitutional Committee.

An examination of the Constitution must consider its effectiveness in practice as well as its intentions. How far was it successful in providing a legal framework and a viable system of government and administration for the society for which it was intended? The document, divided into two main sections subdivided into articles (§) deals firstly with the organization of the state and secondly with the position of the individual within the state, the fundamental rights and duties of the German people.

The Reich

The preamble to the Constitution proclaimed Germany to be a democratic state: supreme power and authority was formally vested in the people. The state was, however, nowhere referred to as a republic, a term felt by many non-Socialists to smack too much of revolution. Unhappily, in an attempt to create an impression of continuity, the title Reich (Empire), despite the autocratic, imperialist overtones of the term, was retained. Against Preuss's advice the Constitutional Committee advocated the establishment of a quasi-federal structure, comprising the former states of the Empire, renamed provinces, *Länder*. Opposition to the unitary state which Preuss had championed was motivated by a fear, prevalent particularly in south Germany, that a unified Reich would in practice be nothing other than an enlarged Prussia. The new federal structure did little, however, seriously to challenge the preponderance of Prussia which already controlled three-fifths of the territory and population of Germany. This structural weakness could have been remedied only by the dismemberment of Prussia into smaller units – a decision enforced by the Allies in 1945. In 1919 a similar suggestion was successfully rejected by those who had a vested interest in maintaining the unity of Prussia.

The Organs of Government

The autocratic system of government provided for in Bismarck's Constitution was replaced by parliamentary institutions. The formerly powerful Federal Council, Bundesrat, was replaced by the Reichsrat, a body which pursued the interests of the Länder but which exercised no legislative and administrative power over the Reich as a whole. Executive power, formerly vested solely in the Kaiser, was shared between the Reich president and the Reich government. The Reichstag, previously merely participant in the legislative process, found itself with vastly increased power. It became the central authority and enjoyed normally both legislative and administrative superiority over all other organs of government.

The Reichstag

The Reichstag, composed of popularly elected representatives, had two functions: it was the supreme legislature and it exercised parliamentary control over the government and the president. This contrasted starkly with its former rôle which had been confined to drafting legislation and controlling the budget. Apart from formulating legislation on all but the minor domestic matters, the Reichstag was exclusively responsible for controlling the government's policy in foreign affairs, defence, finance, trade and communications (§ 6). In internal affairs it bore sole responsibility for the formulation of a civil and criminal code of law, judicial procedure, police affairs, social security and transport (§ 7). Reich legislation was deemed superior to that of the Länder parliaments, a provision which ensured that the central government retained overall control (§ 13).

Electoral Procedure

The Reichstag was elected for a period of four years (§ 23) by universal suffrage (§ 22). Unlike its predecessor which was convened by order of the Kaiser, the Reichstag under the Weimar Constitution possessed the right and the duty to convene itself (§§ 23, 24) by holding popular elections.

The electoral procedure was cumbersome. The sovereign people were to elect their parliamentary representatives equally and directly. All citizens over the age of twenty were eligible to vote (previously women and men under twenty-five had been denied the franchise). It was decided to adopt proportional representation as the electoral system, since it accorded equal validity to each vote and assured the representation in parliament of minority groups. Without proportional representation the smaller, middle-class parties feared that they might lose their identity. The country was divided into thirty-five large constituencies in which the electors were required to cast votes not for individual candidates, but for a political party.

One representative was elected for every sixty thousand votes cast and lists of party candidates drawn up by the local party committees, determined who was to receive a seat in parliament. Compared with the system of majority vote as used, for example, in the United Kingdom, proportional representation is in one sense more democratic in that it reflects with greater arithmetic accuracy the wish of the electorate. However, without built-in safeguards – such as that embodied in the electoral law of the German Federal Republic which decrees that no party shall enjoy representation in parliament unless it polls at least five per cent of the total vote – it tends to produce a multiplicity of minor and splinter parties. During the fourteen years of the Republic no single party was returned with an overall parliamentary majority. This inevitably resulted in the formation of a succession of coalition governments whose composition was always subject to party-political compromise. The intensive inter-party horse-trading which necessarily preceded the formation of a viable coalition cabinet allowed opponents of the régime to maintain a sustained attack on the system on the grounds that it encouraged party-political self-interest at the expense of the state. The stability afforded by a two-party parliamentary system was thus denied to the Republic. Ironically, the drafters of the Constitution had included no reference to political parties and decreed that Reichstag deputies were to follow the dictates of their conscience, as representatives of all the people. They were not to feel bound by specific mandates, allow themselves to be lobbied by pressure groups, or be coerced by party whips (§ 21).This impractical, if laudable, ideal had blinded the Constitutional Committee to the necessity within the parliamentary system of party discipline and willingness to compromise.

Between 1919 and 1930 thirteen cabinets held office of which only six could count on a parliamentary majority. Paradoxically, broad coalitions (i.e. those which enjoyed a parliamentary majority) often proved in practice to be no more effective than minority cabinets (those without a parliamentary majority) for their constituent members frequently failed to reconcile their conflicting interests. The continual formation of minority cabinets testified to the widespread disinclination of parties to involve themselves in the responsibility of government. Some parties, in particular the Social Democrats, preferred often to 'tolerate' a cabinet rather than to enter a coalition which they knew would force them to agree to compromises, to which their electorate would object. The parties' unwillingness to collaborate in the functioning of government lessened considerably the authority and, ultimately, the viability of the parliamentary system.

The system of voting from party lists had a further disadvantage: it prevented the electorate from participating in the choice of candidates, who were selected by party organizations. This opened the way for ambitious, self-seeking but not always competent party favourites. Independent politicians without the financial support of wealthy sponsors or the backing of a party machine had no prospect of entering the Reichstag. The system also precluded the establishment of a personal relationship between the electorate and its representatives; the population felt alienated from the machinery of government and the representative felt little sense of responsibility or accountability towards his electorate.

The Reich Executive

The executive body comprised the Reich president and the cabinet, headed by the Reich chancellor. It was the president's responsibility to appoint and dismiss the chancellor and, acting on the chancellor's advice, to appoint cabinet ministers (§ 53). While appointed by the president, the cabinet was responsible solely to parliament whose confidence it required to hold office (§ 54). This somewhat anomalous arrangement was intended to provide parliament with a safeguard against the president's becoming too powerful. In fact it was rendered ineffective by the emergency powers granted to the president under article 48 which allowed him to overrule parliament if necessary. Nevertheless parliament's right to pass votes of no confidence in a government was a weapon which it used with damaging frequency against several minority cabinets.

The chancellor enjoyed considerable executive power as the supreme formulator of government policy (§ 56). He bore overall responsibility to parliament for collective cabinet decisions, an arrangement which could cause him considerable embarrassment since chancellors often had little effective control over coalition parties other than their own. This provision caused frequent cabinet crises, and provided further palpable evidence to the general public of the instability of the parliamentary system. The second member of the executive, the Reich president was also elected by direct, universal suffrage and not, as several socialist members of the Constitutional Committee had advocated, by the Reichstag. Preuss considered that popular election of the president would provide a counterbalance to the dangers inherent in the election of members of parliament by proportional representation. Election to the presidency was open to any German over thirty-five years of age. The normal period of office was seven years (§§ 41, 43). Membership of the Reichstag was forbidden to the president (§ 44). Presidential election by popular vote once again presupposed a degree of political maturity on the part of the electorate which they simply did not possess, as the election in 1925 of an aged, anti-republican, field-marshal to the presidency clearly demonstrated.

In effect the office of president was conceived of as a republican substitute for the dissolved monarchy, a compromise between constitutional monarchy and parliamentary democracy (Eschenburg). Considerable authority was vested in the president by the Constitutional Committee which foresaw the need for an impartial head of state who would, if necessary, coerce recalcitrant political parties into participating in viable coalitions. In their determination of the president's duties and powers the Constitutional Committee appear to have been subconsciously inflenced by the character and ability of the provisional head of state. The office of Reich president was in effect tailor-made for Friedrich Ebert and did not suit the personality of his successor, Hindenburg. The middle-class parties, steeped in the authoritarian tradition, and unsure of their own ability as parliamentarians, welcomed the provision of a strong head of state, who would act as an arbiter to settle differences of opinion. They wanted a substitute Kaiser, an *Ersatzmonarch*, a desire shared also by many right-wing Socialists.

The president enjoyed both a representative function and considerable executive authority. He formally represented the nation in foreign affairs, concluded alliances and treaties and declared war and peace in the name of the people (§ 45), and, as head of state, it was his function officially to ratify and promulgate legislation passed by the Reichstag (§ 70). With the endorsement of a popular referendum he could exercise a right of veto over a specific piece of legislation (§ 73). It was also the president's duty to appoint and dismiss the chancellor and government ministers (§ 53), and under article 25 he was empowered to dissolve the Reichstag over the head of parliament and call for a general election. Dissolution of the Reichstag could not be invoked twice for the same reason but in practice this limitation proved ineffective since a pretext could always be found to justify a second dissolution (on 12 November 1932, for example, Hindenburg dissolved the Reichstag 'because of the danger that the Reichstag may demand the repeal of my emergency decree of 4 September', a flagrant breach of the spirit if not the letter of the Constitution). The Constitutional Committee had intended of course to provide for the substitution of normal parliamentary procedure by presidential rule only in exceptional circumstances, and as long as the president remained truly the defender of the Constitution and upheld parliamentary democracy, his comprehensive powers were acceptable. Though no dictatorial use of these powers was made until 1932 when Hindenburg dismissed Brüning for holding views contrary to his own, their very existence was a flaw in the Constitution.

His most extensive powers were embodied in the notorious article 48. This decreed that 'if public safety and order are seriously disturbed or endangered' the president was empowered to 'take the necessary measures to restore public safety and order, intervening, if necessary, with armed force.' The singularly imprecise wording of the article in effect granted the president unlimited powers, including the suspension of all civil liberties. Ebert made frequent use of these powers. Between 1919 and 1925 over a hundred emergency decrees were enacted. His grounds differed from those of his successor; whereas Ebert fought to secure the foundation of the Republic, Hindenburg, subconsciously or not, aided and abetted its collapse in the belief that rule by presidential decree was in some way more efficient and orderly than democratic government.

While the chancellor was formerly required to countersign emergency decrees, this safeguard was neutralized by the president's right to dismiss him. While article 48 further empowered the Reichstag to repeal emergency decrees, the president had the considerable advantage of immediate powers. Article 43 gave the Reichstag the right to appeal directly to the electorate for the dismissal of the president, another element in the elaborate system designed to counter-balance executive forces, but the practical procedural difficulties were such that the implementation of this article was virtually impossible.

The Länder

The individual German states, demoted to the status of Länder, and united in a quasi-federal structure, lost their former supremacy over the Reich when in 1919 their financial and legislative privileges were subordinated to the Reich government. Their former right to levy taxation and collect customs and excise duties was transferred to the Reich (§ 82) and after Erzberger's finance reforms were introduced later in 1919, the Länder became financially fully dependent on the Reich treasury. Länder parliaments, *Landtage*, were popularly elected, were limited in their legislative competence to those fields in which the Reich had not previously legislated (§ 12). In the event of controversy Reich law was deemed to have precedence over Land law (§ 13). The main function of the Länder governments, however, was organizational and administrative: they were to implement and enforce Reich legislation in their own territories and, while enjoying considerable administrative independence, they were subject to supervision by Reich officials. If necessary, the Reich government had the right to undertake armed intervention against a Land which failed to perform its constitutional obligations (§ 14).

The Reichsrat

The Länder were represented at national level by the Federal Council, *Reichsrat*, composed of delegates drawn proportionately from the popularly elected representatives of the various Länder governments. To avoid perpetuating the former hegemony of Prussia, no Land was allowed to occupy more than two-fifths of the total number of seats (§ 61).

The function of the Reichsrat was primarily advisory: it informed the ministers about the implementation of Reich legislation in the Länder and assisted the special committees of the Reichstag (§ 67). While it retained the right to initiate legislation and to participate in the revision of parliamentary bills, its legislative powers were severely curtailed in that only the Reichstag could implement laws.

Popular Legislative Initiative

The Constitution provided for popular legislative initiative from two sources: from the Reich Economic Council (§ 165) – to be discussed below – and from the whole electorate (§ 73). Ten per cent of the electorate could initiate an ordinary parliamentary bill or propose an amendment to the Constitution by petitioning the Reichstag which was then obliged to organize a plebiscite which would decide whether the bill was to become law (§ 73). In fact little use was made of these provisions since the process for holding plebiscites was extremely cumbersome. The over-emphasis on popular democracy in the Weimar Constitution did little to further the cause of parliamentary government in Germany. Opponents of the régime made great capital out of plebiscites and referenda, ironically designed to safeguard democracy. Seven referenda and plebiscites were held during the fourteen years of the Republic and each occasion was used as a weapon by the opposition to discredit the government.

The Judiciary

The seventh section of the Constitution dealt with the functions of the judiciary. The independence of the judiciary from the executive and the legislature was guaranteed, and was subject only to the codified law of the Reich (§ 102). Judges were appointed for life and could be suspended or dismissed only on the decision of the judiciary itself (§ 104). While these guarantees for the independence and integrity of the judiciary were rightly recognized as an essential safeguard against governmental interference, the Constitutional Committee failed to realize the implications of granting such independence to judges who, for the most part, had been appointed during the monarchy and who were to prove unsympathetic to the Republic. Only a wholesale reorganization of the judiciary in the early stages of the revolution could have prevented the anti-democratic bias in the legal profession.

The Rights and Duties of the German People

The second half of the Constitution, containing over fifty articles, dealing with the fundamental rights and duties of the citizen, illustrates well the compromise implicit in the document, with its unhappy mixture of innovatory socialist principles and the liberal ideals of 1848. Liberal guarantees for the fundamental rights of the citizen were listed anew. Several provisions were genuinely reformatory, such as the introduction of equality for women (§ 109); others included equality before the law (§ 102) and protection against illegal arrest and retrospective legislation (§ 108). The freedom of the individual was guaranteed by the provisions for freedom of expression in the press and elsewhere (§ 118), secrecy of the postal and telephone services (§ 117), freedom of assembly and association (§ 124), the right to practise any religion (§§ 135, 136) and the integrity of religious communities (§ 135).

The basic duties of the citizen to the community included the citizen's duty to lend the state his personal services in time of national need and his duty to perform military service if necessary (§ 153). The 'integrity and social advancement' of the family, the basis of the social structure of the state, were to be assured (§ 119), as were the rights of parents and children – legitimate and illegitimate (§§ 121, 122). Social measures to be introduced included the revision of the taxation system which would provide for the levying of taxes in accordance with the means of each citizen (§ 135). Less sensible was the decision to abolish all orders and decorations in an overzealous desire to establish absolute equality (§ 109), confirmation for many of the gratuitous puritanism of the Republic. This decision deprived the state of one of the cheapest and most effective methods of rewarding its citizens, which while appealing perhaps to selfish instincts in the recipients would none the less have appeased many otherwise anti-republican, middle-class citizens.

The failure to declare personal rights and freedom inviolable proved disastrous for the Republic. In fact a presidential decree could suspend them as any other section of the Constitution, and while it is futile to suggest that constitutional rights have any value beyond that accorded to them by the population, Hitler would not have been able subsequently to declare that he had come to power by legal means if he had been obliged to observe the principles contained in this section of the Constitution.

Education

In educational matters the Constitution showed scant imagination. Compulsory free education until the age of eighteen was prescribed for all (§ 45) in state schools (§ 144), after the anti-clerical Socialists and Democrats had overriden the Centrists' desire for confessional schools (renewed inter-party conflict on this issue was to bring down Marx's coalition in 1928). Neither the Constitutional Committee nor succeeding governments considered further educational reform desirable and, as a result, German schools with certain notable exceptions continued in the Imperial tradition as centres of instruction which virtually ignored progressive educational theory. Teachers, for the most part politically conservative – they were employed as civil servants – neglected to explain to their pupils the workings of parliamentary democracy and the relationship of the individual citizen to the Republic.

In 1920 the *Deutsche Hochschule für Politik*, an independent political institute, was established at the suggestion of a number of progressive politicians and public figures. It was dedicated to the political education of its students, men and women drawn from all social classes, and to research into political theory and practice. The institute was unique in Germany but, while excellent within its terms of reference, was too small to make a significant impression on Germany's political life. Mass political education which could well have prevented the widespread hostility to politics and the Republic demonstrated by German youth in the 1920s was not undertaken.

Similarly, failure to reform the universities, havens of right-wing ideology, was a serious omission. Apart from guaranteeing academic freedom for university teachers (§ 112), the Constitution made no reference to higher education. The universities provided a platform for the ultra-conservative, anti-republican attitudes of most university teachers, and encouraged the activities of reactionary student fraternities, *Burschenschaften*. These comprised both undergraduates and graduates and functioned as an 'old-boys' network in industry and the professions, assuring their members of favourable discrimination in their careers. Moreover, since university education was available only to those who could afford the expense, few children from working-class families were able to attend. In this way the position of privilege of the old order was preserved.

Economic Provisions

The concluding section of the Constitution outlined the economic reorganization of the country. In its attempt to please everyone and to accommodate the agreement reached by the Community of Labour in November 1918 the Constitutional Committee produced a mixture of capitalist and socialist principles. At the insistence of the middle-class parties, private property and the right of inheritance were guaranteed (§§ 153, 154), while the SPD demanded the inclusion of a clause which exhorted property owners to use their wealth 'for the common good' (§ 153), two demands which were virtually mutually exclusive. Further socialist provisions included the possibility of nationalization, provided compensation was paid in full for any property confiscated (§ 156). In fact the opportunity to nationalize sections of the German economy had been compromised by the Community of Labour agreement and now that a coalition government was in power there was little possibility of further industries being taken over by the state. Several undertakings were, of course, already in state ownership. These included local transport, the national railways, telecommunications and the gas and electricity supply. State intervention in industry was, moreover, frequent and accepted.

While the decision not to introduce further nationalization of industry and land prevented an immediate industrial and agrarian crisis, it created an unassailable position of power for major industrialists and granted the impoverished Junkers of north-east Germany a further reprieve.

Further articles embodied the concessions granted by the employers to the trade unions under the terms of their agreement of November 1918. These included the right to work (§ 163) and an extensive scheme of social security (§ 161). Neither of these provisions was effective in 1930 with the outbreak of the Depression and the increase in unemployment. A guarantee of workers' rights was given (§ 165) and they were invited to participate equally with the employers in Economic Councils which would negotiate wages and working conditions. Local and Reich Economic Councils were also to be established, empowered to initiate economic and social legislation (§ 165). Whereas such councils had flourished spontaneously in 1918 as a popular democratic force, they had been destroyed by the armed intervention of Noske's troops in January and March 1919 and any attempt now to revive the councils would prove impossible. Even in July 1919 the article was little more than an obeisance to the left wing of the MSPD.

The Shortcomings of the Constitution

The defects of the Constitution become increasingly apparent in the examination of Germany's economic, social and political development up to 1933. Basically, the Constitution failed in that it attempted to determine the form of the ideal state without recognizing the existing structure of power or attempting to regulate its relationship to the state. As critics have shown, Preuss and his colleagues failed to realize that effective power in Germany lay not with the Reichstag but with the president and the Reichswehr, as its rôle in the revolution had already indicated and the events between 1919 and 1933 were to confirm. No mention was made in the Constitution of the function of the army and no attempts were made to purge the army High Command of its predominantly anti-democratic officers. The trade unions were likewise ignored by the Constitution despite their important rôle within the state, as were the employers' organizations whose clandestine anti-republican operations went unchecked. The press and other mass media, whose rôle developed into one of supreme importance in the years between 1928 and 1933, also received no mention. The relationship of the civil service, the main administrative body in the Reich, to the government and parliament was not prescribed and the higher civil service, appointed under the monarchy, was not purged of its anti-democratic elements. Likewise the judiciary was allowed by default to maintain its anti-republican bias; anti-democratic judges were allowed to remain in office. Neither the Provisional Government nor the National Assembly was willing to enact such reforms since, as Eschenburg has pointed out, they wished to end the revolutionary period and to return to 'normality' as early as they could. Their desire, though wholly sincere, was none the less misguided: they clung to their erroneous belief that hostility to the régime would soon evaporate and that a new generation, nurtured in democracy, would quickly replace the old guard.

Worst omission of all was the failure to define the function of political parties in a document which intended to provide the legal basis for the maintenance of parliamentary democracy. It might well have been advisable to include a clause which would allow anti-democratic parties to be outlawed, as for example in the Basic Law of the German Federal Republic. The failure of the Republic was due in no small measure to the continuous hostility of the extreme right and left and the failure of the Constitutional Committee to realize that the Republic would be prey to such difficulties.

Throughout the life of the Republic the extremist parties maintained vigorous opposition to the régime. It is important to remember that the Nationalists and later the Communists and Nazis in opposing successive governments did not consider themselves as a 'loyal opposition' in the style of Westminster politics. The régime in fact had no parliamentary opposition, only opponents. Right-wing extremists fostered popular belief in their *national*, i.e. nationalistic, political philosophy, while left-wing extremists rejected 'bourgeois democracy' out of hand. The republican parties, squeezed between the two totalitarian extremes, were faced with the formidable task of promoting the cause of moderation.

Domestic Dissatisfaction 1919–20

The internal unrest in Germany which continued throughout the period of office of the Bauer cabinet presented further grave threats to the integrity of the Republic.

Discontent was widespread among the workers. They felt that although political democracy existed in form, its introduction had not materially altered their position in society. The old guard remained entrenched in its position of power, especially those in the armed forces and the civil service. The electorate had not been consulted in the drafting of the Constitution, no nationalization of private property had been undertaken, and the workers' councils had proved unsuccessful. In short, the policy of the Majority Socialists had become increasingly discredited and workers by the thousand transferred their political allegiance to the Independent Socialists.

Their mistrust of the MSPD was not unfounded. The maintenance of law and order, the sacred cow of the Majority Socialists, assumed pride of place before traditional Socialist doctrine, an inversion of priorities which gave rise to continuous industrial unrest.

The *malaise* was, if anything, even greater among the middle classes, who were, unfortunately, not impressed by the government's attempts to maintain law and order. Any enthusiasm they had felt in 1918 for the introduction of the Republic was quickly evaporating – they, too, felt that little had changed for the better and began to see in the Republic a scapegoat on which they would blame the vicissitudes of everyday life. Their dislike for the Republic was focused on the MSPD which was the mainstay of the National Assembly and which had appointed the President and the Chancellor from within its own ranks. They saw the delay in calling for new elections after the acceptance of the Constitution as a deliberate Socialist ruse to keep power in their own hands. As the workers moved further left, the middle classes shifted towards the right-wing parties, the People's Party and the German Nationalists. The Social Democrats' dilemma could not be resolved. By preserving the support of their middle-class colleagues they inevitably alienated the more radical members of the party. If they had not accommodated the Centrists and Democrats they would not have been able to participate in the Provisional Government.

Matthias Erzberger, leader of the Centre Party and Minister of Finance in the Bauer government, incurred unusually widespread hostility, the result in part of his controversial and outspoken career in the Reichstag. He had exposed the predecessors of the German Nationalists for the part they played in a colonial scandal in 1906, he had instigated the Peace Resolution in 1917, he had signed the Armistice in 1918 and now, by lending the support of the Centre Party, he was helping to keep a Socialist government in power.

Antagonism towards Erzberger grew in the summer of 1919 when he introduced his radical reform of the Reich finances. Reforms were necessary to meet not only the Allied reparation demands but also to cover the debts incurred at home during the war. There was also the growing danger of currency depreciation: the mark was now worth less than a third of its 1914 value. The aims of the financial reform were twofold, both organizatory and social. Taxes in future were to be levied by a central Reich authority and the heavily increased taxation burden was to fall more heavily on the shoulders of the wealthy. The right wing denounced the proposals as a ruse to soak the rich, while the Länder decried their loss of financial independence. A smear campaign against Erzberger was launched in the extremist press.

Karl Helfferich, a former Imperial Minister of Finance who, as Vice-Chancellor, had been forced to resign after the acceptance of the 1917 Peace Resolution, led this witch-hunt. He accused Erz-berger of dishonesty and impropriety, forcing him to institute legal proceedings against his detractors. Such a move played straight into Helfferich's hands for it gave him a public forum from which he could continue his attack. The trial, which had begun on 19 January 1920, and had been interrupted by an attempt on Erzberger's life, ended on 12 March, with judgement in Erzberger's favour, but also with the court convinced of the truth of several of Helfferich's allegations. Erzberger's political career was ended. His premature retirement was a considerable loss to German political life, for it deprived the government of its able Minister of Finance, and the Centre Party of its leader. Although the extent to which Erzberger was guilty of unprofessional conduct remains doubtful, the wider implications of the trial were clear: the contest between Helfferich and Erzberger had also been one between the *ancien régime* and the Republic. The result was a blow to democracy, and a sign to the right wing that its recovery had begun.

The Failure of German Labour

In 1919 Germany's numerous trade unions amalgamated into three large groups: the socialist-dominated General Trade Union, the Catholic Christian Trade Union and the liberal Hirsch-Düncker Trade Union with seven million, one million and two hundred thousand members, respectively. The concentration of the unions provided German workers with potentially powerful representation and influence. However, the new unions found themselves compromised by the failure of their predecessors in the Central Community of Labour to press in 1918–19 the workers' claim to full and equal participation in industrial management.

In January 1920 the National Assembly debated the proposed legislation on works' councils which was intended to grant participation to workers, albeit in a form acceptable to the employers. In an attempt to rescue the failed revolution, left-wing socialist and communist workers held a mass demonstration outside the Reichstag building on 13 January, demanding greater powers for the councils. On government orders contingents of the pro-republican Prussian police intervened against the demonstrators, killing over forty men. The incident was harmful to both sides: the workers failed to achieve their aim of full participation in industry and the government parties had to suffer the accusation that they had wilfully murdered working men.

The renewed internal unrest was cynically welcomed by the extreme parties on the left and right. Now that the National Assembly had performed its formal duties, general elections, they maintained. should be held at once to choose deputies to the first

Reichstag. The government parties were understandably reluctant to call early elections since their popularity had clearly been adversely affected by recent events: the MSPD had appeared to betray the working class while the DDP and the Zentrum were accused by their followers of failing to restore order to the streets. Inter-party differences became irrelevant within a couple of weeks when a determined right-wing Putsch was staged in Berlin with the aim of deposing the government.

The Kapp Putsch

Noske's dictum that the function of the army was to safeguard the security of the Reich frontier and ensure the maintenance of internal order under the command of the civilian government, was not shared by many army leaders. Several of them decided to stage a revolt against the Bauer government in March 1920. They wished to overthrow the Republic and establish in its place a military dictatorship. Victims and propagators of the stab-in-the-back legend had many grievances: they were outraged by the severity of the peace treaty, taking particular exception to the War Guilt Clause and the provision for the extradition of so-called war criminals.* Worse still, the government was bound to reduce the strength of the army and navy to a provisional maximum force of one hundred thousand and fifteen thousand men, respectively, by 10 March 1920. Demobilization orders had already been issued to several brigades including the naval brigade under the command of Captain Hermann Ehrhardt, a well-known Freikorps leader, which was stationed in Döberitz near Berlin.

The military commander in the Berlin area, General von Lüttwitz, shared the dislike of his colleagues for the MSPD which, since it had accepted humiliating peace terms, he considered unfit to govern. His concern about the reduction of the armed forces was not purely one of selfish conservatism, for he was convinced that a strong military force was necessary to protect the country against a possible Bolshevik intervention from Russia. His solution was to mount a *coup*, a decision which displayed considerable

* The Allies had agreed that these criminals could be tried in German courts of law under the supervision of an Inter-Allied Commission. Of nearly nine hundred cases only twelve were tried and only six of these ended in the conviction of the accused. Nevertheless they had assumed the aura of martyrs, and the Weimar Coalition which agreed to conduct the trials was further vilified by the right wing.

political *naïveté*. His fellow conspirators included Ludendorff's former adjutant, Max Bauer, and the Provincial Director-General of East Prussia, Wolfgang Kapp. Lüttwitz tried in vain to force Noske, the Minister of Defence, to withdraw the order to disband Ehrhardt's brigade. He therefore decided to defy the government and prevent the enforcement of the minister's decision. The Ehrhardt brigade which was to lead the attack against the government, recently returned from Weimar to Berlin, set out for the capital on the evening of 12 March.

The same night an emergency meeting of the cabinet was called. Of the military leaders present only General Reinhardt, Chief of Army Command since the previous autumn, advocated military resistance to the Putschists. General von Seeckt, Chief of the *Truppenamt*, the body which had replaced the former Supreme General Staff, spoke for the majority of his fellow officers when he stated that 'Troops do not fire on their comrades'. Seeckt then tendered his resignation and disappeared to his flat in Berlin until events decided his future.

Since military defence of Berlin was ruled out the government decided to take refuge in Dresden and set out in the early hours of the morning. Before leaving they appealed to the population to participate in a general strike. The strike which began on the following day proved to be a decisive factor in crushing the revolt.

An hour after the government had left Berlin by car Ehrhardt's brigade passed under the Brandenburg Gate in the city centre. There they were met by Lüttwitz and Kapp. Ludendorff, who maintained that he was out for a night stroll, was also there to greet them. The first stages of the Putsch were successfully completed. The troops seized the government offices in the Wilhelmstrasse without encountering resistance. A military government was announced: Kapp was declared Chancellor and Lüttwitz Minister of War. The new government had not, however, reckoned with the general strike. The response to the legitimate government's call was all but universal. The Independent Socialists chose temporarily to overlook their disagreement with the MSPD, and together with the Centrists, the Democrats, and later even the Communists, they supported a strike which paralysed the gas, electricity and transport undertakings of the whole country.

Non-cooperation with the Putschists was not confined to the

working classes. Germany's senior civil servants took the unprecedented decision to refuse to perform their duties. Further difficulties were encountered by Kapp's government when the officials of the *Reichsbank* refused to finance the revolutionary régime without authorized signatures. By 14 March the strike was almost complete. The public services, the administration and the financial centres were at a standstill. The civil servants had been encouraged to take this action by the lack of support for the Putschists shown by the right-wing People's Party and German Nationalists, who, while sympathizing with many of Lüttwitz's aims, had little respect for Kapp's ability to govern and scant faith in the success of the *coup*. Not wishing to be compromised in the event of its failure, they preferred to stand aloof until the outcome was beyond doubt. They were finally dissuaded from supporting the *coup* by the decision of the legitimate government to announce that a general election, which they had demanded for some time, would be held as soon as the revolt was put down. Equally damaging was the reaction of the army whose support was less than Lüttwitz and Kapp had confidently expected. On the whole, the forces in the south and west remained loyal to the legitimate régime and only those east of the Elbe and in the Ruhr and Thuringia joined the revolt. All prospect of success was thus destroyed and on 17 March the leaders of the Putsch were obliged after only six days to flee the capital they had tried to dominate.

The failure of the Putsch was politically significant for it demonstrated that the proletariat and their political organizations were willing to unite in the face of a common anti-democratic threat. It proved also that at this time only a small minority of the middle classes and the army favoured the introduction of a military dictatorship and that the counter-revolutionary circles could not reimpose an authoritarian régime at will. But while the Putsch was a political failure, it had scored a considerable, if short-lived, military success which had seriously threatened the elected government. Equally disturbing, the army leadership had been discredited in the eyes of many republicans.

The Trial of the Putschists
The trial of the leaders of the Putsch and their supporters betrayed the double standards of justice which were applied on

many occasions under the Republic. On 21 May 1921 the Democratic Minister of the Interior in Wirth's cabinet, Eugen Schiffer, reported to the Reichstag that of the 705 offences recorded during the Putsch, 412 cases had been amnestied, 109 had for various reasons not been pursued, the trial of a further 176 had been halted, 7 were not yet completed and there had been 1 conviction. Ultimately 3 of the conspirators were convicted of treason. Lüttwitz retired to the country, Ehrhardt was able to continue his subversive activities in Munich and Kapp, on his return from Sweden where he had temporarily sought refuge, died in prison while awaiting trial. Of the 775 officers who participated in the Putsch 13 were punished, 48 temporarily suspended and 6 dismissed; the sum total of their prison sentences was 5 years. In contrast, after the overthrow of the soviet régime in Munich in 1919 52 defendants were sentenced to a total of 135 years' imprisonment.

A comparison of the sentences imposed on left- and right-wing political assassins is even more alarming. Between 1919 and 1923 22 political murders were perpetrated by left-wing supporters. Of these 18 were punished with an average prison sentence of fifteen years, and 10 were executed. During the same period 354 political murders were committed by right-wing sympathizers of whom 326 were not convicted. The 28 sentenced served an average period of 4 months' imprisonment.*

The Failure of the General Strike

The occurrence of the Putsch and the government's handling of the crisis deeply concerned the left wing which had done much to ensure the solidarity of the general strike. The Independents had not organized the strike merely to help the MSPD back into power and to restore the *status quo ante*. On 20 March they declared their unwillingness to return to work until at least some of their demands had been met by the government. These included the punishment of the Putschists and the dismissal of Noske, long the target of criticism from the left. They also stipulated the introduction of economic and social equality for the working classes, by means of a redistribution of wealth, and the democratic reform of the civil service, industrial management and the army leadership. An agreement was reached

---

* Statistics taken from *Die Zerstörung der deutschen Politik* ed. H. Pross, pp. 139-41.

between the government parties and the trade unions to implement their demands in return for their undertaking to return to work.

This agreement, if it had been carried out in full, could have strengthened the stability of the Republic for it dealt with some of its basic weaknesses. Only three months later this opportunity was lost when the Weimar Coalition was replaced by a bourgeois government after the general election of 6 May.

The failure of the trade unions to capitalize on the successful overthrow of the Kapp régime discredited them in the eyes of many workers. The employers regained the upper hand as the added burden of inflation and unemployment was imposed on workers in the following few years. Sectional interests produced tensions within industry which could no longer be resolved and Ebert's attempt to create a national state by means of industrial partnership was finally destroyed.

Noske's Resignation and Seeckt's Appointment

The main victim of the affair was Noske. Scheidemann, prompted doubtless by the attitude of the Independents and Communists and by the suspicion of many of his party colleagues, called for Noske's resignation, in a parliamentary debate on the Putsch. This was tendered and accepted on 22 March. General Reinhardt, Chief of the Army Command, resigned in sympathy and out of respect for Noske. The Vice-Chancellor, Eugen Schiffer, the sole member of the cabinet to remain in Berlin, nominated von Seeckt to succeed Reinhardt. Thus the one army leader who had advocated military opposition to the insurgents was replaced by a man whose attitude to the *coup* had been decidedly ambiguous. As Heiber remarks, it was not simply a question of troops refusing to fire on comrades, as Seeckt had maintained, but of government troops refusing to oppose mutinous comrades. Significantly only after long heart-searching was Ebert able to ratify Seeckt's appointment

Noske was succeeded by Otto Gessler, a member of the Democratic Party. Gessler, a former judge and mayor of Nürnberg, accepted the post, one of the most formidable in the cabinet, with the greatest misgivings. He remained Minister of Defence in successive governments until January 1928. The SPD had thereby lost not only one of their most able politicians, but control of the Ministry of Defence and, thereby, influence over the Reichswehr.

Control of the armed forces rested henceforth with the middle-class parties and the army leadership and the survival of the old order was finally ensured.

The Reichswehr under Seeckt

Seeckt's appointment in 1920 inaugurated a period of development for the armed forces which transformed them into a virtually autonomous 'state within a state', responsible only to itself. However honourable the intentions of the leadership, and these were by no means always beyond reproach, the disturbing anomaly could not be overlooked that army policy was formulated and executed largely without the sanction of either the Ministry of Defence, the responsible government body, or the elected parliament. There are four main reasons for this unsatisfactory situation, namely, Seeckt's professional ambition, the unsatisfactory personal relationship between him and Gessler, the army's inherited tradition and the restrictions imposed by Versailles which encouraged clandestine evasion.

The Armed Forces Laws, passed in 1921, formally regulated the rôle of the Reichswehr and ratified the reorganization which had been carried out after the Versailles limitations had come into force in April 1920. Conscription had been abolished and a professional army of 100,000 volunteers and a navy of 15,000 volunteers had been formed. These figures included 4,000 army and 1,500 naval officers. Officers and men were selected almost exclusively from the ranks of the provisional Reichswehr with the exclusion of participants in the Kapp Putsch. The leaders of the Reichswehr were for the most part men who had served in the Imperial army and navy. They brought with them a military and naval tradition and ethos which contradicted the principles of a democratic state. Nurtured in the spirit of Prussian militarism, the leaders of the armed forces sought to restore and preserve the social prestige of the *élite*. High-ranking officers belonged for the most part to social classes acceptable to the leadership. Recruitment had been Seeckt's responsibility since his appointment in July 1919 to the Truppenamt, the body which had replaced the compulsorily disbanded General Staff. From the outset the Reichswehr was moulded by Seeckt's personality and political views. Had conscription not been banned by the Allies the German government could have supervised recruitment from all social classes and thereby created a truly republican Reichswehr.

Seeckt, a product of the Prussian military tradition, was born in 1866, son of a Pomeranian aristocratic family. He was proud, autocratic, ambitious and highly intelligent. Well-versed in all aspects of military life, he commanded widespread respect and loyalty from his officers and troops. His relations with politicians remained cool: a convinced monarchist, he could not come to terms with the concept of a democratic Republic governed by commoners.

His conception of the rôle of the armed forces differed significantly from that generally accepted by democratic states. He maintained that the Reichswehr should be *überparteiisch*, that is, it should be above party politics; proof of the dangers inherent in dabbling in politics had been provided by the fiasco of the Kapp Putsch. Seeckt's contention was valid in the sense that armed forces should demonstrate no party-political bias in the execution of their duties. His conception of impartiality was, however, less straightforward, for he maintained that the Reichswehr was responsible only to the Reich and not to the government of the day. While this view had been tenable under the autocratic Empire, when the army and navy had sworn an oath of allegiance to the Kaiser, it could hardly be applied to current circumstances. The Constitution required the Reichswehr to swear an oath of allegiance to the Republic, that is, to defend its integrity and the freedom of its elected government against attack from whatever quarter. Imperceptibly allegiance was transferred from the Republic to the person of Seeckt *vice* the deposed monarch. The Reichswehr's reaction to internal unrest depended to a great extent on Seeckt's personal attitude, and this, as events proved, varied according to the political colouring and social standing of the insurgents. Under the cloak of political impartiality Seeckt became an active politician, who worked constantly to further the interests of the Reichswehr as an autonomous body.

While it would be inaccurate to claim that the Reichswehr under Seeckt was outwardly hostile to the Republic, its attitude remained at best lukewarm. Indicative of its indifference was the campaign launched by the officer corps for the restoration of the former Imperial colours, black, white and red, as the ensign of the Reichswehr, the *Reichskriegsflagge*. Their request was sanctioned in 1920. The republican colours, black, red and gold, were relegated to the status of an insert in the top inner corner of the flag, as if to symbolize the relative importance of the Republic and the Reichswehr.

According to the Constitution and the Reichswehr laws, supreme command of the Reichswehr was vested in the president. He delegated his power to the minister of defence, *Reichswehrminister*, who was responsible to parliament for all matters concerning the armed forces. The day-to-day running of the Reichswehr clearly had to be supervised by the service leaders themselves. This arrangement functioned smoothly under Noske and Reinhardt who enjoyed mutual respect and who had reached an understanding concerning the function of the armed forces in the Republic. Their replacements, Gessler and Seeckt, did not enjoy such close personal relations nor did they share a common view of the rôle of the Reichswehr. It was unfortunate, to say the least, that Gessler did not possess the personal authority to impose his will on Seeckt and thereby to prevent the creation of the 'state within a state'.

The Reichstag was further deprived of democratic control over the Reichswehr by the need to promote illegal military activities abroad. In order to evade the strict limitations on arms and men imposed by Versailles, Seeckt inaugurated negotiations with foreign powers who were willing to collaborate secretly with Germany. Like many right-wingers, Seeckt was able to overlook his fervent anti-Bolshevism when it was in his interests. In September 1921 he held successful secret talks with Russian military experts in his flat in Berlin. Forbidden equipment was to be made in Russia under the auspices of *Gefu, Gesellschaft zur Förderung gewerblicher Unternehmungen*, Company for the Promotion of Industrial Undertakings, which opened offices in Berlin and Moscow. Gefu supplied government finance for the construction of arms factories for German concerns such as Junkers, Krupp and Stinnes. There and in several other European countries prototypes of forbidden equipment, tanks, aeroplanes, submarines and other armaments were constructed and tested by the Reichswehr. A new department in the Truppenamt, the Special Russian Section, called *Sondergruppe R* (i.e. *Russland*), was created to co-ordinate the clandestine operations. It also organized the establishment of an illegal army, *Schwarze Reichswehr*, which trained short-term recruits, specifically banned at Versailles since the Allies wished to prevent Germany from building up a military reserve. Seeckt's programme was approved by Wirth and Stresemann. Clearly, since parliamentary discussion of such activities was out of the question, the Reichswehr was allowed a free hand and, moreover, was relieved of the burden of public accountability, for if the illegal activities came to light the minister of defence would have to shoulder responsibility before parliament.

Faced with an army and navy which, by the standards of the day, were diminutive, Seeckt resolved to compensate for numerical weakness with technical and logistic superiority. As well as the Russian activities he submitted regulars at home to intensive training in modern warfare. Training was made as realistic as possible by the substitution of wooden dummies whenever real equipment was lacking. He evolved an *élite* skeleton force of specialists which could quickly and efficiently be enlarged if necessary into a sizeable army and navy. The value of Seeckt's plan was subsequently proved by the Nazis.

Müller's Caretaker Cabinet

Noske's departure from the cabinet provoked the government's fall, since many of his colleagues resigned in sympathy. On 26 March Hermann Müller, a leading Social Democrat and Foreign Minister in the retiring government, accepted Ebert's request to form a cabinet which would govern the country until new elections were held. These, he announced, would take place on 6 June. The implementation of the social, administrative and military reforms which had been promised to the trade unions would now have to be postponed until after the general election. Unfortunately, the results of the election effectively prevented them from reaching the statute book.

4

Continuing Instability 1920–1923

Character of the Period 1920-23

THE ELECTION of June 1920, conducted in the shadow of recent disturbances, inaugurated a period of further instability which culminated late in 1923 in the near dissolution of the Republic. The difficulties to which the country was exposed were many and varied, deriving from both foreign and domestic sources. The instability of successive governments – six cabinets held office in the three and a half years – stemmed from the indecisive election result which failed to produce a party capable of forming a government alone or of imposing its authority on coalition partners. The situation was aggravated by the hesitation of the Socialists to assume government responsibility and by their doctrinaire refusal to collaborate with right-wing parties in the national interest.

The Allies' London Ultimatum on reparations provoked outrage within Germany and undermined further the standing of the Republic. A policy of fulfilment, *Erfüllungspolitik*, inaugurated and pursued by Wirth's governments, miscarried on account of French germanophobia. Germany's failure to comply to the letter with her obligations gave France and Belgium a suitable pretext to invade the industrial region of the Ruhr in order to exact a 'productive pledge' from Germany. Germany replied by ordering workers and civil servants in the Ruhr to offer passive resistance to the occupying forces. Stalemate in the Ruhr encouraged galloping inflation and brought Germany's industry to a standstill.

On the credit side, Germany succeeded in concluding a treaty of friendship with Russia at Rapallo. The assassination soon after of Walther Rathenau, the Foreign Minister responsible for reaching agreement with the Russians, was one of a series of political acts of violence, largely committed by right-wing extremists, which testified further to the precarious existence of German democracy.

The years 1920–23 saw also the rise of the National Socialist Party under Adolf Hitler, to a position of considerable political power in Bavaria. The period ended with an abortive counter-revolutionary putsch staged by the Nazis in November 1923, and successfully put down by the Reichswehr.

The political saviour of the Republic in the crisis year of 1923 was Gustav Stresemann, leader of the People's Party. He managed within a remarkably short time to bring internal revolt under control, to introduce a new currency and to negotiate the withdrawal of the occupying forces in the Ruhr. His policy of fulfilment and international understanding, *Verständigungspolitik*, was to prove unusually effective in the five years until 1929.

The Electoral Campaign

The electoral campaign in 1920 centred on the record of the Provisional Government. The MSPD in particular sustained bitter attacks from both right- and left-wing parties. The Nationalists campaigned on the issue of the acceptance of the Versailles Diktat, which, they maintained, was an act of treason against the Reich. The Independent Socialists, for their part, condemned the government's social record. The misery of post-war Germany had, they contended, hardly lessened and the government's promise of social reforms had not been fulfilled. Its record in combating internal disorder was hardly to the credit of a so-called socialist party. The DVP campaigned with an anti-republican, anti-clerical, anti-marxist manifesto with which they hoped to poach supporters from the Democrats who had collaborated with the Catholic Centre and the Marxist Socialists. Waving the patriotic flag – the Imperial colours, black, white and red – they joined in condemning those who had signed Versailles, forgetting that they had had no alternative solution to offer at the time.

The election, as is shown by the table of results on the following page, produced a Weimar Coalition to the extreme left and right wings, and confirmed the widespread popular dissatisfaction with the government's handling of the country's affairs since the revolution. The Democrats suffered the most severe reverse in fortunes. Their vote was reduced by over fifty-five per cent, a result which reflects the disillusionment of middle-class liberals with life under the Republic. Their former supporters deserted in millions to the DVP and DNVP. Their coalition partners, Socialists and Centrists, likewise suffered badly with a reduction in votes of nearly one half and over one third respectively (much of the former support for the Zentrum having been transferred to the Bavarian People's Party whose candidates were standing for the first time). The SPD was now paying for its half-hearted socialism, and lost several million votes to the Independents.

THE ELECTION OF 6 JUNE 1920
The results of the election were as follows:

		Votes cast (to nearest thousand)		Number of seats		Percentage of total vote	
		1919	1920	1919	1920	1919	1920
KPD	Communist	—	590,000	—	4	—	2·1
USPD	Independent Social Democratic	2,317,000	5,047,000	22	84	7·6	17·9
MSPD	Majority Social Democratic	11,509,000	6,104,000	163	102	37·9	21·6
DDP	Democratic	5,642,000	2,334,000	75	39	18·6	8·3
Z	Centre	5,980,000	3,845,000	91	64	19·7	13·6
BVP	Bavarian People's	—	1,239,000	—	21	—	4·3
DVP	People's	1,346,000	3,919,000	19	65	4·4	13·9
DNVP	Nationalist	3,121,000	4,249,000	44	71	10·3	14·9
Others		209,000	870,000	3	9	0·8	5·4
Total (to nearest hundred thousand)		30,400,000	28,500,000	421	459		

79·1 per cent of the electorate voted compared with 82·7 per cent in 1919.

The two anti-republican parties on the right, the People's Party and the Nationalists, benefited handsomely by the middle-class flight from moderation. The former increased its support nearly twofold, the latter by thirty-five per cent. On the left the Independents inherited over three and a half million votes from their moderate Socialist rivals while the Communists, participating for the first time, managed to secure over half a million votes out of a total turnout of twenty-eight million.

The elections to the first Reichstag had thus produced a situation which rendered the formation of a viable coalition almost impossible. The majority enjoyed by the former coalition parties was destroyed – they now controlled only 205 out of 459 seats compared with 329 out of 421 in the National Assembly. The addition of the Bavarian Party's seats produced a total 226, which would create an unacceptably precarious majority of three votes.

Ebert asked the Majority Social Democrat, Hermann Müller, as leader of the largest party, to form a government. He in turn approached the Independent Socialists with an invitation to participate in a coalition together with the three Weimar parties (Majority Socialists, Centrists and Democrats). Only with Independent support could the anti-republican parties of the right be excluded from government. The Independents, concerned with their domestic problems which were soon to culminate in the dissolution of the party, and still smarting from the effects of the SPD's recent opposition to their followers and their cause, spurned the overtures from the 'antirevolutionary, capitalist and militarist' Majority Socialists. Despite Ebert's attempts to persuade his former colleagues to include the People's Party in a widened Weimar Coalition Müller refused in his turn to collaborate with a party which had recorded its opposition to the régime, despite assurances that the DVP if included in a government would formally announce its acceptance of the Constitution.

The results of the election had been widely interpreted as proof that the Reich was a 'republic without republicans'. The attitude of the SPD encouraged the claim that the Reichstag was a parliament without parliamentarians. Socialist distaste for the right-wing ethos of the People's Party was understandable, as was their fear that by collaborating with the representatives of big business they would accelerate the defection of their left-wing supporters to the Independents. However, their refusal, purely on grounds of party-political expediency to participate in the government of a state which was largely their creation, and which needed the active support of the SPD's one hundred and two deputies, displayed an ostrich-like reaction to an unpleasant situation. After only eighteen months in office the Social Democrats were to join the ranks of the parliamentary opposition, and they surrendered their power to a succession of coalition governments which proved to be largely incompetent to deal with the admittedly overwhelming series of difficulties which occurred during the following three years. They remained in opposition, apart from two short periods at times of national crisis, until June 1928. Having cut themselves off from political power they resumed their traditional pre-war rôle of parliamentary opposition. As Mann observes, the Republic, inasmuch as it was a Social Democratic Republic, ended in 1920.

As the formation of a large coalition seemed to be impossible, the unhappy compromise of forming a government without a parliamentary majority was adopted. The elderly politician, Dr Konstantin Fehrenbach, a progressive Centrist and President of the last Imperial Reichstag, was approached and on 25 June succeeded in forming a coalition of three bourgeois parties: the Democratic Party, the Centre and the People's Party which, at Stresemann's instigation, now declared itself willing to collaborate in republican government. With a combined total of one hundred and sixty-eight seats it became the first of many minority coalitions to be created during the life of the Republic. Depending for their survival, as they had to, on the benevolent tolerance of other parties outside the government they constituted another unstable institution in an already vulnerable régime. The Social Democrats in the hope of gaining the best of both worlds agreed to support the Fehrenbach government on condition that it introduced no anti-socialist legislation. In fact they emerged with the worst of both.

At the insistence of the Democrats, the Populists declared their intention to uphold the Constitution. However, despite this public avowal of conversion to republicanism, many adhered in private to their former nationalist and monarchist ideals. Stresemann was an important exception within his own party. Though a monarchist by nature he became increasingly convinced in the early 1920s of the need to accept the Republic since it was now an established fact. He became archetypal of the *Vernunftrepublikaner*, the republican not of inner conviction but of rational appraisal of Germany's situation.

Fehrenbach's cabinet announced a programme which was progressive in its aims – broadly it undertook to continue the policies of the previous government. However, its policies remained largely unimplemented at the end of its period in office. The promised purge of anti-republican elements in the Reichswehr were carried out half-heartedly. Two socialist measures, the introduction of unemployment insurance and plans for further nationalization, were shelved, the latter at the insistence of the People's Party which, as the representative of big business, was naturally opposed to the introduction of any social legislation inconsistent with the interests of their particular electorate. The main preoccupation of the government was with the prickly problem of reparations which, as they rightly argued, had to be settled before many pressing domestic issues could be tackled.

The Realignment of the Left and the Modification of Party Political Tactics

The election success of the Independent Socialist Party in May 1920, though a clear indication of popular faith in orthodox Socialism, concealed the existence of an ever-widening split within the party. At the Party Conference held in Halle in October 1920 the left wing under the leadership of the shop stewards, Obleute, the instigators of much of the revolutionary fervour in the early months of the Republic, decided to work towards unity with the newly constituted Communist Party, in the common endeavour to establish a dictatorship of the proletariat.

The Heidelberg Conference in 1919, at which the KPD had been formed out of the tattered remnants of the Spartacist League, had decided to follow Lenin's advice to exclude from the party the Utopian left wing and those who despite the abortive revolt of January 1919 still advocated the Putsch as the only means of seizing power. They were to work towards the proletarian revolution from within the established organs of government, especially parliament and the trade unions. Comintern, the Third Communist International, established in Russia in 1919, had advocated a union between the KPD and the Independents provided that their right wing, who sympathized with the aims and methods of the 'revisionary' Majority Socialists, was excluded. Accordingly in October 1920 the bulk of the USPD joined forces with the KPD to form a second left-wing party of considerable strength, having a membership of half a million. The Independents brought to the union their press, their valuable party organization and a network of powerful shop stewards in many branches of industry. Despite the bankruptcy of the policy of revolt the KPD, acting on orders from Moscow, pursued the policy throughout the 1920s.

In September 1922 the right-wing rump of the Independents finally joined the Majority Socialists at their party conference in Nürnberg. There now existed in Germany two Socialist parties accurately reflecting the ideological divergence of the left wing: the Communists whose ultimate aim was still revolutionary and the Social Democrats with their belief in the evolutionary development of society towards egalitarianism.

There was a similar change of tactics on the right. The Nationalist Party was convinced after the fiasco of the Kapp Putsch that the Republic was for the time being firmly established. Impressed by the benefits bestowed on the DVP by their declaration of support for the Constitution, they decided likewise to announce their support. This was an act purely of political expediency which they believed would allow them to work – like the Communists – within the system to achieve their aim, the restoration of the *ancien régime*.

Thus the Republic now possessed two, possibly three, extreme parties which, while paying lip-service to parliamentary democracy, were in fact working insidiously for its overthrow. This situation was in some respects more difficult to tackle than overt opposition to the régime which could at least be recognized by all for the threat it contained.

The Allied Reparation Committee Reports

At Versailles the German delegation had made an offer of reparations for 'all damage done to the civilian population': one hundred thousand million gold marks to be paid interest free over a period of fifty or sixty years. This would have allowed Germany to invest a lump sum of thirty thousand million marks and pay the annual instalments from the interest on the capital (assuming a rate of interest of at least six per cent). The offer was rejected out of hand and Germany was forced to sign a blank cheque, the amount of reparations to be decided by an Allied Reparation Committee which was to submit its report by May 1921. In the interim Germany was required to pay twenty thousand million in advance, mainly in kind.

During 1920 and 1921 several discussions were held between representatives of the Allied and German governments to attempt to reach agreement on the amount Germany was to pay. The inclusion of German delegates at the conferences displayed a certain improvement in the Allied attitude towards Germany but the thaw in the diplomatic climate was not matched by any more realistic appraisal of Germany's ability to fulfil the demands made of her. While Britain attempted to settle an amount which Germany was capable of paying without incurring economic ruin, the French were equally determined to demand reparations which would prevent Germany from undertaking industrial reconstruction. The withdrawal of the U.S.A. from European affairs into isolationism following the election of Warren G. Harding in 1920, and the refusal of Congress to ratify Versailles, had aroused widespread *Schadenfreude* in Germany for they expected this dissension in the Allied front to work in their favour. In fact the reverse proved to be the case since the departure of Wilson deprived Germany of her most lenient victor and France of Wilson's personal guarantee to defend her integrity. The French government was thus encouraged to intensify its intransigence. Nor did the separate peace treaty concluded between Germany and the U.S.A. in August 1921 produce the anticipated alleviation of the peace terms for the Americans insisted that Germany should fulfil her obligations to the Allies.

Successive conferences at Paris and London failed to produce any agreement between the two sides: Allied proposals of a total payment of two hundred and twenty-six thousand million gold marks was countered by a German proposal which, when stripped of its window dressing, amounted to little more than the thirty thousand million already offered at Versailles.

On 27 April 1921 the Commission produced its report. Largely as a result of British influence the sum demanded had been reduced to one hundred and thirty-two thousand million gold marks.* The sum was to be paid over a period of thirty years, beginning with instalments of two thousand million. An immediate down payment of one thousand million marks was demanded. The British economist, John Maynard Keynes, an ardent opponent of the economic aspects of the Versailles Treaty, estimated that one hundred and thirty-two thousand millions exceeded three-fold Germany's capacity to pay. In addition, Germany was to make an annual payment equalling twenty-six per cent of the value of her exports, whereby the Allies would both benefit from and circumscribe any economic recovery in Germany.

* i.e. £6,600,000,000, approximately $32,000,000,000.

The Fehrenbach government refused to accept the Commission's decision and accordingly resigned on 4 May. On the following day the Allies, in conference in London, issued their so-called London ultimatum. Germany was given six days to accept the plan. She was further required to comply with former demands concerning the disbanding of irregular armed forces in Germany and the bringing to trial of named war criminals. Failure to comply with the ultimatum would result in the occupation by Allied forces of the Ruhr (the Rhine ports of Düsseldorf, Duisburg and Ruhrort had already been occupied in March on a flimsy pretext) and also in a reintroduction of the shipping blockade. The situation depressingly resembled the dilemma produced by the Allied ultimatum over Versailles. It was felt, justly, that the Allies' demand far exceeded those imposed by the victors in previous peace treaties. Not only was the sum enormous, but the period over which it was to be paid, thirty years, would keep international hostility alive until 1951. Any politician who acceded to the ultimatum would incur the odium of the population and encourage the stab-in-the-back legend, for few bothered to reflect that they were being required to pay for the war adventures of the Kaiser and the army High Command. Fehrenbach's cabinet, unwilling to accept the findings of the Reparations Commission, resigned on 4 May 1921. On the following day the Allies issued the by now traditional ultimatum: Germany was to accept the Reparations Plan within six days; failure to do so would result in Allied occupation of the Ruhr, Germany's main source of raw materials and major industrial centre. The Reichstag was flung into confusion; the Nationalists, true to their hyper-patriotic blustering custom, advocated rejection, a wholly unrealistic suggestion in terms of practical politics. The Socialists and Centrists considered the country to be faced with Hobson's choice: occupation of the Ruhr by foreign troops would not only aggravate Germany's severe financial difficulties, but also encourage the supporters of Rhineland separatism, and therefore their only option was to agree once more to an Allied Diktat.

The Wirth Cabinet

The interregnum was ended on 10 May when Joseph Wirth, Minister of Finance since Erzberger's resignation in March 1920, succeeded in resurrecting the Weimar Coalition. Wirth, born in

1879, was like his predecessor, Erzberger, a South German Catholic and member of the progressive left wing of the Centre Party. Like Erzberger and Fehrenbach, he was regarded with suspicion by his right-wing, agrarian party colleagues. The Social Democrats felt themselves able to resume governmental responsibility. The realignment of the Independents and the Communists allowed the SPD greater flexibility in that it diminished the risk of mass defection of party supporters to the left. The People's Party, on the other hand, not wishing to incur the blame for having to underwrite a debt of one hundred and thirty-two thousand million marks, refused to collaborate further in the government. Thus, now that the Reich had once more become acutely vulnerable it was the republican parties which assumed the unenviable task of guiding the country through troubled waters. On the following day, twenty-four hours before the expiry of the Allied date-line, the Reichstag debated and accepted under duress the Reparations Plan by two hundred and twenty to one hundred and seventy votes, on the understanding that the integrity of Upper Silesia within the Reich was to be preserved. Socialists, Democrats and Centrists (together with several Independents) voted in favour while the right-wing People's Party and Nationalist Party sanctimoniously opposed the bill.

The Policy of Fulfilment of Wirth and Rathenau

Wirth chose Walther Rathenau to serve as Minister of Reconstruction in his cabinet. He was promoted to the Foreign Ministry in January 1922. The choice was courageous for Wirth was aware that Rathenau's Jewish descent would make him the object of attack from anti-semitic groups in Germany. He was an industrialist of outstanding ability, son of the founder of Germany's large electrical concern, A.E.G., and its managing director from 1915. During the war he had demonstrated his administrative skills in organizing the country's supply and distribution of raw materials. The author of several politico-philosophical works, he was an outspoken critic of capitalism and advocated the elimination of the 'hereditary servitude' of the working classes by severely limiting the right of inheritance. He was one of the few industrialists who supported the Republic with enthusiasm.

Germany's foreign policy of the 1920s was primarily concerned with a gradual revision of Versailles and with improving relations with the West and, subsequently, with Soviet Russia. It resembled the labours of Sisyphus (Herzfeld) in that any consistent policy was frequently overruled by events outside the control of the government whether they were domestic problems or the ever-recurrent problem of reparations. Together Wirth and Rathenau were responsible for adopting a policy of fulfilment, *Erfüllungspolitik*, towards the terms of Versailles. In reality they had no practical alternative: failure to comply with the terms of Versailles would have invited invasion of the Reich. But the aim of the Erfüllungspolitiker was more subtle: they wished to convince the Allies of Germany's good faith and readiness to comply with the treaty but they hoped that by trying to fulfil Allied demands to the best of their ability they would demonstrate that they were impossible. The Nationalists did all they could to discredit the policy, without being able to produce a workable alternative. They ignored its subtleties in favour of deriving maximum party-political benefit out of the situation. Ultimately the policy failed as a result of the unshakeable intransigence of the French who insisted on their pound of flesh, a demand which was encouraged by the revanchist protestations of the German Nationalists.

Organization 'C' and the Assassination of Erzberger

Though the Nationalists at no time openly advocated armed opposition to the régime, their anti-republican, anti-semitic, jingoist tirades succeeded in arousing violence in others. One such anti-republican group to be formed at this time was the Organization Consul founded in July 1921 by Captain Ehrhardt and several other members of his brigade who had participated in the Kapp Putsch. It was based in Munich, the haven of counter-revolutionaries, and thrived under the benevolent eye of the Bavarian Premier, Gustav von Kahr, an ultra-right-wing monarchist and particularist. The aims of the organization were desperate: they pledged themselves to rid the Reich of its leading Socialists and Jews, to bring parliamentary democracy to a swift end and to establish secret courts to try and execute 'traitors' by which they meant supporters of the Republic. Their first prominent victim was Matthias Erzberger, condemned for his promulgation of the Peace Resolution in 1917, his signing of the Armistice, and his financial reforms. On 28 August 1921 two former officers in Ehrhardt's Marine Brigade and veterans of the Kapp Putsch shot and killed him at a summer resort in the Black Forest. The two assassins escaped to Hungary via Munich where, it would appear, they received semi-official assistance. The assassination – which followed that of Kurt Eisner in February 1919, and Karl Gareis, leader of the Bavarian Independent Socialists, in June 1921 – provoked widespread dismay and outrage in republican circles. The DNVP likewise expressed its anxiety, as if blind to the vicarious moral guilt it had incurred. The conduct of the Bavarian government was widely condemned and Kahr's resignation was prised out of him in September 1921. He was replaced by Count Hugo von Lerchenfeld-Köfering, a republican and supporter of the Wirth government, but rational government in Bavaria was not to endure for long for in the following year Lerchenfeld was replaced in November 1922 by Eugen von Knilling, a nationalistic member of the Bavarian People's Party.

The Upper Silesian Plebiscite

In October 1921 the Allies presented Wirth's coalition with a further problem of overwhelming proportions by their interpretation and implementation of the Upper Silesian plebiscite which had been held in March of that year.

Other clauses contained in Versailles, which dealt with territorial adjustments had already been implemented in various ways. Eupen and Malmédy were surrendered in 1920 to Belgium since the population had – under considerable pressure from the Belgian occupation forces – opted for union with Belgium. Instead of the plebiscite laid down in the treaty, the population was required to indicate its decision in open lists. The plebiscite held in Schleswig in July 1920 was conducted correctly: the northern zone of the plebiscite area voted for union with Denmark while the southern, smaller zone decided to remain part of the Reich. Memelland, which had been placed under the trusteeship of the League of Nations as an independent state, was on 12 January 1923 annexed by force by Lithuanian troops. The violation of the treaty was ratified by the League in the following year. The situation in Upper Silesia was more complicated. The region possessed extensive coal and mineral deposits and contained much heavy industry. It was becoming increasingly imperative to reach a decision about the future of the territory since armed clashes between Polish and German irregulars grew daily more serious, not least since the French forces of occupation, stationed in the area to maintain peace, patently favoured the Poles at a time when strict impartiality was essential.

The plebiscite was held on 20 March 1921. 433,574 votes were cast in favour of Polish rule, while 707,122 voters preferred to remain within the Reich, on the face of it a German majority of over sixty per cent. Accordingly, the German government claimed its right to the whole area, pointing out the need to preserve its economic unity. The Poles for their part claimed those communes which had voted for union with Poland. A strict division according to the decision of each commune was clearly impossible since those (699) with a Polish majority were largely rural areas, while those (754) with German majorities were for the most part urban and more often than not enclaves surrounded by Polish speaking districts. The indecisive result led to further clashes. In an attempt to force the hand of the Allied Commission which had been instructed to determine the line of the frontier, Korfanty, a Polish Upper Silesian, entered the plebiscite area with an armed band of Polish volunteers, unhampered by the French peace-keeping force. The government dared not risk incurring Allied wrath by sending regular army troops into the area and had to content itself by giving tacit support for a detachment of Freikorps who successfully countered Korfanty's troops.

The Allied Commission failed to agree on a frontier because the French continued to champion the Polish claims while the British supported the Germans. To resolve the deadlock the Allies decided to refer the problem to the League of Nations. The report of a committee set up by the League to draft a frontier was accepted on 20 October. It appeared largely to disregard the results of the plebiscite. The frontier was drawn to give Poland nearly half the disputed territory which included three-quarters of the region's industry and mines, a large German minority of three hundred and fifty thousand and two wholly German towns, Kattowitz and Königshütte. Since the latter was situated on the new Polish-German frontier it had clearly been given to Poland for reasons other than geographical convenience.

The loss of the industrial regions threatened to cripple further the already unstable German economy, and the widespread resentment of the German public found political expression in the resignation of the Wirth government on 26 October. At a time when Germany was actively pursuing a policy of fulfilling the terms of Versailles, the Allies had decided to mete out further injustice to the Reich which made fulfilment both economically and politically more difficult. It appeared to the German population that compliance with the treaty was binding on only one signatory.

Wirth's Second Cabinet and Inflation

At Ebert's request Wirth offered to form a new cabinet on 30 October, having made his gesture of protest to the Allies. He took advantage of the opportunity to redistribute the ministerial portfolios, taking over the Foreign Ministry himself in order later to put it in the charge of Walther Rathenau. The new coalition, however, emerged considerably reduced in voting strength since the Democrats, fearing further alienation of their supporters, refused to participate, while they allowed their two party members, Rathenau and Gessler (Minister of Defence), to continue in office in a purely private capacity.

Wirth's second cabinet was presented with further intense domestic difficulties caused by the resumed devaluation of the mark. Inflation had its roots, of course, in the economic strains imposed on Germany by the war. The Allied blockade on German shipping, which had wholly disrupted Germany's export trade, and the transformation of Germany's industry into a war machine had been the main contributory factors between 1914 and 1918 when the value of the mark fell by two-thirds from one shilling to four pence (from twenty-five to eight cents). A further decline in the currency was occasioned by the swingeing impositions of Versailles: loss of colonies, loss of Reich territory rich in raw materials, and above all the extortion of reparations, combined with the external and internal consequences of a lost war and a failed revolution – continuing internal anti-republican strife and an almost universal loss of confidence. By the early months of 1920 the exchange rate against the pound sterling had dived to 300 marks (approximately 82 marks to the dollar).

The successful suppression of the Kapp Putsch and, more important, the deflationary effects of Erzberger's tax reforms produced a temporary respite but this was accompanied by less salutary effects of Erzberger's squeeze: a rapid increase in unemployment and the growing stagnation of industry which led to a decline in the real wealth of the country. The improvement was to be short-lived. The London Ultimatum of May 1921 with its demand for an unexpectedly large total reparation debt, followed in October by the dubious partition of Upper Silesia, produced further abrupt devaluations. During the month of January 1922, for instance, the rate plunged from 770 to 860 marks to the pound (approximately 210 and 247 marks to the dollar, respectively).

The Crisis Over Reparations and the Cannes Conference

Germany had been able to pay the first instalment of reparations, one thousand million marks, on schedule in August 1921 but this was to be her last payment in currency for three years. By December financial advisers assured the government that further payments were out of the question. Only foreign loans would allow Germany to meet her debts and no investor was likely to place funds in a sinking ship. Wirth accordingly approached the Allies with a request for a moratorium on the payments due in January and February 1922. Lloyd George and the French Premier, Aristide Briand, both comparatively moderate in their attitude towards Germany, called a European conference in Cannes in January 1922 which would discuss the general economic situation as well as reparations. Germany and Soviet Russia, both outcasts from the European congress of nations, were invited to send representatives.

Rathenau, who had represented Germany in earlier economic discussions with the Allies, headed the German delegation. He all but convinced the British and French that Germany wished to fulfil her obligations even if she could not meet her immediate commitments – they were impressed by his intelligence, realism and sense of proportion. But on 11 January in the middle of the conference the French parliament toppled Briand from power and he was replaced on 15 January by the inveterate Germanophobe, Raymond Poincaré, President of France during the war and a former chairman of the Allied Reparations Commission. While forced to accede to those decisions already reached – a postponement of the reparation instalments due in January and February, and the holding of a second European economic conference in Genoa in April – Poincaré made it clear that he intended to wrest the last *Pfennig* from Germany. In a diplomatic note he informed the German government that her stay of execution must be bought at a high price. This included the imposition of tax increases, currency restrictions and economies in government spending, none of which, if accepted, was likely to enhance the standing at home of the Wirth coalition. Naturally the German government rejected the French note which was seen as an impudent intrusion into Germany's domestic affairs. It was an accurate expression of Poincaré's primitive revanchism. The maintenance of peace in western Europe consisted in keeping Germany subservient, and his policy of obstruction unquestionably contributed much to Germany's internal chaos in the early twenties. That this policy was likely in the future to ricochet on to France was a subtlety lost on Poincaré's essentially simplistic philosophy of politics.

Germany's Foreign Policy under Rathenau

Rathenau, who had few positive results to bring home, had nevertheless won a reputation as a skilled negotiator and diplomat. On 31 January Wirth appointed him Foreign Minister. His subsequent career was marred and cut short by the incessant flow of abuse from the extreme right wing. To attack him for his pursuit of a policy of fulfilment lay within the realm of 'legitimate' political debate, but to attack him on purely racial grounds was typical of the excesses in which the anti-semitic fanatics of the age indulged.

Rathenau was faced with a formidable task. He had to attempt to formulate a foreign policy which adhered to the principles of Erfüllungspolitik and at the same time improve Germany's international standing. Rathenau was by nature pro-Western and he argued that an alliance between the two outcast nations of Europe, Germany and Russia, which was advocated by many political observers, would be seen by the Allies as posing the threat of world Communist revolution. This view was shared by the Social Democrats and, not surprisingly, opposed by the KPD who regarded *rapprochement* with Russia as a first step to the introducton of Soviet government in Germany. They were supported, curiously, by several Nationalists, motivated not of course by any sympathy with the principles of Marxist-Leninism but by the conviction that stable relations in the east would enable them eventually to exact retribution from France. Their view was shared by Seeckt, leader of the

Reichswehr, who regarded a *rapprochement* with Russia as the only sphere in which Germany could pursue an active foreign policy. He saw in Russia a potential ally in the destruction of Poland and the restoration of the pre-war Russo-German frontier. Germany had already shown sympathy to the Soviet régime by remaining neutral in the Russo-Polish war of 1920 and by according the Soviet government diplomatic recognition which was withheld by many Western nations including Britain and the U.S.A. Now that Lenin had revised party doctrine by allowing Soviet collaboration with capitalist régimes, Seeckt hoped for closer economic political and, most important to him, military collaboration with Russia, which he regarded as a more effective method than Erfüllungspolitik of evading the restrictions of Versailles. He had welcomed the signing of the Russo-German Commercial Treaty of May 1921 as a useful preliminary measure. In the following September he opened secret negotiations about the expansion of Russia's armaments industry with German financial and technical assistance.

Diplomatic relations between the two states were encouraged in Berlin by one of Germany's most able diplomats, Baron Adolf von Maltzan, head of the eastern European division of the Foreign Ministry. He favoured a formal political alliance with Russia and initiated informal negotiations in Berlin which produced agreement on many issues. These contacts had received the blessing of Chancellor Wirth, who, since his overtures to the Western powers had been rebuffed, was curious to ascertain Russia's attitude. Rathenau remained unconvinced of the value of further *rapprochement* with Russia but in view of the lack of Allied response to his policy of fulfilment, he encouraged Russo-German economic links and supported Seeckt's military programme. On the Russian side, the Soviet government had regarded Germany as a potential ally for some time. At the Soviet Congress held in December 1920 Lenin had voiced the opinion that Germany, oppressed by Versailles, would naturally seek to form an alliance with Russia, a view which was greeted with considerable warmth by the German Foreign Office Minister, Walter Simons.

The Treaty of Rapallo
On 10 April 1922 the International Economic Conference opened inauspiciously at Genoa in an atmosphere of considerable Franco-

German hostility, aggravated by the worsening monetary crisis in the Reich. Ostensibly the main item on the agenda was the reintegration of Russia into the European economic sphere, the result of a suggestion which Rathenau had made the previous autumn to Lloyd George, in return for a British undertaking to reopen discussions on reparations. The delegates at Genoa, especially the British, were eager to affect a *rapprochement* with Russia but the French characteristically vetoed the inclusion of reparations on the agenda. Economic ties with Russia would, it was hoped, accelerate the economic reconstruction of eastern Europe and present the Allies with an opportunity of coercing the Soviet government into honouring the debts incurred with Western countries by the Czarist régime and into compensating foreign investors in Russia who had suffered financial loss since the Revolution.

The German delegation, accorded equal status at an international conference for the first time since the war, included three of the country's leading politicians: Wirth, Rathenau and von Maltzan as well as government advisers on reparations. They hoped despite French intransigence to inaugurate discussions on reparations, if only on an informal basis, for these nevertheless were central to any consideration of the European economic system. The delegations sent by the other three main powers reflected the importance which their respective governments attached to the conference. Great Britain was represented by her Prime Minister, Lloyd George, Soviet Russia by the People's Commissar for Foreign Affairs, Georgy Chicherin, while Poincaré deliberately snubbed the conference by sending his deputy, Louis Barthou, as the French delegate.

Some progress had already been made between the Germans and British in private talks. Lloyd George, influenced by Keynes' indictment of Versailles *The Economic Consequences of the Peace* which convincingly argued Germany's inability to meet more than a third of the reparation debt which the Allies had demanded, appeared to show sympathy with Germany's problems. The French, however, continued to refuse either a further moratorium on payments or a reduction of the total sum.

The situation was confused by Germany's exclusion from Lloyd George's discussions with the Russian delegation. Wirth and Rathenau feared that Russia was being encouraged to collaborate with the Allies and, in return, to be allowed to claim reparations from Germany under article 116 of Versailles. In fact the discussions between the Allies and Russia were less threatening than the ill-informed German delegation feared, for the French refused categorically to contemplate any understanding with the Soviet government unless they agreed to meet in full the debts incurred by the Czarist régime. Nevertheless the German delegates were left wholly in the dark about the nature of the talks and not unnaturally they conjectured about the subjects under discussion. Whether or not Lloyd George discussed the possibility of Russia's benefiting from article 116, which would have set the seal on Germany's economic ruin and isolated her on both her eastern and western frontiers, the mood of uncertainty and apprehension it produced in the German delegation was all too real.

In the small hours of 16 April 1922, Easter Sunday, von Maltzan wakened Rathenau with a telephone message from Chicherin: unless Germany accepted the Russian offer of a political and economic treaty, Russia would conclude a pact with the Allies. Rathenau, the pro-Western, staunch defender of the policy of fulfilment, reluctantly agreed to meet his Russian counterpart in the neighbouring Mediterranean resort, Rapallo, to negotiate a Russo-German treaty. The negotiations were completed within the day for a draft had already been formulated by Maltzan and Chicherin, who had broken his journey in Berlin *en route* to Genoa. It is not clear whether Chicherin's ultimatum was a ruse to win over the reluctant Rathenau.

The terms of the treaty of friendship were of considerable value to both states. They agreed to restore full diplomatic and consular relations. In return for a renunciation by Russia of all rights to reparations from Germany under article 116 of Versailles, Germany relinquished all claim to indemnification for loss of German-owned property in Russia which had been nationalized since the revolution. Trading regulations between the two states were to be strengthened with the granting of mutual trade preferences.

In terms of international affairs the details of the treaty were unimportant though the announcement of its conclusion caused a world-wide diplomatic sensation and provoked sentiments of outrage from several Allied governments. What was significant was the association of the two outcast nations of Europe, a union which had been produced by the intransigence of the Allies, in particular the French and Belgians, and one which the West viewed with misgivings and distrust. In reality it represented no reorientation of Germany's foreign policy which under Rathenau, and later Stresemann, remained essentially pro-Western. By concluding an alliance with Russia they sought to demonstrate to the West that Germany was capable of pursuing an independent foreign policy despite Allied attempts to dictate to Germany and keep her diplomatically isolated. One definite result of Rapallo was the immediate refusal of the Allies to countenance any reduction of reparations but their willingness on that score had never been very credible. A greater fear was that the treaty contained secret military clauses which posed a threat to Western security. In fact Rapallo contained no such agreement because, as Heiber points out, that had already been catered for elsewhere. At all events Great Britain and France were thrown into each other's arms once more and for the present the Allies presented a united front.

Bavaria Becomes the Centre for Right-Wing Extremism

After the failure of Eisner's government and the suppression of the Communist régime by the Freikorps, Bavaria and, in particular, Munich became the centre for right-wing anti-republican groups. The widespread antipathy of the Bavarians for the Weimar state resulted not only from the popular, if unfounded, fear of a Marxist *coup* in Berlin which, they believed, the Social Democrats in the government would encourage, but equally from their ingrained particularism and hostility to the predominance of Prussia. They regretted their incorporation into the German Empire in 1871, and bitterly resented the demotion of the State of Bavaria to the status of a federal Land, and the accompanying curtailment of their former sovereignty, which had been imposed on them by the new Constitution. Subsequent legislation, introduced by the Weimar Coalition, had, they believed, brought further disadvantages to Bavaria. Erzberger's reform of the taxation system, which deprived the Länder of any remaining fiscal independence irreparably split the Centre Party.

Under the leadership of such men as the Landtag deputy, Gustav von Kahr, and the Munich Chief of Police, Ernst Pöhner, the presence of political extremist groups, composed largely of former

1 Kaiser Wilhelm II

2 Paul von Beneckendorff und von
Hindenburg

3 Erich von Ludendorff

4 Hindenburg, the Kaiser
and Ludendorff

6 Rosa Luxemburg

5 Karl Liebknecht

7 Matthias Erzberger

8 Friedrich Ebert

10 Philipp Scheidemann

9 Wilhelm Groener

11 Scheidemann proclaiming the Republic before the Reichstag, 1918

12 Gustav Noske and Friekorps troops

13 Sailors in revolt in Berlin

14 Spartacist guards during the Berlin Rising 1919

15 DDP election poster (1920) advocating moderation and condemning extremism of the right and left

16 Spartakus election poster (1920) condemning the proposed introduction of parliamentary democracy

17 Kurt Eisner

BERLIN

MÜNCHEN

II/6

BAYERN, DER BOLSCHEWIK GEHT UM!
HINAUS MIT IHM AM WAHLTAG!
BAYERISCHE VOLKSPARTEI

18 BVP election poster (1919) warning against intervention in Bavarian affairs by the Bolshevik, i.e. SPD, government

19 Clemenceau, Wilson and Lloyd George in Paris

20 Captain Ehrhardt (left) with officers during the Kapp Putsch

21 Wolfgang Kapp

22 General
Hans von
Seeckt

23 Walther Rathenau

24 Adolf Hitler

25 Ernst Röhm

26 French Occupation troops in the Ruhr, 1923

27, 28 Bank notes during the Inflation, 1923

29 Gustav Stresemann

30 Men and women searching for coal during the Inflation, 1922

32 Hjalmar Schacht

31 Wilhelm Marx

33 SA troops arriving in Munich before the Hitler Putsch, 1923

34 NSDAP election poster (1924) appealing to the workers and attacking capitalists

35 Racialist block (NSDAP) election poster (1924) attacking the parliamentary system

36 SDP election poster (1924) equating Nazism with militarism and hostility to the working class

37 Hermann Müller

38 Alfred Hugenberg

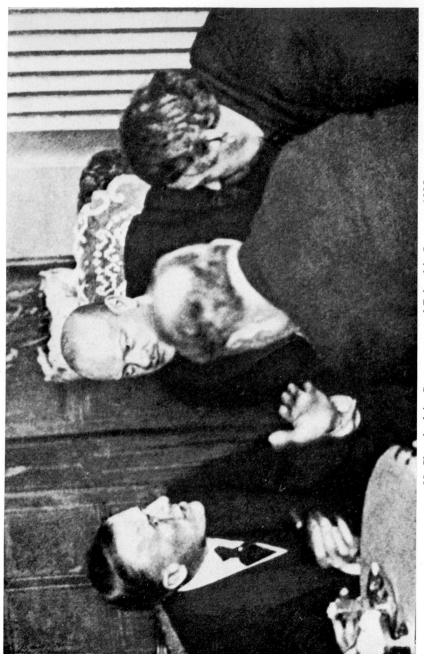

39 Chamberlain, Stresemann and Briand in Lugano, 1925

40 Kurt von Schleicher

41 Heinrich Brüning

42 DVP election poster (1930) showing Stresemann and the Rhine, an allusion to his successful policy towards the West

43 DNVP election poster (1932) calling for increased presidential powers and an end to the parliamentary process

45 Franz von Pap

44 Papen and Schleicher

46 SPD election poster (1932) showing a worker crucified on a swastika

47 Zentrum election poster (1932) proclaiming Brüning as the last bastion of freedom, law and order against left- and right-wing extremism

48 NSDAP election poster (1932) proclaiming Hitler as the workers' last hope

49 Hitler shaking hands with Hindenburg

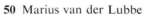
50 Marius van der Lubbe

51 The Reichstag on fire, 1933

52 Hermann Goering

53 Joseph Goebbels

Ein Volk, ein Reich, ein Führer!

54 One People, one Reich, one Leader: poster which hung in offices and schoolrooms throughout Germany until 1945

members of the disbanded Freikorps who had been unable to enter the Reichswehr, was openly tolerated. The para-military activities of the self-styled Patriotic Leagues, *Vaterländische Verbände*, which they formed, were encouraged by the authorities. In this milieu, wholly permissive towards right-wing extremism, the small German Workers' Party, *Deutsche Arbeiterpartei*, came into being, later to be transformed by Hitler into the National Socialist Party.

The Origins of Adolf Hitler

Adolf Hitler was born on 20 April 1889 in Braunau-am-Inn, Upper Austria, a small town on the frontier between the Austro-Hungarian Empire and Bavaria. He was the son of a fifty-two-year-old customs official, Alois Hitler, and his wife, Klara, aged twenty-nine. Alois Hitler, the illegitimate son of a Graz servant woman, Anna Maria Schicklgrüber, received his surname from his foster-father. The suggestion, often made, that Hitler's father was Jewish has been neither proved nor disproved. This, as Nolte points out, is unimportant compared with the possibility of Hitler's believing that he might be quarter-Jewish, which, given his views on racial purity, would account for the virulence of his anti-semitism. Hitler's early family life, though materially relatively comfortable, seems to have been far from happy. 'Alois Hitler was not only very much older than Klara . . . but hard, unsympathetic and short-tempered. His domestic life – three wives, one fourteen years older than himself, one twenty-three years younger; a separation; and seven children, including an illegitimate child and two others born shortly after the wedding – suggests a difficult and passionate temperament. (Bullock: *Hitler, a Study in Tyranny*, p. 25f.)

After attending a number of primary schools Hitler entered the *Realschule* in Linz where the family had settled in 1897, a secondary school specializing in technical and commercial education. His progress was undistinguished. He showed little aptitude for sustained study and was obliged to transfer at the age of fourteen to the Realschule in the near-by town, Steyr. He despised his teachers with the single exception of Leopold Pötsch, who taught history and whose ardent German nationalism aroused Hitler's interest and, he maintained in his autobiography, *Mein Kampf*, that of his fellow pupils who 'often aflame with enthusiasm, sometimes even moved to tears' (p. 13) listened to Pötsch relating heroic tales of German history, using 'our budding nationalistic fanaticism as a means of educating us'. (*Mein Kampf* p. 14.)

In 1905, without obtaining his school leaving certificate, a necessary qualification for entry into the Austrian Civil Service, a career which his father had chosen for his son, Hitler left school. He subsequently blamed his lack of academic success on the poor relationship which existed between him and his father and his refusal to follow his father into government service. The decisive reason would seem to be the limitations imposed on him by his personality: he was prone to short-lived bursts of enthusiasm for projects but was prevented from sustaining interest and application by his lack of self-discipline and a dominant trait of inertia. Two years later he left his mother's home and moved to Vienna, the capital of the Austro-Hungarian Empire. He took with him the inheritance, which was made over to him at the age of eighteen, left to him by his father who had died five years earlier.

Hitler's Years in Vienna

Hitler had abundant faith in his artistic abilities and confidently expected to be accepted as a student by the *Kunstakademie*, the Academy of Fine Arts in Vienna. The rejection of his application for admission in 1907, on the grounds that his drawing ability was insufficient, deeply embittered him. He spent the following seven years pursuing a totally aimless existence in Vienna: having rapidly exhausted his capital in indulging his extravagant tastes, he was reduced to living in the appalling conditions of Viennese working-men's hostels and lodging-houses for the unemployed. During this period he had no regular employment but drifted constantly from one job to another undertaking a variety of casual work from labouring to painting picture post-cards. It was not, however, the misery of his living conditions which made the deepest impression on Hitler during his stay in Vienna, but the political ideas which he assimilated from his conversations with fellow inmates, from innumerable booklets and pamphlets and, in particular, from the anti-semitic gutter press, which he read in his not inconsiderable spare time. 'Vienna remained for me the hardest, though most thorough, school of my life', he wrote in *Mein Kampf*, 'In (Vienna) I obtained the foundations for a philosophy in general and a political view in particular ... which never left me.' (p. 114.)

The Foundations of Hitler's Political Creed

In 1924 Hitler maintained in *Mein Kampf* that he had been revolted by the cosmopolitan, internationalist society which he discovered in Vienna, capital city of an empire which embraced a dozen nations in central Europe. 'I was repelled by the conglomeration of races which the capital showed me,' he maintained, 'by this whole mixture of Czechs, Poles, Hungarians, Ruthenians, Serbs and Croats, and, everywhere, the eternal mushroom [literally, *fission fungus*] of humanity – Jews and more Jews.' (*Mein Kampf* p. 119.) Whether at that time anti-semitism occupied such a pre-eminent position in his philosophy is doubtful. More likely, he ascribed greater significance to his Viennese apprenticeship in retrospect when he discovered the virulence of post-war German racialism. The chronology is, however, relatively unimportant in a discussion of his recorded opinions.

Hitler stated that his racialism owed much to the policies of two contemporary Austrian politicians, Georg von Schönerer, leader of the Austrian Pan-German Party, and Karl Lueger, Mayor of Vienna and leader of the Christian Socialist Party, the largest in the Austrian Parliament. He was attracted by Schönerer's fanatical German nationalism, his opposition to the multi-national Austro-Hungarian Empire, his anti-semitism and his vision of a regeneration of the German people, but condemned his anti-clericalism as tactically unsound in a staunchly Catholic country. He admired Lueger, on the other hand, as an astute political tactician, for his success in winning over large sections of the electorate, the *petite bourgeoisie*, minor civil servants and workers, with policies which transcended traditional class barriers and which he expounded in eloquent, sentimental speeches. Lueger's anti-semitism differed from that of the Pan-Germans in that it was based on economic rather than racialist grounds but was none the less effective. He offered to protect the 'little man' from the threat of economic exploitation by usurious business interests which he ascribed to Jewish *entrepreneurs*. He won further support by introducing civic improvements and social reform, and while these good works were not motivated by socialist convictions, for Lueger was avowedly anti-Marxist and a supporter of the Catholic Church, they were successful in attracting the votes of the workers. Hitler later wrote in *Mein Kampf* that an amalgam of the policies of the two parties, the racialism and nationalism of the Pan-Germans and the social and economic programme of the Christian Socialists, could have produced 'a movement which . . . might have successfully intervened in German destiny'. (Ibid. p. 112.)

The corollary of Hitler's anti-semitism was his idealization of the Aryan, a term used by contemporary racialist theorists to describe the Germanic or Nordic tribes of northern Europe, the *Herrenrasse* or master race. Hitler deduced from his view of history which saw the development of Western culture in terms of a continuous battle between Aryans and Jews, that, 'If we were to divide mankind into three groups, the founders of culture, the maintainers of culture, the destroyers of culture, only the Aryan could be considered as the representative of the first group.' (Ibid. p. 263.) For this reason racial 'purity' was essential. Intermarriage, or 'blood mixture' in the vocabulary of the racialists, was abhorred as it contradicted 'the iron logic of nature . . . Blood mixture and the resultant drop in the racial level is the sole cause of the dying out of old cultures.' (Ibid. p. 269.) The Aryans, therefore, had to maintain their dominance by means of constant vigilance and struggle against society's subversive elements.

His hatred for Social Democracy, the only rival to his anti-semitic fervour, in fact sprang from the same source. Emulating Lueger's simplistic, and erroneous, equation of economic exploitation with Jewish business interests, he monomanically identified Socialism with an international Jewish conspiracy to conquer the world. 'Meanwhile, I had learned to understand the connection between this doctrine of destruction (Social Democracy) and the nature of a people of which, up to that time, I had known next to nothing. Only a knowledge of the Jews provides the key with which to comprehend the inner, and consequently real, aims of Social Democracy.' (Ibid. p. 47.)

His profound, petit bourgeois fear of a Marxist-Jewish proletariat conspiracy produced in him unbounded hatred for both Jews and Social Democracy and a messianic mission to attack both with unrelenting, fanatical zeal. 'If with the help of his Marxist creed, the Jew,' whom he considered to be 'the mightiest counterpart to the Aryan,' (Ibid. p. 272) 'is victorious over the other peoples of the world, his crown will be the funeral wreath of humanity. . . . Hence today I believe that I am acting in accordance with the will of the

Almighty Creator: by defending myself against the Jews I am fighting for the work of the Lord.' (Ibid. p. 60.) After 1933 he all but achieved his appalling aims in the *Endlösung*, the final solution to the 'Jewish Question', their extermination.

The Austrian Social Democrats, though hated for their internationalism, won Hitler's admiration for their efficient party organization. He learnt much by observing the nature of their popular appeal: mass meetings, street marches, smart uniforms, party songs and the combination of social and political activities. Here was the direct forerunner of the Nürnberg rallies, the Brown Shirts, the Horst Wessel Song and the slogan 'Strength through Joy', (*Kraft durch Freude*), the Nazi organization which provided cheap recreation and holidays for working families. He also profited, as Nolte shows, from his study of another political group, the German Workers' Party, *Deutsche Arbeiterpartei*, DAP, which enjoyed a considerable following in pre-war Austria. Steeped in romantic notions about the nobility of the German craftsman in medieval times, it was critical of the workings of early twentieth-century capitalism. Its *raison d'être*, however, was to protect German workers from the threat of cheap Czech labour and, as such, was essentially non-Marxist. It placed its faith in the concept of the German nation and was, therefore, willing to collaborate with other classes in society in its attempt to ward off the threat from without. Nazi tactics owed much to this model especially to the *conditio sine qua non* of the external threat. The omission from *Mein Kampf* of any allusion to the DAP suggests, as Nolte convincingly argues, that Hitler deliberately wished to conceal the similarities between the DAP and the Nazi Party.

Hitler's Character

His racialist theories are also significant in illuminating his intellectual limitations. Hitler, ever critical of reason and logic, demanded that issues with which he had to deal should be immediately intelligible; if they appeared complex he reduced them to simplistic terms which he could readily grasp. Nolte attributes this to Hitler's dominant trait of infantilism which, present in all people, was exaggerated in him to a psychopathic degree. He indulged in frequent day-dreaming and wishful thinking often within the context of a Wagnerian Germanic Utopia. Plans of pretentious monuments which he made in his adolescence were executed thirty years later when he came to power. He harboured grudges permanently: a year after coming to power, in the Night of the Long Knives, he directed the elimination of hundreds of people, influential and unimportant alike, to whom at some time in his life he had with or without justification taken exception. His infantile appreciation of life enabled him to convince himself of the practicality of wholly impractical schemes, and with his air of supreme self-confidence and outstanding gift of oratory to convince others. His infantilism accounts also for his inability to compromise his views or to accommodate others and for his frequent outbursts of anger. 'Hitler's rage', writes Nolte, 'was the uncontrollable fury of the child who bangs the chair because the chair refuses to do as it is told; his dreaded harshness, which nonchalantly sent millions of people to their death, was much closer to the rambling imaginings of a boy than to the iron grasp of a man, and is therefore intimately and typically related to his profound aversion to the cruelty of hunting, vivisection, and the consumption of meat generally.' (*Three Faces of Fascism* p. 289.)

Hitler Moves to Bavaria

In May 1913 Hitler decided to leave Vienna, apparently to avoid conscription into the Austrian army. He settled in Munich where, at the outbreak of war in August 1914, he enlisted in the Bavarian army. The war promised him, and many Austrians and Germans, release from a humdrum existence and offered the prospect of personal adventure in a patriotic cause: the defence, and for some, the aggrandizement, of the Imperial Reich. His wartime experiences in the trenches deepened his bitterness towards life, though he valued the companionship of his fellow troops. He was twice denied promotion to the officer corps on account of his fanaticism and despite his having been decorated twice with the Iron Cross (second and first class), one of Germany's highest military awards, he rose no higher than the rank of corporal. When the Armistice was signed in November 1918, Hitler was a patient in a hospital in Pasewalk in Pomerania, receiving treatment for temporary blindness caused by mustard gas which British forces had used in attacking his division near Ypres in October.

Hitler was outraged by the terms of the Armistice and was convinced, as were many of his comrades, that the military had been betrayed by the civilian government which was headed, significantly, by a Socialist. At the end of the year he returned to Munich and witnessed the establishment of the Bavarian Socialist Republic under Kurt Eisner who, conveniently for Hitler's conspiracy theory, was an intellectual, a left-wing Socialist and a member of the Jewish faith. It reinforced all his previously held prejudices and appeared to confirm the propaganda he had recently read in the 'Protocols of the Elders of Zion', a tract which, while purporting to be of Jewish authorship, was in fact undisguisedly anti-semitic but whose authenticity Hitler unquestioningly accepted. He decided to engage in politics in order to rid Germany from the grips of this imaginary international conspiracy.

Military service had satisfied Hitler's desire for action and had provided him with the security of community life. With the end of the war he became unemployed once more. He disliked the prospect of returning to his fatuous peacetime existence and looked for an occupation which would satisfy his megalomanic ambition. He did not have long to wait. In May 1919, after the combined forces of the Reichswehr and Freikorps had overthrown Levien's and Leviné's Soviet régime, army authorities established a commission to inquire into the activities of Communist suspects. Hitler, called before the Commission to give evidence, impressed its members with his opinions and eloquence and was offered employment in its propaganda division. His function was twofold: he was to assist in compiling a list of those who had collaborated with the Soviet régime and, when his superiors had discovered his talent for rabble-rousing, he was appointed 'education officer' whose task it was to indoctrinate the troops and assure that they remained loyal to the military command.

In September 1919 he investigated a small political group, the German Workers' Party, *Deutsche Arbeiterpartei*, which had been founded six months previously by a local railway mechanic, Anton Drexler. The military authorities regarded the party as a potential mouthpiece for their propaganda since it was opposed to Marxism and dedicated to the *embourgeoisement* of the working and lower middle classes. It advocated improvements in the working conditions of the 'little man' while laying great stress on the virtues of nationalism and patriotism. In the late Autumn of 1919 Hitler joined the party as its 555th member; his subsequent claim that he was its seventh member referred, as Watt shows, to his membership of the executive committee. Early in 1920 Hitler was placed in charge of creating the party's publicity machine, an office for which he was well qualified. Under his guidance the party, which until this time had been little more than one of the many groups of malcontents which were formed during the revolution, developed into a sizeable political force, limited at first to Munich and Bavaria but within a decade to become a mass movement. The immediate aim of the party at this time was to overthrow the *Judenrepublik* and eliminate the November Criminals, the Jewish conspiracy of Liberals, Democrats and Socialists who had stabbed Germany in the back.

Hitler's monomanic attacks on the Republic sprang from his particular objection to democracy, to the notion of compromise, and the need to comply with the will of the majority (provided, that is, that the majority disagreed with his philosophy) inherent in the parliamentary system. His vehement rejection of the Weimar Republic, motivated by this genuine fear of democracy, conveniently provided him with a plausible *rationale* for the humiliating defeat which the German army had sustained and the events of the winter of 1918 to 1919. The Republic became a popular scapegoat on which every minor dissatisfaction could be blamed, and Hitler's monomania persuaded the gullible likewise to concentrate their aggression and hatred onto this single foe.

The question has to be asked: how did the Nazis and Hitler succeed in winning the minds of large numbers of people where other racialist groups and fanatics failed? Nolte, among others, suggests convincingly that their success may be ascribed to Hitler's peculiar gifts of oratory, both to the content and the technique of his public speaking:

Time and again his speeches contained passages of irresistible force and compelling conviction, such as no other speaker of his time was capable of producing. There are always the places where his 'faith' finds expression, and it was obviously this faith which induced that emotion among the masses to which even the most hostile observer testified. But at no time do these passages reveal anything new, never do they make the listener reflect or exert his critical faculty: all they ever do is conjure up magically before his eyes that which already existed in him as a vague feeling, inarticulate longing. (Ibid. p. 292.)

It was this ability to articulate feelings of which the audience had previously been only subconsciously aware, what Nolte calls his mediumistic faculty, combined with his evangelistic style of speaking which distinguished him from other politicians. He relied not on rational political argument, whose effect he recognized to be limited, but on arousing an emotional response in his audience, a technique for which he had an innate and seemingly unfailing psychological understanding. The combination of powerful rhetoric and the emotional appeal of racialism and patriotism induced a state of hysteria in his audience which no logical political argument could ever achieve. Truth in political argument was, he maintained, irrelevant; the efficacy of a speaker lay in his ability emotionally to arouse audiences by whatever means were most successful. 'The scantiness of the abstract knowledge they possess directs their sentiments more to the world of feeling. That is where their positive or negative attitude lies. . . . Their emotional attitude at the same time conditions their extraordinary stability. Faith is harder to shake than knowledge . . . and the impetus to the mightiest upheavals on this earth has at all times consisted less in a scientific knowledge dominating the masses than in a fanaticism which inspired them and sometimes in a hysteria which drove them forward. Anyone who wants to win over the broad masses must know the key that opens the door to their hearts. Its name is not objectivity (read weakness) but will and power.' (*Mein Kampf* pp. 306–7.) This belief in the credulity of the masses, subsequently borne out by events, dictated Hitler's strategy in disseminating his views: 'Propaganda must be adjusted to the broad masses in content and in form, and its soundness is to be measured exclusively by its effective result.' (Ibid. p. 311.) 'It should limit itself to a few points, emphasized frequently for only if the simplest ideas are repeated thousands of times will the masses finally remember them.' (Ibid. p. 169.) Truth was not considered by Hitler to be even a *desideratum* of politics: 'If truth is to be falsified for the sake of greater efficiency the lie should be enormous for such a falsehood will never enter the heads [of the masses] and they will not be able to believe in the possibility of such monstrous effrontery and infamous misrepresentation in others; yes, even when enlightened on a subject, they will long doubt and waver and continue to accept at least one of these causes as true. Therefore, something of even the most insolent lie will always remain and stick.' (Ibid. p. 211.) This advocacy of consciously unscrupulous methods testifies further to Hitler's remarkable ability to understand the psychology of his mass audiences and also to his shrewd estimation of his political opponents whose faith in the democratic system, he accurately supposed, would prevent them from using the same political weapons as himself.

Party Organization

In April 1920 the party's title became the National Socialist German Workers' Party, *Nationalsozialistiche Deutsche Arbeiterpartei*, NSDAP, an attempt to widen the party's appeal particularly among the working classes. It borrowed many of the trappings of Socialism, including, as Broszat has shown, the red colour of the party's flags and armbands, now emblazoned with the racialist emblem, the swastika, and Socialist songs with, naturally, revised texts. The new title, however, aroused misgivings among the bourgeoisie about the Nazis' attitude to the capitalist system and later in the year Hitler was obliged to deny that the party was anti-capitalist. National Socialism implied no condemnation of capitalism as such, but of the 'tyranny' of Jewish capital in the German economy. Any suspicion of capitalism harboured by other party leaders in the early years of Nazism was quickly dispelled when they realized that the financial and political support of big-business was essential if they were to obtain power. The title of the party was, as Heiber shows, wholly misleading. It was only National when it suited its purpose, preferring for example in 1923 to attack the German government than to blame the French for the Ruhr occupation. In 1920 it could hardly be regarded as a German party, restricted, as it was, to Munich. Neither can it be maintained that the Nazis aimed to be a working-class party for they deliberately appealed to a broad spectrum of the population. For similar reasons the term 'party' was an inaccurate description of an essentially extra-parliamentary force, pledged to the creation of a dictatorship which excluded all political opposition. Subsequently the Nazis referred to themselves as a movement, *Bewegung*, which, like Mussolini's

Fascist *movimento*, purported to transcend vulgar, decadent party politics.

Hitler was determined from the day he joined the party to become its leader. Only leadership of the party would satisfy his megalomania. This lust for supreme power and control of the state – of which his fear of democracy and parliamentarianism is symptomatic – accounts for his particular conception of the ideal social structure. Its form was in essence pyramidal: the leader, the creator of the new *national* culture at the apex would head an organization of command. The leader would issue orders to his immediate inferior who would, in turn, supervise the activities of those below him and so on down to the lowest forms of human existence at the base, the Jews.

In 1921 Hitler succeeded in ousting Drexler from the party leadership. As his grip on the party organization became stronger he fostered the personality cult of the *Führer*, the National Leader, encouraged by Mussolini's success as Italy's *Duce*. Italian Fascism provided further inspiration to the Nazis in military matters. In November 1921 Ernst Röhm, the leader of a group of Bavarian officers and an amateur politician, with the connivance and tacit encouragement of his superiors in the Munich Army Command, founded the SA, *Schutzabteilung*, Defence Division, later changed significantly to *Sturmabteilung*, Storm Division. The SA was the party's private army, moulded on the *Squadre d'azione*, the Fascist para-military organization in Italy which had scored considerable successes. Its members, drawn from the recently demobilized Freikorps units, including the unsuccessful Putschists of Captain Ehrhardt's brigade and the Organization Consul, which had been responsible for Erzberger's assassination, formed an impressive, intimidating force of zealots and thugs, eager to engage with political opponents. They fulfilled a secondary rôle by appealing to the popular love of military pomp: smart aggressive uniforms, organized marches and stirring, martial music. As Bullock observes, as many people were attracted by displays of violence, in which the SA indulged, as were repelled by them. Hitler relied on their presence at public meetings not only to create a bogus atmosphere of pomp and circumstance but also to silence hecklers, for his strategy of persuasion through emotional appeal presupposed non-interference from the audience.

The Party Programme

At one of the party's first mass meetings held on 25 February 1920 in the Hofbräuhaus, a Munich beer-hall, Hitler proclaimed the Programme of the National Socialist Party. The twenty-five points of the Programme, designed to attract the largest following, were an amalgam of the views of several leading party members, in particular Drexler, Hitler and Gottfried Feder, the party's economic theorist, and presented a mixture of socialist, nationalist, economic and racialist theory. The first four points, which closely reflect Hitler's philosophy, are historically the most significant in that they contain the basic Nazi principles, namely, rejection of Versailles, territorial expansion and racial purity. Since the treaties of Versailles and St Germain failed to grant the German people equality with other nations, they were to be abrogated (point 2). Germans were to be granted the right to self-determination (point 1), an appeal to Pan-Germanism, clothed in Wilson's liberal terminology. Although Hitler was later to maintain in *Mein Kampf* that: 'One must not allow existing political frontiers to distract attention from what ought to exist on principles of strict justice', those principles had little in common with Wilson's ideals. Indeed, Germany's right to acquire new colonies 'for the nourishment of our people and the settlement of our surplus population', was claimed in point 3. The areas to be colonized were defined in *Mein Kampf* where Hitler wrote: 'If land was desired in Europe [i.e. during the First World War] it could be obtained by and large at the expense of Russia, and this meant that the new Reich must again set itself on the march along the road of the Teutonic knights of old, to obtain by the German sword sod for the German plough and daily bread for the nation' (pp. 128–9). Their expansionist aims, he maintained, remained unaltered, and were outlined in the two principles of the Nazis' *Ostpolitik*: the acquisition of *Lebensraum*, Living Space, by means of the traditional *Drang nach Osten*, Thrust to the East, into the Slav territories. The exponents of the expansionist policies sought to justify their lust for colonial gains by arguing that the eastern territories would provide the *Herrenrasse* with the raw materials and agricultural produce essential for a solution to their economic problems. Point 4 deals with racial and specifically anti-semitic matters: 'Only members of the nation (*Volksgenosse*) can be citizens of the state. Only those of German blood, whatever their creed, can be members of the nation. Therefore no Jew can be a member of the nation.' Those who were not citizens of the state were to be subject to special alien laws (point 5), to be deprived of the right to vote in popular elections and denied appointment to official posts (point 6). The programme argued that the Jews were the source of all Germany's ills and pledged the Party 'to combat the Jewish-materialist spirit within us and outside us' in the conviction 'that a lasting recovery of the nation can be achieved solely from within, based on the principle of "common interest before self-interest"' (point 24). The *rationale* for this Utopian – and patently false – racialist theory was that the German nation could be reborn and restored to its rightful position of strength and dignity only if it achieved 'racial purity'.

The remaining points deliberately wooed the support of various sections of the population. The Programme exploited the widespread popular discontent with the Republic, by discrediting the parliamentary régime with its 'corrupting parliamentary practices' (point 6), and proposing a new, quasi-socialist system. It was the duty of the state to provide employment for its citizens (point 7), an appeal to the unemployed, which in the years between 1930 and 1933 acquired new relevance. The aged – a valuable source of votes – were to be given generous financial aid (point 15). The principles of Feder's and Drexler's anti-capitalist crusade were expounded under the heading, printed in large, bold type, 'Abolition of the tyranny of interest', deliberately challenging Marxism on its own ground. The Nazis undertook to abolish interest on capital (point 11), to nationalize large concerns (point 13) and to introduce profit-sharing for workers in industry (point 14). The Nazis' anti-capitalism differed fundamentally from Marxist doctrine: while exploiting the *petite bourgeoisie's* fear of the power of big business, the 'little man' was encouraged to remain a petty capitalist in order to 'create a healthy middle class' (point 16). Large departmental stores (i.e. specifically those in Jewish ownership) were to be leased to small traders (point 16), who became a reliable source of support for the party. The small farmers were also catered for: under the terms of a radical land reform, landowners were to be expropriated and their estates given to the peasants, who since the war had suffered from acute financial difficulties (point 17).

The Programme gave details of a radical reorganization which the

Party intended to impose on the structure of the state. The quasi-federal structure of the Republic was to be replaced by a 'strong, central Reich power' which would control administration throughout the country (point 25). This is not to be understood simply as an attack on separatism or particularism, which, in Bavaria at least, was by no means wholly unsympathetic to the Nazis, but was basic to Hitler's philosophy of organization. If all power within the state was to emanate from the top, from the Führer, then a unitary system of government was essential. Other conditions necessary for the establishment of dictatorial rule were listed: the future Nazi régime would replace Roman Law, condemned for its support of the 'materialistic world order', with a German law (point 19) which, undefined in the Party Programme, was to secure the existence of a totalitarian police state. Freedom of expression was to be severely curtailed by the provisions of point 23 which demanded the banning of newspapers owned by non-Germans (i.e. Jews) and the creation of a German press. It threatened to proscribe 'those newspapers which are not conducive to the national welfare' and to prosecute 'artistic and literary tendencies which have a destructive influence on the life of the nation'. Legal action was to be undertaken against 'the conscious political lies, disseminated in the Press', a principle flagrantly contradicted by Hitler in *Mein Kampf*. The indoctrination of the youth was openly advocated at 'schools [which] must aim to teach the idea of the state as soon as the pupil can comprehend it' (point 20). Following Lueger's careful avoidance of opposition from organized religion, the Programme vouchsafed freedom of conscience to all religious denominations – with the exception of course of Judaism – 'as long as they do not endanger the existence of the state, or offend against the morality of the German race' (point 24).

The Programme was declared inviolable by the party conference held at Bamberg in 1926. Many of its basic principles remained official party policy: territorial expansionism, Pan-Germanism, anti-semitism and the Aryan cult, and the establishment of a totalitarian, unitary state. Other points, in particular those dealing with economic principles, underwent considerable modification. In April 1928, in an attempt to appease agrarian interests, Hitler declared that the expropriation of land, referred to in point 17, applied only to those who had obtained land 'in an illegal manner', that is, 'primarily to Jewish land speculators', the traditional scapegoat. In fact the party ideology, apart from its basic anti-Marxist, anti-semitic, nationalist and expansionist principles was deliberately fluid, adaptable and often self-contradictory. In this way new supporters were attracted by a programme which appeared to accommodate and confirm their private prejudices.

The Slow Growth of the Party

In the early 1920s the party's progress was slow, failing to make the impression on Bavarian politics which Hitler with his customary over-confidence had expected. It contrasted with the situation of Fascism in Italy. The reasons for the comparative weakness of Nazism lay, as Nolte demonstrates, in the different *raisons d'être* of the two parties. While the Italian Fascist Party was essentially a middle-class movement opposed to a real Marxist threat, National Socialism was founded in reaction to a lost war and from fear of a Bolshevik revolution, as the heterogeneous composition of the membership at this time shows: demobilized soldiers, disillusioned intellectuals, especially students, apolitical workers and *petite bourgeoisie* and a motley of malcontents. As Nolte further shows the Party was obliged to create constant agitation in order to foster the impression that left-wing revolution was imminent. This accounts for the Nazis' equation of Bolshevism with Social Democracy and the Jewish community, a combination with sufficient superficial plausibility to convince the gullible. The need to create civil disturbance to give an impression of impending – Bolshevik – revolution was met by the disruptive terrorist activities of the SA.

The acquisition in December 1920 of a newspaper, *Völkischer Beobachter*, Racialist Observer, with money raised by Ernst Röhm, much of which was donated secretly and illegally from Reichswehr funds, allowed Hitler's propaganda to reach a wider audience and brought a moderate increase in membership. In the early 1920s the Party suffered from a chronic shortage of funds although several local *entrepreneurs* offered financial support to Hitler. Lack of adequate capital prevented the Nazis from successfully exploiting the instability of the Republic in the many crises which occurred in the first years of its existence. It was obliged *pro tempore* to collaborate with other right-wing, racialist groups and with the Bavarian authorities if it was to exploit Bavarian particularism and hostility to the democratic central government in Berlin, as preparation for the overthrow of the Republic and the establishment of a Nazi dictatorship. For this reason the Nazis joined the racialist organization, the Union of Fatherland Leagues, *Vaterländische Verbände*, in November 1922 and succeeded in 1923 in gaining the sympathy of the Bavarian Commissioner, Gustav von Kahr, and General von Lossow, Reichswehr leader in Bavaria, on whose support the success or failure of their projected Putsch against the Republic would depend. Given that the Party depended for its very existence on civil agitation and political unrest, the crisis year 1923 presented Hitler with an opportunity which he could not ignore.

The Assassination of Rathenau

The government's success at Rapallo did little to moderate extreme right-wing passions. Hostility to the Erfüllungspolitiker grew more virulent throughout 1921-2. The disgrace of Versailles had been followed by the enormity of the Allied demand for reparations, the injustice of the Upper Silesian plebiscite and the continuous depreciation of the currency. Their discontent demanded a scapegoat, preferably a politician, on whom they could vent their splenetic rage, a man to whom they could attribute their ills, real and imaginary. Such a man was Walther Rathenau for he possessed several vulnerable qualities. To be a liberal republican was condemnation in itself, Rathenau, however, combined this with further undeniable faults, not the least of which was his Jewish faith – 'race', to use the extremists' term – a feature which provoked the blind hatred of many, from the wealthy Nationalist to the impoverished *petite bourgeoisie*, *Spiessbürger*. During his period of office as Foreign Minister, Rathenau had become the object of a parliamentary smear campaign organized by the Nationalists under their fanatically anti-semitic party leader, Karl Helfferich, a politician who could already boast of having destroyed Erzberger's career and who bore the moral guilt for his assassination. Helfferich, a zealous opponent of Erfüllungspolitik, regarded Rathenau as a member of an international Jewish conspiracy whose intention it was to bring disaster to the Reich. Had it not been Rathenau who had conducted negotiations on reparations with the Allies in Cannes and London, which had condemned Germany to financial servitude for thirty years? Moreover, had it not been at Rathenau's instigation that the Treaty of Rapallo had been concluded with the Bolsheviks? That the second accusation did not accord strictly with the facts of the situation and that it contradicted the notion that Rathenau intended to fetter Germany to the Allies, were regarded by the right-wingers as hair-splitting objections.

On the morning of 24 June 1922, the day after a Reichstag debate in which Hellferich had indicted Rathenau with having caused the galloping depreciation of the mark, Rathenau left his home in Grunewald, in western Berlin, for his office in the Wilhelm-strasse in the city centre. His open car was followed by another vehicle carrying three men, members of 'Organization C' and former officers in Ehrhardt's Marine Brigade. They drew within range and one of them lobbed a hand grenade into Rathenau's car while a second peppered it with sub-machine-gun fire. He was killed instantly.

Assassination had become the order of the day for political extremists. It was regarded by many opponents of the régime as a legitimate political weapon; only three weeks earlier an attempt had been made on the life of Philipp Scheidemann. The same afternoon Wirth addressed a crowded session of the Reichstag praising Rathenau's efforts and exhorting supporters of the Republic, Socialists and liberals, to oppose by all legal means the further spread of terrorism in the country. 'The enemy', he stated, 'is to be found on the Right.' Helfferich, at whom the remark was primarily addressed, was all but thrown out of the chamber.

The Emergency Decree 'for the Protection of the Republic'

On the same day Ebert made use of his emergency powers under article 48 of the Constitution to promulgate a presidential decree 'for the Protection of the Republic' obliging the Länder governments to suppress organizations hostile to the Republic and to prosecute those who worked for its downfall. A special supreme court, *Staatsgerichtshof*, was established to deal with all matters affecting the security of the Republic. On 18 July the decree was confirmed by a large majority of the Reichstag. Opposition came from the Communists, the Nationalists and their new bed-fellows, the Bavarian People's Party, whose Land harboured many of the illegal groups.

Right-wing deputies in the Bavarian Landtag forced the moderate but weak Premier, Lerchenfeld, to issue an emergency decree to counteract the Reich law, a constitutionally illegal act. Ebert threatened to order military intervention in Bavaria in order to impose the Reich law but indicated also that he was willing to negotiate with the Land government. A compromise was reached: Bavaria agreed to rescind their unconstitutional decree while the Reich undertook to grant special rights to the Bavarian government in matters concerning the police and the judiciary. Once again a head-on conflict between the two had been avoided by the Republic's backing down before Bavarian, illegal, obstruction. Though the immediate crisis was resolved, holding the candle to the devil merely postponed the day when the Reich would have to deal firmly with Bavaria.

The seeds of further conflict were sown almost immediately. The Bavarian right wing, dissatisfied with the terms of the Berlin-Munich agreement, demanded the resignation of the 'weak' Lerchenfeld. The BVP and the Bavarian branch of the Nationalists, now unified in all but name, chose as his successor the malleable politician, Eugen von Knilling. He could be relied upon to dance to the tune called by the monarchist leader, Kahr, who had been forced to work behind the scenes since his dismissal from the premiership in September 1921.

The Deterioration of the Economic Situation

Severe financial repercussions resulted from the public disquiet aroused by Rathenau's assassination, and confidence in the mark was severely shaken by the repeated outbreaks of thuggery which followed his death. Since 1918 Germany had suffered from increasing financial difficulties, rapid inflation and an adverse trading balance, caused by the infirmity of the German economy and industry which had been geared for several years to a war-machine. The economic and financial distress inherited by the Republic was aggravated by the penalties imposed at Versailles. Monthly payments of reparations rapidly depleted the Reichsbank's holdings of gold. This encouraged further speculation against the mark, which in turn led to an increasing lack of confidence abroad and a mass withdrawal of foreign capital from Germany.

There was moreover a crisis in agriculture which the government had failed to solve. The war had imposed severe strains on farmers: under-investment, depletion of livestock and deterioration of equipment. The crisis had been aggravated by Versailles with the loss of agricultural land and the demand for livestock from France and Belgium. Landowners, now reassured that nationalization of their estates would not take place, displayed a defiant attitude towards the government and did little to restore German agriculture.

The difficulties in industry were of a different nature. There Rathenau's policy of industrial rationalization led to a remarkable increase in efficiency. Small firms were amalgamated into large concerns and industrial productivity rose sharply. Increased efficiency was accompanied by increased unemployment, already swollen by demobilized troops who had not been able to find work. A plentiful supply of labour allowed employers to resume their despotic influence on the economy and prevent governments from introducing further social welfare. The truce between employer and employee, already severely strained, was irreparably broken. The plight of the workers was aggravated by inflation. As Vermeil points out, whereas wages had risen between 1918 and 1922 fifteen times, prices had increased fifty times over the same period. In real terms the worker's wage had decreased by seventy per cent.

The economic situation raised serious doubts about the future of Erfüllungspolitik, especially since with Rathenau's death Wirth would be obliged to pursue the policy alone. It was doubtful whether he had the political authority to uphold Erfüllungspolitik in the face of increasing inflation, the overwhelming opposition of the DNVP and the intransigence of the French which had done so much to exacerbate the financial crisis.

Poincaré remained wholly unwilling to show understanding for Germany's economic problems as long as France still owed large sums of money to the U.S.A., a debt incurred during the war. It is plausible to argue that Poincaré derived more than a little satisfaction from the knowledge that if Germany continued to fail to meet her obligations he would have a sound pretext to demand a 'productive security' from Germany, that is, he would be justified in occupying and exploiting one of Germany's industrial areas. In this way not only would France be able to obtain her full share of reparations, but also, more important, Germany would be prevented from rivalling France economically. Only by enforcing Versailles to the letter, he argued, could France be protected from a resurgent Germany.

Though obliged by the agreement concluded between the Reich

and Briand, his predecessor, to allow the deferment of the reparation instalments due in January and February 1922, Poincaré refused to countenance any further postponement. The entrenched attitudes of both parties produced stalemate. France and her Allies demanded the stabilization of the mark as a pre-condition for discussions on reparations – the French believed that Germany had fostered inflation in order to cheat them of their dues. Germany, on the other hand, maintained that financial stability could not be achieved without an extended moratorium and, in addition, a sizeable foreign loan. Both standpoints were erroneous in substance. It was untrue, even naïve, for Poincaré to maintain that the German government had encouraged inflation and, as Heiber points out, events subsequently proved that the currency could have been stabilized without further relief from reparation payments. The policies of the two states were naturally dictated in part by the mood of mutual suspicion which existed between them and by a genuine concern on the part of the German government lest the Nationalists should be given further opportunity of making cheap, anti-Republican propaganda.

Wirth's Resignation

The deepening financial crisis demanded strong government at a time when Ebert's tenure of the presidency was about to expire and when Wirth's Erfüllingspolitik lay in ruins.

The political ferment which would arise from a presidential election – for the Constitution prescribed the holding of a popular election – would aggravate an already highly unstable political climate. Despite opposition from the Nationalists a large majority in the Reichstag, comprising all parties from the SPD on the left to the DVP on the right, voted in October 1922 to extend Ebert's term of office until 25 June 1925, and thus avoid the upheaval of an election.

Ebert was now able to turn his attention fully to the impending government crisis. Conscious that Wirth needed wider support in the Reichstag to allow him to combat the anti-government forces at home and to deal effectively with foreign pressure, Ebert suggested that the cabinet should be enlarged to include members of the People's Party to form a Grand Coalition, that is one including both right- and left-wing parties. His suggestion met with immediate opposition from his former colleagues in the SPD who refused on ideological grounds to participate in a coalition which contained DVP members. Their refusal was motivated as ever by their fear of antagonizing the party rank and file and in particular the party's new left wing which it had inherited from the defunct Independent Social Democratic Party. The DVP, as the representative of big-business interests, would, they contended, inevitably counter those of the working class on such vital issues as wages and working conditions. Wirth declared himself unwilling to continue in office without the support of the SPD and resigned on 14 November.

Public dissatisfaction with the workings of parliament led to a widespread demand for a cabinet of businessmen who, free from party political control, would, it was felt, govern the country more successfully. The right wing argued that Germany was being destroyed by inter-party squabbles and government by compromise. They advocated a return to the system of paternalistic, autocratic government which had existed under the monarchy. It was fortunate for the Republic that the extremists on the right and, equally, those on the left were at that time insufficiently organized to exploit the crisis and impose a totalitarian régime, Fascist or Communist.

Cuno's Cabinet of Businessmen

In choosing a new chancellor Ebert attempted to accommodate popular demands as far as possible while remaining consistent with his beliefs and faithful to the spirit of the Constitution. On 16 November he requested Dr Wilhelm Cuno, managing director of Hapag, the Hamburg-America shipping line, to form a government. Cuno, a member of no political party, held moderately right-wing views. He succeeded in forming a Bourgeois Coalition of the DDP, the Zentrum, the BVP and the DVP. His ministers were all men who enjoyed a reputation for integrity in the business world, *Männer mit diskontfähiger Unterschrift*, as they were described. Their professional reputation and expertise would, it was hoped, provide the solution to Germany's difficulties where professional politicians had failed. The Nationalists continued to refuse the responsibility of office and together with the Socialists and Communists controlled two hundred and sixty-five votes against the coalition's one hundred and ninety-seven.

Cuno, not wishing to prejudice his position, continued to fulfil the monthly payments, while attempting to arrange a conference to re-examine the whole question of reparations. Allied reaction to the request was mixed. The U.S.A., pursuing their isolationist policy, did not wish to become embroiled in European affairs. Britain's new Conservative Prime Minister, Andrew Bonar Law, who had succeeded Lloyd George in October 1922, proved, contrary to Cuno's assessment, to be no match for his French colleague. Moreover he had no intention of endangering the already strained Anglo-French relations. The French Premier, Poincaré, predictably showed no more sympathy to the new coalition than he had shown to Wirth's cabinet. If anything a cabinet of businessmen confirmed his suspicions that Germany's industry was flourishing and that she was deliberately defaulting while concealing her real wealth behind a smoke-screen of inflation. He would grant a moratorium on payments only if Germany's major industrial region, the Ruhr, were pledged to France as a guarantee. He was, of course, eager to occupy the Ruhr to prevent it from becoming too powerful a threat to French industry and *sécurité*.

Though her plans met with strong opposition from the British government, France decided to impose sanctions on Germany if she defaulted further. On 27 December 1922 the Reparations Commission disclosed that Germany had failed to deliver a consignment of a hundred and forty thousand telegraph poles to France and had therefore broken her treaty obligations. The German government maintained that the non-delivery of the telegraph poles was the result of an oversight – in the circumstances a most unfortunate oversight – but the French were not to be deprived of the opportunity they had been waiting for. On 11 January 1923 five divisions of French troops and one Belgian division invaded the Ruhr. Ostensibly their task consisted in granting protection to the Belgian and French technical staff who were occupying German mines and industry. Supported on this occasion by the U.S.A., Britain delivered a strong protest to the French and Belgian governments. While contesting their decision to seize a productive security from Germany they undertook no further action when their note was rejected.

As German military opposition was out of the question, Cuno ordered the workers and government officials in the Ruhr to adopt a policy of passive resistance. No work was to be undertaken which might benefit the occupying forces and all deliveries of reparation goods to France and Belgium were to cease at once. The French retaliated by introducing several measures designed to hinder everyday life. These included the setting up of customs frontiers and passport formalities within German territory.

The policy of the government was endorsed by all the major political parties, for the belief was widespread that Poincaré intended to disrupt the unity of the Reich by encouraging the creation of a separatist Rhineland state. Whether this assessment of French aims was accurate or not remains unclear, but, as Herzfeld has pointed out, Cuno's policy towards the French was formulated on the assumption that they did in fact harbour ulterior motives. Otherwise the continuation of passive resistance, which caused considerable domestic hardship, would have made little political sense. Poincaré's avowed intention of seizing a productive security had been thwarted by passive resistance and France received less from Germany during the Ruhr occupation than in the comparable period the year before.

Not surprisingly, passive resistance developed frequently into active resistance and clashes between the civilian population and French troops often occurred. Senseless acts of violence and sabotage became matters of course. In one such incident at the Krupp factory in Essen several workers attempted to prevent French officers from removing vehicles belonging to the firm. They were machine-gunned by French troops and fifteen workers were shot dead. In the whole period of Franco-Belgian occupation more than a hundred German civilians were killed and over a hundred thousand arrested, including many civil servants and police officers who refused to compromise their sworn oath of allegiance to the Republic.

The climate of widespread violence brought with it the threat of a Putsch by right-wing anti-republican groups. The extreme right, pacified at first by the establishment of the cabinet of businessmen, whom they trusted would implement a nationalist, anti-Marxist policy, soon became disenchanted with their new leaders. The Nazis, in particular, lost no opportunities of fomenting political unrest, ascribing blame for the Ruhr occupation to the 'November Criminals' (and as Halperin has commented, not to the French, an indication of the quality of Nazi patriotism). Despite the government's fears, no right-wing *coup d'état* was staged, largely, it would appear, on account of the ambivalent attitude of the Reichswehr whose active support would have been essential. The leading army officers, although undeniably right-wing in their political beliefs, were unwilling to back the would-be Putschists, while their supreme commander, Seeckt, remained unwilling to precipitate the downfall of the Republic. Seeckt saw in the crisis a welcome justification for his view that the Reichswehr should be increased in size. He argued plausibly that the presence of French troops in the country might be seen by the Poles – who had recently concluded a treaty with France – as a suitable opportunity to invade the Reich. The force of one hundred thousand men, allowed under Versailles, would be wholly inadequate to counter invasion from the east. The only solution, Seeckt argued, was to form a second, clandestine force – the so-called Schwarze Reichswehr – a plan to which Ebert reluctantly agreed. His misgivings were well-founded for not only did the formation of such a force contravene Versailles, worse, its existence would strengthen the army's position as a state within a state.

Galloping Inflation

The deterioration in Germany's balance of payments, the continuing depletion of her gold reserves and a popular growing suspicion of paper money now rendered the eventual collapse of Germany's currency inevitable. Domestic and foreign lack of confidence in the mark was well-founded. Dr Rudolf Haverstein, Governor of the Reichsbank, the government-controlled, central bank which issued Germany's paper currency, did much to aggravate the situation. A conservative financier of the old school, Haverstein had little understanding of economic theory. He answered the needs of succeeding governments for increased finance by printing more and more notes. No attempts were made to discover the real causes of inflation or to find a possible cure. Successive budgetary deficits were covered simply by increasing the face value of the currency. This produced further inflation and, in turn, further deficits. Paper mills and printing presses worked twenty-four hours a day in a vain attempt to satisfy the ever-increasing demand for currency.

Political unrest aggravated the situation: on 23 June 1922, the day before Rathenau's death, the exchange rate stood at 1,450 marks to the pound sterling (approximately 330 marks to the dollar) Within two months of his assassination it plunged to 5,450 marks (1,240 marks to the dollar). French occupation of the Ruhr and

Cuno's policy of passive resistance dealt the death blow to the mark. On 1 January 1923 the rate stood at 32,750 marks to the pound (7,090 marks to the dollar); by the end of May, when the disruption of industry had become acute, the mark had fallen to a tenth of its value six months previously and now stood at 335,000 to the pound (73,000 marks to the dollar).

The day-to-day life of the man in the street was severely disrupted by the effects of inflation. In 1923 the rate of exchange of the mark against the U.S. dollar was announced twice daily. At midday all prices were marked up according to the new rate. One of the more bizarre examples of the situation at the end of the year was the convention which operated in restaurants. People taking lunch had to agree to pay their bill at the rate which prevailed when they had finished eating, which would not necessarily agree with the prices shown on the menu. There was a never-ending frenetic race to unload currency as quickly as possible for people naturally preferred to buy goods, however inessential, than be caught with large amounts of worthless marks. Workers and employees received their wages daily – often with a daily increment – and spent them at once. The penalty for not doing so could be enormous. At the height of the crisis a newly-married couple who had received a gift of cash with which to furnish their flat discovered when they came to spend the money that it would buy no more than a few items of clothing. Barter frequently replaced normal commercial transactions and those firms who continued to accept paper money frequently insisted on payment in foreign currency. Foreign tourists were able to live lives of luxury for small sums of hard currency.

Inflation did not affect all sectors of the community equally, of course. Large property owners were protected against the effects of inflation because their wealth was invested in real estate. Similarly speculators, especially those who incurred large debts, profited handsomely. Despite high interest rates levied by banks the inflationary process inevitably benefited the borrower. To the benefit of the rich, taxation could be paid in devalued currency. During this period many industrialists such as Hugo Stinnes, proprietor of one of Germany's largest coal and steel companies, were able to increase the size of their concerns by buying out their ailing competitors and re-equipping their factories at minimal cost. Many industrialists in their own interest encouraged inflation.

The middle classes were economically ruined when their savings became worthless overnight, and those living on fixed incomes and pensions were made destitute. The traditional middle-class virtue of thrift was negated; they felt socially *déclassé* and deprived of their self-respect. Workers were little better off. Wages rose relatively more quickly than salaries but in real terms declined in purchasing power. Relations between employers and employees deteriorated further. The destruction of the economic basis of the middle classes and the gradual impoverishment of the workers, intolerable for the human misery it produced, was politically dangerous. It encouraged disaffection for the Republic and produced a marked drift towards political extremism, as the results of the election held in 1924 show. The huge proletariat created by inflation was easy prey for the anti-democratic forces in the Reich.

The Fall of Cuno's Government and the Creation of Stresemann's Grand Coalition

A situation of stalemate was soon reached in the Ruhr, with Poincaré's refusal either to evacuate the occupied territory or to discuss reparations until passive resistance was abandoned and Cuno's refusal to end passive resistance before the French had withdrawn. The unequal trial of strength ensued for eight months and the longer the crisis endured the more vociferous criticism of Cuno's government became. The barrenness of his policy was patent: the French remained in the Ruhr and, as a direct result of passive resistance, the mark had become virtually worthless. Galloping inflation in its turn had brought industry to a standstill since it was unable to buy raw materials abroad, and had demoralized the population. On 9 August the Socialist leader, Müller, in a speech before the Reichstag demanded the resignation of the cabinet of businessmen, and two days later Cuno complied. Ebert once more had to face the odious and hazardous task of finding a successor. He was all too conscious of the gravity of his duty. The country clearly needed to be governed by a strong personality at the head of a broadly based coalition, if it were to be rescued from its perilous political and economic situation. Gustav Stresemann, leader of the People's Party, seemed to Ebert to have the qualities necessary to fulfil the demands of the chancellorship. Would the Socialists be willing to enter a coalition with the People's Party with which they had refused to collaborate nine months previously? Would they agree to serve under Stresemann, a man who had never enjoyed the sympathy of the SPD?

After considerable discussion within the Party, the SPD finally agreed to renounce their former objection to the DVP and to participate in the formation of a Grand Coalition which embraced a broad political spectrum. It contained four Socialist, two Democrat, three Centrist and two Populist ministers. Furthermore they accepted Stresemann's appointment as Chancellor and Foreign Minister, for he had now abandoned his nostalgia for the monarchy and shown his loyalty to the Republic.

Stresemann's First Cabinet Takes Office

On assuming power Stresemann was faced with a task of immense proportions: a solution had to be found to the Ruhr crisis, inflation had to be halted and the danger of revolt by extreme right- and left-wing anti-republican groups needed swift attention. It was clear, too, that political stability could not be achieved without financial stability, and that a cure for Germany's currency crisis depended on an immediate settlement of the Ruhr problem.

On 14 August he introduced his cabinet to the Reichstag and outlined his policies. His task, he stated, was to preserve the very existence of the Reich, according to the principles of the Constitution. It was a task which required the co-operation and support of all sections of the community. Any attempt to usurp power would be crushed: at stake was government by parliamentary democracy. His cabinet obtained a decisive vote of confidence by two hundred and forty to seventy-six. The opponents came as ever from the two extreme parties, Communists and Nationalists, while several right-wing members of Stresemann's own party and many left-wing Socialists abstained from voting, in open defiance of Stresemann's call for unity.

The End of Passive Resistance

The first task of the new government was to resolve the Ruhr *impasse* which was now in its ninth month. Passive resistance had sorely depleted the country's already rapidly disappearing gold reserves, which had been used as social security payments to the victims of the Franco-Belgian invasion. The subsidy paid in one month alone, forty million gold marks, would, if continued at that rate over twelve months, amount to a quarter of the annual reparation instalment. Stresemann argued that passive resistance had been introduced in an attempt to drive out the French and, secondly, to force the Allies into granting Germany a reduction in the amount of reparations demanded from her. Hopes that the British government would exert diplomatic pressure on the French to withdraw were dispelled when, on 19 September, the British Prime Minister, Stanley Baldwin, openly voiced support for Poincaré's uncompromising attitude. Poincaré, determined to derive maximum satisfaction from Germany's deepening crisis, refused to grant any concession to Germany which would have allowed her to save face, let alone cash. Confronted by French intransigence Stresemann's decision to end passive resistance was all the more courageous, and it is an indication of his popularity and political ability that he was able to undertake such a course of action. His decision was based on a realistic appraisal of Franco-German relations. While France continued to regard 'politics as the continuation of war by other means' (Hermann), Germany would remain economically and politically fettered. The only foreign policy likely to succeed was one of international understanding, *Verständigungspolitik*, whose immediate aim would be *rapprochement* between France and Germany. On 26 September Stresemann ordered passive resistance to be abandoned and authorized industry to comply with the demands of the occupying forces that all industrial products should be handed over to them and that taxation should be paid directly to them. His decision provoked the customary chorus of outrage from the extreme right.

In October the President of the U.S.A., Calvin Coolidge, suggested that a non-political committee of cconomic experts should be set up to examine the whole problem of reparations. The Reparations Commission, reassured of German good faith by the abandonment of passive resistance, adopted his suggestion on 30 November and convened the Dawes Committee. The French occupation of the Ruhr continued until the Committee's recommendations were adopted the following year.

Bavarian Revolt

The ending of passive resistance met with little opposition from the electorate and in the occupied Länder normal working was quickly resumed. In Bavaria, however, the right-wing BVP government reacted with hostility to Stresemann's decision. On the same day, the Bavarian Prime Minister, Eugen von Knilling, protested by declaring a state of emergency. He appointed one of his predecessors, Gustav von Kahr, to the position of General State Commissioner, investing him with full executive power within the Land, an action which was wholly unconstitutional (under article 13 of the Constitution). This move amounted to an act of open rebellion against the central government in Berlin. It was provoked by the objection of the right-wing particularist régime in Bavaria to the inclusion of Socialists in Stresemann's cabinet, whom they considered to be subversive Marxists. It had become Bavaria's mission to attack what they called Communist-infested, internationalist Berlin with the Christian, patriotic forces of Bavaria, under the slogan '*Durch Bayern zum Reich*' (through Bavaria to the Reich). Kahr was chosen for his considerable power: he was a member of the triumvirate in control of the *Kampfbund* (Militant Union), a united front of rightwing racialists, together with his two colleagues, Hitler and Ludendorff. Invested with new power, Kahr set about replacing constitutional parliamentary government with a cabinet of businessmen.

The Bavarian revolt forced Stresemann reluctantly to request Ebert to declare a state of emergency which was to apply to the whole country (under article 48 of the Constitution). He further vested the Minister of Defence, Otto von Gessler, with full executive power which, however, effectively passed into the hands of the supreme Army Commander, General von Seeckt, on whose goodwill the civilian minister had to depend.

Earlier in the year Ludendorff had approached Seeckt with the proposition of an amalgamation of the racialist Freikorps and the Reichswehr. They would deploy this force to march on Berlin in the style of Mussolini's march on Rome, and overthrow the Republic. Seeckt refused to collaborate because he despised the political motives and methods of the racialist para military force and because he adhered as ever to his dictum that the army had above all to remain apolitical. He thereby incurred Ludendorff's implacable displeasure.

The conflict between Berlin and Munich soon came to a head: on 19 October Gessler ordered General von Lossow, the Bavarian military commander, to suppress the *Völkische Beobachter*, the national daily newspaper controlled by the Nazis, which had launched a libellous attack entitled 'The Dictators Stresemann and Seeckt'. On Kahr's advice Lossow ignored Gessler's command and he announced the transference of his allegiance from the Berlin government to Kahr's régime. On 22 October Gessler dismissed Lossow but Kahr ordered him to remain in office. There were now two armies in the Reich. Seeckt advised those obeying Lossow that they were violating their oath.

Stresemann's Second Cabinet and the Enabling Bill

Normal parliamentary procedure was considered by all coalition parties to be too cumbersome to deal sufficiently quickly with the deteriorating internal situation; the government would have to act boldly and decisively. When the Reichstag convened on 27 September after a six-week recess it was suggested that an enabling act be passed to allow the government temporarily to legislate without parliamentary consent.

An unexpected difficulty was encountered when the majority of the Socialist deputies refused to allow the government freedom to tamper with the sacred eight-hour day which they had laid down in November 1918 as one of the first fruits of the revolution. The DVP, representative of the employers, regarded the limitation as a severe handicap for German industry in international competition. Compromise proved for the moment impossible, and, accordingly, Stresemann announced the dissolution of his cabinet on 3 October. Ebert requested him to form a second cabinet. He refused to invite the DNVP to participate, objecting to their hostile attitude towards the Republic. The formation of a minority cabinet was also impossible since the DNVP would certainly have voted it out of power. The only solution was to attempt once more to accommodate the Socialists. On 6 October compromise was reached: an enabling act would be introduced which excluded regulation of the working day, simultaneously the eight-hour limitation would be temporarily suspended by normal legislative procedure. A new Grand Coalition presented the enabling bill to the Reichstag on 13 October where it was passed with the constitutionally necessary two-thirds majority. The law would lapse with a change in the composition of the government.

Separatist Threats and Left-Wing Land Governments

The new government had to deal with several threats to the integrity of the Reich in several Länder. In the Ruhr and the Rhineland French occupation forces openly encouraged separatists in Aachen and Speyer to proclaim a Rhenish Republic and an autonomous Palatinate which, they hoped, would serve as buffer states between France and the Reich. The attempt failed as a result of lack of popular support, but nevertheless remained a potential threat to national unity.

Further internal threats were posed by the existence since October of coalition governments of left-wing Socialists and Communists in the two Länder of Saxony and Thuringia, which opposed the moderate policy of the Reich Socialist Party. They advocated a return to the original tenet of socialism, proletarian supremacy, and judged the contemporary political situation ripe for revolution. Events in Bavaria presented them with further evidence which assisted their cause: they pointed to the danger of a right-wing seizure of power in Munich. The situation was further aggravated by the disclosures by Erich Zeigner, Prime Minister of Saxony, of the secret operations of the Schwarze Reichswehr, proof, he maintained, of the corruption of the army command. Events came to a head on 23-4 October when Communist supporters staged an abortive Putsch in Hamburg. Stresemann feared that events in Hamburg would encourage the Saxon and Thuringian régimes to stage a Communist *coup d'état* directed against the Reich, and attempted to persuade his cabinet colleagues of the need to send in the Reichswehr. The Socialists had misgivings about deposing a government which had been constitutionally elected, while Kahr's unconstitutional régime continued unchallenged in power. Stresemann felt obliged to act when he learnt that Bavarian troops, including regulars under the command of Captain Ehrhardt acting on Kahr's orders, had assembled on the frontier with Saxony and Thuringia. Their plan was to conquer these two Länder and then to march on Berlin where they intended to usurp full control of the Reich. The argument in favour of armed intervention in Saxony became incontrovertible. On 29 October Stresemann anticipated the Bavarians by ordering Reichswehr troops under the supervision of the former Populist Minister of Justice, Rudolf Heinze, to depose the Zeigner government. Dresden was taken without resistance later that day. The

Thuringian government was likewise forced to relinquish office.

The Resignation of Socialist Ministers

The Socialist members of the Reich cabinet, who had not been informed beforehand of the intervention, protested strongly at Stresemann's action, which they considered unconstitutional. Sauce for the Saxon goose should be sauce for the Bavarian gander, they argued. Stresemann disagreed for two reasons: he did not consider that a right-wing, particularist government presented such a threat to the Reich as an internationally promoted extreme left-wing government. Armed intervention in Bavaria could well provoke a civil war and separatism. Gessler had already warned the cabinet that while Seeckt did not sympathize with the racialists, he was unlikely to support the deployment of the army against the Bavarian rebels. When in September Stresemann had asked Seeckt for his support, Seeckt had replied, 'The Reichswehr stands behind you if the German chancellor goes the German way'. He was determined as ever to maintain the unity of the Reichswehr whatever the political colour of the government of the day. Moreover it was known that Hindenburg had tacitly bestowed his patronage on the Kahr–Lossow régime which already had the full support of his former comrade Ludendorff. The Socialists refused to modify their demand for government intervention in Bavaria and on 2 November resigned their portfolios.

In one sense the resignation of the Socialists strengthened the government's hand, in that it alleviated the fears of the Kahr–Lossow régime, which albeit wholly unfounded were none the less all too real, namely that Berlin was in the hands of hard-line Marxists. On the other hand the remaining rump cabinet of Democrats, Centrists and Populists was parliamentarily weak and would doubtless be out of power as soon as the Reichstag, in recess since the middle of October, reconvened. Moreover, with the change in the coalition, the enabling law had automatically lapsed. There followed a week of intense party-political, internecine warfare in which several interested groups attempted to unseat Stresemann. They were overtaken in their machinations by the events of 8–9 November in Munich.

The Hitler–Ludendorff Putsch

In Munich, news of the deposing of the Saxon and Thuringian

governments and of the resignation of the Socialists from the Reich government, weakened Kahr's resolution to move against Berlin, an undertaking which now would prove almost certainly to be an utter fiasco, a view shared by Lossow. The Racialists and Nazis were of a different opinion. Hitler decided to force Kahr's hand in the belief that otherwise the opportunity to seize power would be lost for ever.

On the evening of 8 November Kahr addressed an anti-Marxist meeting on the fifth anniversary of the Republic, in the *Bürgerbräukeller*, a popular Munich beer-cellar. While he was speaking, Hitler entered the hall with a number of Storm Troopers armed with machine-guns. Hitler mounted the speaker's platform and proclaimed a National Revolution. Under duress, Kahr, Lossow, Ludendorff and Seisser, the Bavarian chief of police, agreed to join with Hitler in forming a revolutionary government: Hitler was to be the head of the government, Lossow the Army Minister, Seisser the Minister of the Interior and Ludendorff Commander-in-Chief of the Reichswehr, while Kahr was to remain first in command in Bavaria. With the exception of Ludendorff their agreement was feigned – they had no intention of taking part under Hitler's doubtful leadership in a revolution against the central authorities – and, moreover, Kahr and Lossow had already decided to try to settle their differences with Berlin. Later that evening Hitler naïvely allowed them to return to their homes, believing that he had secured their support.

After leaving the hall Kahr and Lossow formally dissociated themselves from the 'agreement' they had been forced to sign, and ordered the mobilization of the police and the Reichswehr to oppose the Racialists should they persist in their plans for revolt. Berlin was informed of the impending putsch. That night Ebert declared a state of emergency and the cabinet transferred executive power and supreme command of the Reichswehr to Seeckt. Vested with dictatorial powers, Seeckt found himself obliged to defend the Republic and the Constitution, an ironic situation.

Hitler and Ludendorff, though aware that they would not be widely supported, nevertheless decided to organize a march on Munich the following morning in the hope that this would revive Kahr's enthusiasm. When they arrived at the city centre they found their way blocked by detachments of police and loyal troops.

The police opened fire on the demonstrators who dispersed at once. Hitler escaping in a car. Ludendorff marched on alone towards the armed force which blocked his way and was arrested.

Neither Kahr nor Lossow, who shared much responsibility for the putsch, in that they had created between them a climate for revolt, was prosecuted by the Reich. Kahr's treason and Lossow's mutiny were quietly forgotten by Berlin after they had shown that they would no longer collaborate with the Nazis. On 26 February 1924 the trial of Hitler and Ludendorff began. It presented the defendants with an ideal opportunity to launch a comprehensive and wholly irrelevant attack on the Republic and to indulge in anti-semitic propaganda. The judgement indicated the benevolent attitude of the judiciary towards crimes committed by right-wing Nationalists. Ludendorff was acquitted in spite of ample evidence offered which conclusively proved his guilt, Hitler was found guilty of high treason and given the minimum sentence, five years' imprisonment, of which he served less than nine months, in comfortable quarters in the fortress at Landsberg.

The régime had displayed its double standards once again. Right-wingers who committed unconstitutional acts were let off lightly while legal left-wing governments were forcibly dissolved. The implementation of government policy was, moreover, seen to depend, as ever, on the support of the Reichswehr and its equi-vocal leader, Seeckt. Nevertheless, Seeckt had introduced several beneficial measures: he banned the National Socialist Party and brought the Bavarian army divisions firmly under Reich control.

Currency Reform

Stresemann's last achievement as Chancellor was to introduce a new currency. The continuing financial distress of the country could no longer be blamed, as many who gained most from the situation previously asserted, exclusively on the Ruhr crisis. In mid-August, when Stresemann became Chancellor, the exchange rate had stood at 15 million marks to the pound (3.3 million marks to the dollar). By the end of the month it had declined further to a new low of 46 million (10 million marks to the dollar) and by the end of October to 850,000 million (190,000 million to the dollar). Immediate reform of Germany's currency – already long overdue – was now inescapable: the country faced severe food shortages since the farmers were understandably reluctant to exchange their harvest produce for worthless currency. The difficulty of introducing reform was now not one of timing, but of procedure: how to launch a new currency in a country whose faith in paper money had been destroyed, whose gold reserves had been exhausted and at a time when there was little hope of raising a loan abroad.

It had previously been suggested by Karl Helfferich, the war-time Secretary of State to the Treasury, that a new currency should be floated, based not on gold, but on rye, Germany's staple cereal. This suggestion, improbable as it was, was adopted by Stresemann's second Finance Minister, the politically independent, professional administrator, Hans Luther. He introduced a new currency, the *Rentenmark*, backed supposedly by a mortgage of Germany's land and industry. Since such a mortgage could never be redeemed, its backing was, in fact, little more than a bluff. In practice it was of course unimportant whether the currency had any real backing, the essential condition for its success was that the public should have faith in the new mark. Its success was all but miraculous.

On 15 October the government, using its emergency powers, authorized the establishment of a new issuing bank, the *Deutsche Rentenbank*, under the chairmanship of Hjalmar Schacht, founder member of the DDP and a director of the Darmstädter Bank. He was appointed Reich Currency Controller and placed in charge of the issue of the new currency. The government intentionally by-passed Havenstein and when, conveniently, he died two months later his post of director of the Reichsbank also was given to Schacht. Schacht decided to issue a strictly limited amount of Rentenmark and, to the relief of the government, was eagerly accepted as a source of much-needed, stable liquidity by the population. On 15 November the rate of exchange between the old and the new currency was fixed at one million million old marks to one Rentenmark.* The government could now take measures to balance the national budget in the respite provided by the end of inflation. The effect of the new mark's introduction was amazing: goods reappeared in the shops at once and food became plentiful for the first time in months. A semblance of normality returned to everyday life.

* The official rate of exchange was fixed at 4·2 Rentenmark to the U.S. dollar, approximately 20 marks to the pound sterling.

The Fall of Stresemann's Government

Early in November disagreement broke out anew among the Socialist Reichstag deputies over their attitude to Stresemann's cabinet. Thuringian and Saxon representatives convinced their colleagues that the minority cabinet should be ousted. With one hundred and seventy-one seats they were numerically strong enough to force Ebert into ordering the Reichstag to be reconvened (which according to the Constitution required the support of at least one-third of the total representation). Stresemann unsuccessfully tried to extract from Ebert a threat to dissolve parliament if it opposed his government. Such a threat would have forced the SPD into reconsidering its tactics since new elections would certainly reduce their parliamentary strength. On 20 November he asked the Reichstag for a vote of confidence in his government, which, if its record was not unblemished, had achieved remarkable results in a short time. On 23 November the combined forces of the Socialists and Nationalists defeated the motion by two hundred and thirty-one to one hundred and fifty-six. Stresemann resigned after only one hundred and three days in office. Ebert sharply rebuked his former colleagues for their action, saying, 'your reasons for voting the Chancellor out of office will be forgotten within six weeks but you will suffer from the consequences of your actions for the next ten years'. His prediction came true.

5

The 'Golden Years' of the Republic 1924–1929

Character of the Period 1924–29

THE PERIOD 1924–29 was one of apparent political and economic stability which masked the underlying weaknesses of the parliamentary system and Germany's industrial recovery. In the years between 1924 and 1928 Germany was governed by a succession of six bourgeois coalitions of which only two, which included Nationalists, enjoyed parliamentary majorities. The remaining four were wholly dependent for their existence on the parliamentary toleration of the Socialists. It was an unsatisfactory situation for it weakened the authority of successive governments. The Socialists' deliberate avoidance of government responsibility was a poor reflection upon their avowed support of the Republic and further undermined parliamentary democracy. It was not until new elections were held in 1928 that the SPD accepted ministerial posts in Müller's non-party cabinet of personalities.

The Republic's outstanding record in foreign affairs was the product exclusively of Stresemann's Verständigungspolitik and, in particular, of the Franco-German *rapprochement*. His progressive foreign policy was steadfastly supported by successive Centrist chancellors and by opposition Socialists, while the right wing ruthlessly and cynically condemned his capitulation to the French.

Success in foreign affairs tended to hide the fundamental weaknesses of the domestic situation and even created new dangers. The economic prosperity which Germany enjoyed between 1924 and 1929 depended completely on the influx of foreign capital into Germany after the signing of the Dawes Plan. Germany's affluence was essentially illusory, however, for it would collapse if foreign funds were withdrawn. The return of the Reich to the European community, which resulted from the signing of the Treaty of Locarno and Germany's acceptance into the League of Nations, granted her equality among nations and appeared to consolidate the republican régime. As soon as economic difficulties returned in 1929 it became clear that this consolidation was unsound. What was the value of international alliances when faced with economic ruin? Acceptance of democracy was soon shown to be skin-deep. The extremist parties, which had had a lean time in the years of apparent prosperity and international understanding, soon resumed their disruptive activities and exposed the temporarily masked weaknesses of the régime. When the crisis broke in 1929 the two statesmen who could possibly have steered the country through its difficulties, Ebert and Stresemann, had died, hounded to death by the unscrupulous activities of right-wing extremists, and the moderate Socialist, Ebert, had been replaced in the presidency by the authoritarian, monarchist Field Marshal von Hindenburg who was no match for his subversive advisers.

Marx's First Cabinet

Party-political squabbles aggravated Ebert's difficulties in choosing a successor to Stresemann and persuading party leaders to participate in a new coalition. Eventually, on 30 November, Wilhelm Marx, leader of the Centre Party, succeeded in forming a government. Marx, a former judge from the Rhineland, hardly a colourful politician, possessed a strong character and was as competent a chancellor as many of his predecessors. With the exception of the Social Democrats, who continued to refuse government responsibility, the composition of the new cabinet was unchanged, i.e. Democrats, Centrists, Populists and Bavarian Populists. Most important, Stresemann agreed to remain Foreign Minister, a post which he held until his death in 1929. The Socialists, satisfied with their defiant gesture of felling the Grand Coalition, were prepared to tolerate the new government.

The enabling bill, which had been passed in October, had automatically lapsed with the resignation of the Grand Coalition. Marx asked the Reichstag when it reconvened on 4 December to sanction a second law. The government needed special powers, he argued, if it was to deal effectively and quickly with the economic situation and to ensure that the rule of law was enforced throughout the Reich. The Socialists, whose support for the bill was essential, agreed to vote in favour even though it permitted the suspension of the eight-hour day to continue. In return the government agreed to rescind the state of emergency, proclaimed on 26 September, at the earliest opportunity. The enabling bill, which was to remain in force until 15 February, was passed on 8 December despite opposition from the Nationalists, the Racialists and the Communists. Gradually the domestic situation returned to a semblance of normality. The new currency continued to hold its value; the Bavarian government formally pledged its support for the Reich; and in February the ban imposed by Seeckt on 20 November on the extremist parties, Nazis, Communists and Racialists, was lifted. This would allow them to participate in the general election (the term of office of the Reichstag, elected in 1920, would end in June 1924).

Shortly before the enabling law was due to expire Marx appealed to the Reichstag to sanction a further extension so that the government could continue uninterrupted with its measures to restore the economy. The Socialists were no longer willing to comply with the Chancellor's wishes for they had to consider their popularity with the electorate.

Government by emergency decree had proved successful in dealing with domestic unrest: Kahr's régime had been replaced by a government under parliamentary control, and Seeckt had relinquished the executive power that had been vested in him. But the government's economic decisions had been unpalatable to the Socialists. The sacred principle of the eight-hour day, one of the achievements of the revolution, had for practical purposes been wholly abandoned under the terms of an emergency decree promulgated on 23 December when, in an attempt to restore the superiority of German industry in competition with that of other countries, a working-day of ten hours had been introduced. As the government was unwilling to amend its labour policy the SPD refused to sanction a further extension of its emergency powers. Marx had taken the precaution of previously obtaining from Ebert an order to dissolve parliament, to be presented if his request were not granted. Accordingly on 13 March the Reichstag was dissolved and new elections were ordered for 4 May.

The Dawes Committee's Report

The election campaign was bound to deal with the enormous problems which had beset the Republic in the preceding year: French occupation, passive resistance, inflation and the attempted Nazi *coup d'état*.

The issue which dominated the campaign, however, was the report of the Dawes Committee on Reparations presented to the Reparations Commission on 9 April 1924. The Committee, under the chairmanship of the American financier, Charles G. Dawes, had been set up at the insistence of the British and Americans, who overruled Poincaré's reluctance. Its brief was to examine Germany's 'capacity to pay'.

Dawes and his colleagues had drafted their report under the motto 'business not politics', that is they attempted to transfer the reparations issue from the mine-field of post-war European politics to the relatively composed atmosphere of international finance. In sharp contrast to the situation in 1921 when the Allies presented Germany with an ultimatum, Dawes' Committee made the journey to Berlin to consult the German government and Schacht, the new chairman of the Reichsbank.

While not settling the total amount to be paid, the report recommended considerable reductions in the annuities for the next four years, which would provide Germany with an opportunity to restore her economy and stabilize her currency. The first instalment for the period from September 1924 to August 1925 was fixed at a thousand million gold marks of which eighty per cent would be covered by a foreign loan. Thereafter payments were to increase yearly* to the 'normal' annuity, two and a half million marks payable in 1928–9 and subsequent years. Provision was made for larger annuities if Germany's economy prospered beyond the Committee's expectations.

The payments were to be financed from traditional sources, increased taxation and customs dues, and by mortgaging several large industrial concerns and the German National Railways, the *Reichsbahn*, which were to be placed under international control as security to the creditors. The operations of the National Bank, the Reichsbank, were to be scrutinized by a supervisory committee of

---

* Annuities were as follows: 1925–6: 1,220 million, 1926–7: 1,220 million, 1927–8: 1,700 million.

seven German and seven foreign officials. Their function was to prevent a recurrence of galloping inflation which the bank under Haverstein's control had actively encouraged. The Commission would appoint a General Agent for Reparations whose function it was to see that the German government complied with its obligations. Apart from this purely coercive duty he was also to satisfy himself that the payment of annuities would not unduly weaken the German economy, and that the transference abroad of large sums of currency, the major difficulty posed by reparation payments, would not threaten the stability of the mark.

The German government accepted Dawes' recommendations within six days of their submission, on the understanding that the question of the French occupation of the Ruhr should be included in any subsequent discussions. On 26 April the Allied governments gave their acceptance to the proposals though Poincaré persisted in claiming France's right to impose further sanctions if Germany failed to meet her obligations.

Opposition to the report within Germany was widespread. The extremist parties, the Communists, the Racialists and the Nazis, were unanimous in their support for the Nationalists' indictment of the proposals. Helfferich, the DNVP leader, denounced Stresemann's resumption of Erfüllungspolitik which acceptance of Dawes' recommendations implied. Particularly objectionable were, he maintained, the transfer of the Reichsbahn and the Reichsbank to international control. The country would make the most of their opportunity at the forthcoming elections to vote for those parties which opposed the plan. Stresemann countered this attack which, he maintained, grossly distorted the true situation, and indicated the real benefits which Germany would derive from the plan. These included the stabilization of the currency, the removal of the controls and customs frontiers set up by the French in the Ruhr and, most important, the return of political stability to the Reich. Dawes' recommendations would impose a financial burden on Germany which Stresemann too considered to be intolerable as a long-term solution. His acceptance was based on an appraisal of the immediate benefits which it would confer and on the reasonable belief that with the re-establishment of friendly relations between Germany and her former enemies further reductions in reparations could be negotiated within a few years. The Nationalists and the Racialist

Block chose to ignore these arguments for the sake of party-political advantage. The election results bear out the effectiveness of their tactics.

THE ELECTION OF 4 MAY 1924

The results of the election were as follows:

		Votes cast (to nearest thousand)		Number of seats		Percentage of total vote	
		1920	May 1924	1920	May 1924	1920	May 1924
KPD	Communist	589,000	3,693,000	4	62	2·1	12·6
USPD	Independent Social Democratic	5,047,000	235,000	84	—	17·9	0·8
MSPD	Majority Social Democratic	6,104,000	6,009,000	102	100	21·6	20·5
DDP	Democratic	2,334,000	1,655,000	39	28	8·3	5·7
Z	Centre	3,845,000	3,914,000	64	65	13·6	13·4
BVP	Bavarian People's	1,239,000	947,000	21	16	4·3	3·2
DVP	People's	3,919,000	2,694,000	65	45	13·9	9·2
DNVP	Nationalist	4,249,000	5,696,000	71	95	14·9	19·5
(NSDAP)	Racialist Block	—	1,918,000	—	32	—	6·6
Others		870,000	2,186,000	9	25	5·4	8·1
Total (to nearest hundred thousand)		28,500,000	29,700,000	459	468		

77·4 per cent of the electorate voted compared with 79·1 per cent in 1920.

Predictably in such uncertain times the election results were a severe setback for the moderate parties. The Nationalists and affiliated right-wing parties increased their representation from 66 to 106 seats (among these was the newly formed *Nationalliberale Reichspartei*, National Liberal Party, a splinter group which had abandoned the DVP in protest against Stresemann's progressive policies). The Racialists and the Nazis, campaigning as a block, gained 32 seats and entered parliament for the first time. At the other political extreme, the Communists increased their representation from the two seats they had won in 1920 to 62: clearly many former followers of the Independent Socialists who disapproved of the party's merging with the SPD had transferred their allegiance to the KPD. The moderate parties were sharply reduced in strength, an indication of the low esteem which the Republic enjoyed among the electorate. The SPD lost 71 of the 171 seats it had held since its amalgamation with the Independents, a result which reflected the party's vacillation between responsibility and opposition in the preceding year. Its representation of 100 was 2 fewer than the Majority Socialists alone had won in 1920. The DDP's performance was worse: from being the third largest party in 1919 they were now relegated to seventh place, having lost 11 of the 39 seats held in the last parliament. The DVP suffered an even greater reverse. Dissatisfaction with Stresemann's moderate policies had precipitated a flight to the Nationalist block and left the party with only 44 seats compared with their former representation of 66. The Zentrum, receiving 65 seats, only 3 less than in 1920, was the only republican party to maintain its strength. The stability of the Centrist vote throughout the Weimar period is, of course, attributable to its unique position as a confessional party.

The composition of future coalitions was severely restricted by the election results. The Weimar Coalition parties could muster only 193 seats out of a total Reichstag representation of 468. A Grand Coalition would command 237 seats, exactly half of the total representation, while a Bourgeois Coalition totalled 153 seats with the Bavarian Party and 269 with the BVP and the Nationalists. Thus only the latter coalition, with a decided right-wing bias, could enjoy a majority in parliament.

Marx's Second Cabinet

Throughout May Ebert tried to form a coalition government which both commanded a majority in parliament and was prepared to enact the recommendations of the Dawes Committee. The Nationalists, now the second largest party in the Reichstag and strong contenders for office, not only demanded the repudiation of the plan but also chose as prospective Reichskanzler Grand Admiral von Tirpitz, the creator of Germany's navy, an early advocate of unrestricted submarine warfare, and the co-founder with Kapp of the former ultra right-wing Patriotic Party, *Vaterlandspartei* (their former leader, Helfferich, had been killed on 23 April in a railway accident in Northern Italy). Ebert considered these conditions totally unacceptable and he was obliged to ask Marx to remain Chancellor and form another minority cabinet. The composition of the new coalition remained unchanged except for the withdrawal of the BVP delegate, but since the election the total number of party votes on which it could rely had declined to one hundred and thirty-eight out of a total Reichstag membership of four hundred and sixty-eight. The new coalition would, therefore, have to rely even more heavily on the Socialists' one hundred votes if it was to secure the passage of the Dawes Plan through parliament.

The London Conference on the Dawes Plan

On 16 July 1924 an international conference opened in London to formalize the recommendations of the Dawes Committee. Delegates from the Allied countries, the U.S.A. and Germany attended, in contrast to previous conferences in which the German delegate had been kept outside the doors to await the presentation of an ultimatum. The discussions were held in an unusually amicable atmosphere, for in both London and Paris new governments had assumed power which were noticeably more favourably disposed towards Germany than their predecessors. In December 1923 Stanley Baldwin had been succeeded by Ramsay MacDonald, Britain's first Labour Prime Minister and a champion of international understanding. The abortive Ruhr escapade, which had weakened rather than strengthened the French economy, had forced Poincaré to resign the French premiership in May 1924, and he was succeeded by Edouard Herriot, the leader of the Radical Social Party who, like his British counterpart, was eager to reduce international tension.

The main recommendations of the report were accepted by all delegations. The French moreover made an important concession to Germany: it was decided that if Germany failed for any reason to meet her obligations, sanctions would not be imposed unilaterally by any aggrieved power, but the dispute would be referred to a court of arbitration under the chairmanship of the U.S.A. Having obtained this important guarantee against future intervention, the German delegation turned its attention not to obtaining an amendment of the financial recommendations but to securing an undertaking from the French and Belgian delegates that their troops would be withdrawn from the Ruhr immediately. Without their assurance of good faith on this emotive issue, Stresemann in particular and Marx's government in general would be severely criticized by both the Reichstag and the electorate. Although this issue was outside the conference's terms of reference, Herriot agreed under pressure from MacDonald to guarantee complete evacuation of the occupied territory within twelve months. Anti-German sentiment in France prevented him, he maintained, from promising speedier withdrawal but he was willing to concede, as a demonstration of his good intentions, the immediate evacuation of the area around Dortmund and the removal of the customs frontier erected around the Ruhr.

The Acceptance of the Dawes Plan

While the concession granted by Herriot was not as great as Marx and Stresemann had hoped for, the parliamentary passage of the bill to accept the Dawes Plan was comparatively smooth. Socialist support in the Reichstag assured the government of a majority over the Nazis, the Nationalists and the Communists. The bill to mortgage the railways presented a greater problem. A straight majority in the Reichstag was not enough, since it involved a constitutional amendment which required a majority of two-thirds of the members present. At the first vote on 27 August two hundred and forty-eight came out in favour and one hundred and seventy-four against, an insufficient majority. Failure to pass this bill implied rejection of the whole of the Dawes legislation, as agreement to all sections had been stipulated at London. Ebert intervened to rescue the situation: if the plan were not accepted by the present parliament he would call for new elections. The Nationalists had arguably much to lose if a new election were held: they doubted whether they could repeat their success of 4 May. Also they were tempted by an offer made by Marx and Stresemann to include the DNVP ministers in the next cabinet if the party voted in favour of the Railways Bill. Moreover acceptance of the plan would benefit enormously their supporters in industry. At the subsequent ballot forty-eight members of the DNVP voted for the bill, assuring it of the necessary two-thirds majority (311 votes for, 127 against). A couple of days later, on 30 August, the London Accord ratifying the plan was signed.

The Fruits of the Dawes Plan

On 27 October the Reparations Commission confirmed the restoration of Germany's economic unity. The Dortmund area was evacuated and French forces in the territory still occupied received orders to remain unobtrusive. Foreign investors, recognizing that the Dawes Plan safeguarded their investment, eagerly deposited money in Germany largely in the form of loans to local authorities. The injection of foreign credit into Germany allowed the mark to return to the gold-standard as early as October 1924. Prosperity and full employment, admittedly on borrowed cash, returned amazingly quickly. A programme of massive industrial investment and rationalization on the American model of technological and economic expertise was undertaken and productivity was greatly increased. It was at this time that Germany's huge industrial concerns became serious rivals to those in other industrialized nations. These included the formation of the vast steel undertaking, *Vereinigte Stahlwerke*, the expansion of Germany's major electrical firms, A.E.G. and Siemens, and the amalgamation of smaller chemical companies into the giant combine, IG Farben. Trade restrictions imposed at Versailles were ended at the beginning of 1925 and Germany's export trade flourished. However, further rationalization of industry inevitably, as Vermeil points out, increased the number of unemployed. Extra employment could be created only if Germany's output and export markets increased correspondingly. A vicious circle of unemployment and rationalization had been formed which seemed bound to create severe social hardship. In the short term, however, the economy appeared to be healthy even if its restored health had been achieved at a high price in human terms. For the majority able to obtain work the standard of living improved: wages and salaries rose, though the burden of taxation still fell too heavily on the low-paid.

Local authorities indulged in an unprecedented spending spree in an attempt to compensate for the neglect of the previous decade. Hospitals, schools and workers' flats of high quality were built, an extensive network of new roads was constructed and electric power was brought to the whole country. Economic prosperity had provoked near euphoria among the population and the question of when the bubble would burst occurred to few. The fact was, however, that short-term loans could be withdrawn at any time and their remaining in Germany depended on the continuing health of the American economy. Five years elapsed before it failed.

Para-military Groups

A threat to internal security was presented by the existence of a number of para-military organizations whose political influence was disturbing. Four major groups existed under the Republic. Their membership and political complexion varied considerably: some were formed during or immediately after the revolution, others as late as 1924; some had formal links with a political party, others were independent.

On the right wing the largest organization was the National Socialists' SA which has already been described. A further right-wing group, the *Stahlhelm* (Steel Helmet), founded in November 1918 by troops returning from France and composed largely of committed opponents of the revolution, grew quickly. While avoiding direct links with a party, it identified itself politically with the Nationalists. Unlike the Nazi and Communist organizations it did not work actively for the downfall of the Republic, though it did little to strengthen democratic rule in Germany. Among its members were the former Crown Prince and Field Marshal von Hindenburg.

The Communist *Roter Frontkämpferbund* (Red League of Ex-Servicemen) was founded in July 1924. The KPD aimed to create a radical workers' military organization which would ultimately overthrow the Republic and establish a dictatorship of the proletariat. Its secondary aim was to oppose the activities of the Nazi SA which frequently harrassed Communist supporters.

The SPD, with the support of the Democrats and Centrists, founded in 1924 the sole pro-republican force, the *Reichsbanner* (National Flag). Its title, by emphasizing the republican colours, red, black and gold, which were spurned by the other organizations, gave an indication of its aims. It attempted to canalize popular affection for the pomp of quasi-military organizations into a body which would defend the Republic against attack from left and right extremists. Part of its programme was the instruction of its members in citizenship and politics, a belated realization of the need for political education. The Reichsbanner attracted a membership of more than three million.

Apart from the four major organizations, innumerable small

groups, mainly composed of anti-republican desperadoes, existed in the Reich and especially in Bavaria. Such organizations testified to the instability of the Republic and posed a constant threat to its precarious existence; it was intolerable that a democratic state should be obliged to condone such private armies which were answerable neither to the government nor to parliament. Their existence aroused considerable misgivings abroad, particularly in France where the revanchist pronouncements of the right-wing groups were naturally considered a potential menace to her *sécurité*. The creation of the Reichsbanner confirmed the threat implicit in the presence of the groups. It was not sufficiently strong to tackle the problem and indeed its very existence encouraged the situation which it hoped to eliminate. Only the Reichswehr could have enforced a ban and the attitude of the army leadership towards the right-wing groups at least was decidedly ambivalent.

Marx's Cabinet Resigns

On 24 September the DVP reminded Marx of his undertaking to accommodate Nationalist ministers in the cabinet in return for their supporting the Dawes legislation. Inclusion of the DNVP would provide the government with a parliamentary majority and allow Stresemann's foreign policy to be pursued with greater urgency. Marx agreed with the suggestion but had not reckoned with the attitude of the Democrats and members of his own party. There was widespread objection to allowing such men as Alfred Hugenberg into the government. Hugenberg, a fanatical right-wing extremist, had recently made his fortune as an inflation speculator. He invested his gains in a press and film empire which proved subsequently to be not only financially successful but also politically influential as a medium for propaganda. Since there was also no possibility of persuading the SPD to re-enter the government Marx decided to dissolve the Reichstag and order new elections to be held. He argued that the May election had produced a situation which from a party-political point of view was unworkable. The successes of 1924 and the return of domestic stability would encourage the electorate to vote for parties which would form a viable coalition. A strong government would consolidate the country's economic recovery and achieve further international understanding without having constantly to look over its shoulder at the reaction of the opposition parties. The election was arranged for 7 December.

The campaign was without surprises. The Nationalists produced their dog-eared manifesto demanding restoration of the monarchy and a curtailment of parliamentary powers, and proclaiming their chauvinism and anti-semitism. The Democrats and Centrists, while claiming credit for the achievements of their government, demanded further progressive domestic legislation. The Socialists, who welcomed the prospect of new elections which could only benefit their cause, mounted a negative campaign. They attacked the domestic programme of the Marx government for failing to restore the eight-hour day and for not having introduced social welfare. This automatically prompted the question, why they had refused to participate in the government if their policies were so urgent. It was easy to criticize when they had avoided all responsibility.

THE ELECTION OF 7 DECEMBER 1924

The results of the election were as follows:

		Votes cast (to nearest thousand)		Number of seats		Percentage of total vote	
		1924		1924		1924	
		May	Dec.	May	Dec.	May	Dec.
KPD	Communist	3,696,000	2,712,000	62	45	12·6	9·0
SPD	Social Democratic	6,009,000	7,886,000	100	131	20·5	26·0
DDP	Democratic	1,665,000	1,921,000	28	32	5·7	6·3
Z	Centre	3,914,000	4,121,000	65	69	13·4	13·6
BVP	Bavarian People's	947,000	1,135,000	16	19	3·2	3·7
DVP	People's	2,694,000	3,051,000	45	51	9·2	10·1
DNVP	Nationalist	5,696,000	6,209,000	95	103	19·5	20·5
NSDAP	National Socialist	1,918,000	908,000	32	14	6·6	3·0
Others	(including USPD)	2,421,000	2,208,000	25	29	8·1	7·1
Total (to nearest hundred thousand)		29,700,000	30,700,000	468	493		

78·8 per cent of the electorate voted compared with 77·4 per cent in May 1924.

The result was a victory for Stresemann's Verständigungspolitik, for its first success, the Dawes Plan, and for the prosperity which had come in its wake. The two parties who had unrelentingly opposed Stresemann, the Communists and the Nazis, each lost a million votes and 17 and 18 seats, respectively. The end of inflation and the return of financial stability benefited both the Socialists and the moderate bourgeois parties: the SPD increased its representation by a third and the DDP, the Centre, the BVP and the DVP each received a few additional seats. Surprisingly, the Nationalists also increased their share of the vote, albeit by only one per cent, the result, possibly, of their declared intention to enter a government coalition.

The aim of the election, however, had been to produce a result which would facilitate the formation of a viable coalition. Whereas the republican parties had a considerably larger representation than in the preceding 'Inflation Reichstag', the redistribution of seats had produced no obvious solution to the problem of government instability. A Weimar Coalition would command only 247 out of 493 seats. A Grand Coalition, which would have had a majority of 52, was hardly a practical proposition since its two wings, SPD and DVP, as representatives of the two sides of industry, were at each other's throats. A Bourgeois Coalition of all parties from the DDP to the DNVP, which would have commanded 274 seats, was similarly unlikely since the Democrats refused to collaborate with the Nationalists, maintaining their objection to such recalcitrants as Hugenberg whose influence in the party was increasing. The DVP, on the other hand, insisted that any coalition in which they were to serve would have to include members of the DNVP. Not only had this been promised by Marx at the time of the Reichstag debate on Dawes, they also wanted to create a truly conservative government which would benefit the interests of their supporters. Stresemann did not agree with the attitude of his colleagues.

As soon as the election results were declared Marx submitted his government's resignation to Ebert. Ebert asked him to form a new coalition but he was unsuccessful. At Stresemann's suggestion Hans Luther, Finance Minister in the previous cabinet, a member of no political party, was offered the chancellorship. After a month's protracted negotiation a new government was formed, a right-wing Bourgeois Coalition composed of members of the Centre, the Bavarian People's, the People's and the Nationalist Parties as well as several non-party ministers. As ever, the Centre had managed to overcome its scruples, and consented to collaborate with the extreme right.

Overruling Hugenberg, Martin Schiele, the spokesman for the party's agrarian vote and a relatively enlightened Nationalist, had succeeded in persuading his colleagues to accept government responsibility even if this obliged them to pay lip-service to the Republic, the Constitution and Stresemann's foreign policy. Schiele realized that there was little to be gained from maintaining the party's previous unqualified opposition to the Republic. If it was to enjoy any political influence in what promised to be an era of comparative affluence, the party would have to assume government responsibilities.

The coalition did not enjoy a parliamentary majority and was, therefore, obliged to seek toleration from non-government parties. The SPD was implacable in its opposition to the government's domestic policy: it could count on its support only if the eight-hour day were restored, direct taxation were reformed to benefit the lower paid, and protective tariffs – which benefited industrialists and prevented the consumer from obtaining cheaper imported goods – were removed. Not surprisingly, a government which represented the *bourgeoisie* was unwilling to contemplate such demands. The Socialists' opposition to Luther's cabinet was, however, severely weakened by their continued support for Stresemann's foreign policy which they could not oppose simply because they disagreed with other aspects of his government's programme. The Democrats, who allowed Gessler to remain in the new cabinet albeit without the party whip, agreed to tolerate with certain provisos Luther's coalition.

On 19 January 1925 Luther gave his opening address to the Reichstag. He made the customary plea for national unity and the traditional undertaking to uphold the Constitution. The domestic programme, designed to appease the SPD, was unexceptional. While recognizing the need for the introduction of further social welfare, this would, he maintained, have to be funded from an increase in Germany's exports for, while there was no denying the country's increased prosperity, this was due entirely to the influx of foreign loans; Germany's trade balance remained in deficit. In foreign affairs the government intended to build on the foundation of the Dawes Plan and promote international peace and understanding. This would include entry to the League of Nations if the conditions were acceptable. Foremost aim in the government's foreign policy would be the evacuation of the Cologne Zone of Occupation which the Allies had refused to vacate on 10 January 1925, the date specified in Versailles. Luther requested a vote of confidence which was given by two hundred and forty-six to one hundred and sixty votes, the opposition coming mainly from the Socialists who had not been won over by the government's promises of jam tomorrow.

The Death of Ebert

The first weeks of the new government's period of office were overshadowed by the untimely death of the President on 28 February and the need to elect a successor.

For much of his period of office Ebert had been a figure widely misunderstood and underrated even by moderate men, including many of his fellow Socialists. His opposition to the anti-democratic forces at large in Germany had been, they argued, ineffectual, and his attitude towards – admittedly overdue – social reform was also held to be unsatisfactory. His former comrades were, ironically, unwilling to accept that the head of a democratic state should be a commoner in a top hat. What they still subconsciously expected and desired was an Ersatzmonarch, a substitute for the exiled Kaiser, attended by the pomp and circumstance of imperial times. The Anglo-Saxon, Protestant ideal of the self-made man was one foreign to the majority of Germans, workers included. They were nurtured on the belief that the country's leaders should prove themselves by the criteria of noble birth, military prowess or academic ability, During his period in office the members of the saddle-makers' union. to which Ebert had belonged since his youth, expelled him from their ranks and even his expulsion from the Social Democratic Party was discussed at one Socialist conference.

The smear campaign against Ebert organized by right-wing extremists, was even more damaging. The Racialists and the Nazis lost no opportunity of attacking the President by any available means. As far back as 1922 Emil Gansser, a Nazi, had accused Ebert of treason. Their campaign was stepped up in 1924 as the end of Ebert's term of office as President – 1 July 1925 – was coming into sight. They wished at all costs to destroy him politically and prevent his re-election. During the course of the year no less than a hundred and seventy actions for libel were brought by Ebert in the courts. Yet even this does not indicate the full extent of public defamation, as he clearly could not and did not wish to prosecute on every occasion. The defendants, proved guilty, were normally fined a nominal sum of between fifty and one hundred marks. Later in 1924 the Racialist press editor, Rothard, published an open letter to Ebert which renewed the accusation that by supporting the wild-cat strike of Berlin munition factory workers in January 1918, he had been guilty of state treason. Ebert could not ignore this attack which was aimed both at his character and at the office of president, and he brought an action for libel against Rothard at Magdeburg in December 1924. The hearing lasted for two full weeks, in which as much mud was flung at Ebert as the defendant could rake up. The court ruled, on 23 December, that Rothard was guilty of slander and sentenced him to three months' imprisonment. It further declared that Ebert, though possibly morally and politically justified in the action he had taken in 1918, had, according to the criminal code, committed an act of treason. It is difficult to see how a truly impartial judge could have divorced the concepts of criminal and moral guilt while presiding over a case which was patently the product of a witch-hunt. It must, however, be remembered that the judiciary of the Weimar era was not enthusiastic in its support of the Republic, a situation which could be blamed in part on the Socialists' failure in 1919 to reform the administration of the Republic. It was more than ironical that in fact Ebert had done his utmost to dissuade the factory workers from striking in 1918.

Ebert, already a sick man, was spiritually and physically crushed by the judgement. He ignored the advice of his medical advisers, who wished him to undergo an examination for suspected appendicitis, as he was convinced that he had to continue the fight for his personal honour and for the honour of the presidency. He wished to supervise personally the lodging of an appeal against the court's ruling. Unless an appeal were successful, anyone could label him a traitor with impunity. This latest injustice, as he was only too aware, would not simply ruin him politically; it attempted to destroy his moral standing. That he did not immediately resign was due solely to the unprecedented action taken by the cabinet, who – though there was not a Socialist among them – publicly affirmed their faith in the President. Further, much-needed public support for Ebert was given by a number of republican intellectuals.

A deterioration in the condition of his health finally forced him to enter hospital in the middle of February 1925. It was too late to prevent his by now acute appendicitis from developing into a fatal peritonitis, and after an unsuccessful operation, he died on 28 February, aged fifty-two. The immediate cause of death was physical, but it would be more accurate to attribute his death to the hounding persecution to which he had been unrelentingly subjected by unscrupulous political opponents.

His achievement, though not without blemishes, was considerable. He had presided over the transformation of Germany from a bankrupt monarchy into a potentially viable, if still unstable, republic. It is impossible to say how subsequent events would have been affected if he had survived but it is likely that Ebert would have coped more successfully than Hindenburg with the crisis between 1930 and 1933, and that he would have remained true to the spirit of the Constitution. Speculation is, however, a fruitless pursuit. Suffice it to say that Ebert's death deprived Germany of another of its few able statesmen. Stresemann observed after Ebert's death that he had stood above party politics in his desire to serve the whole population in an attempt to unite it among itself – a rare quality in Weimar politics.

Presidential Election

The Republic was faced with the critical task of electing a president by popular vote. The choice of candidates was not made easier by the dearth of eminent public men, a situation which, naturally, could not have been foreseen by the drafters of the Constitution.

The left was split: the KPD refused to support a joint candidate with the SPD. They were wary of electing another Socialist president who would betray the working classes, a charge they had consistently made against Ebert. Disagreement on the left increased the likelihood of a right-wing candidate being elected. As it happened the non-Socialist parties were also in disagreement. The bourgeois parties had sought the nomination of Gessler, the Minister of Defence, but rejected his name under pressure from Stresemann who feared that the election of one of Germany's military leaders would alienate the newly-won support of the Allies and U.S.A. The DVP and the DNVP, supported by the Racialists, finally chose Karl Jarres, a right-wing member of the DVP and the only multi-party candidate. As Mayor of

Duisberg Jarres had acquitted himself courageously during the French occupation of the Ruhr. Between November 1923 and January 1925 he had served in the Stresemann and Marx cabinets as Minister of the Interior. He was clearly a strong candidate. The Nazis insisted on nominating their own candidate, Ludendorff, even though he clearly had little chance of being elected. The BVP likewise chose their own candidate, Heinrich Held, the Bavarian Premier and a staunch federalist. This unilateral decision of the Bavarians indicated their disapproval of the parent party's choice, Wilhelm Marx, the leader of the Centre Party, who had been Chancellor until the previous month. The DDP surprisingly selected their own candidate: Willy Hellpach, the Premier of Baden. With such slender support he could entertain no serious hope of success and his candidature would merely split the anti-Jarres vote. Otto Braun, the capable and respected Prussian premier, was chosen as the SPD candidate, and was clearly Jarres' strongest opponent. The Communists, true to their refusal to co-operate with the Socialists, nominated Ernst Thälmann, who later that year became party leader.

The election, held on 29 March 1925, failed to produce, as predicted, an overall majority for any one candidate, required by the law governing presidential elections. Votes were cast as follows:

	votes to nearest, 1,000	percentage of total vote
Jarres	10,788,000	39
Braun	7,837,000	28
Marx	3,989,000	14
Thälmann	1,886,000	7
Hellpach	1,570,000	6
Held	1,010,000	3·5
Ludendorff	211,000	0·7

A second ballot was arranged for 26 April.

The Socialists realized that if they were to prevent the election of Jarres they would have to support a candidate who was acceptable also to the moderate bourgeois parties. While Braun had come second in the first ballot it was unlikely that many non-Socialists would be willing to transfer their allegiance to him. The Socialist leadership, however, could rely upon the rank and file to accept their nominee, even if he were not a party member. They joined forces with the Centre and the DDP, thus briefly resurrecting the Weimar Coalition, to renominate Marx, a surprising choice of candidate for the SPD, as Marx, a somewhat colourless character, stood on the right wing of his party and, moreover, as a Catholic, was bound to meet hostility in the Protestant areas of Germany. Nevertheless his political competence and ability could not be called into question.

The choice of Marx as a block candidate threw the DVP and DNVP candidature open once again, for it was clear that unless they chose a candidate with a wider appeal than Jarres, Marx would certainly be returned. The DNVP chose as their new candidate the seventy-eight-year-old Field Marshal von Hindenburg. They were relying upon the appeal of the Hindenburg Myth to swell their share of the vote. Hindenburg, who was by no means eager to assume the leadership of a republic with which he had little sympathy, was eventually persuaded by his former colleague, Admiral von Tirpitz, to accept the Nationalists' offer. Stresemann, on behalf of the DVP, attempted to reject the Nationalist's nominee. He argued that Hindenburg, as one of Germany's two military dictators in the war, had incurred the odium of the Allies. His candidature would be a deliberate affront to the Weimar régime and would endanger Germany's recently successful foreign policy. Stresemann's credit with the Nationalists had been exhausted in his earlier objection to Gessler and the DVP was obliged reluctantly to make common cause with the DNVP, *faute de mieux*. Stresemann himself remained unconvinced, and later confided to his secretary that he had cast his vote in favour of Marx. Further support for Hindenburg came predictably from the Nazis and, paradoxically, the BVP. The Bavarian party preferred to back the Protestant, Prussian Hindenburg, than to vote for the Catholic Rhinelander, Marx, who had alienated their support by entering into an alliance with the Socialists. The Communists re-entered Thälmann. As Eyck argues: 'it may well be that the Communist dialectic contains a formula which dissolves every distinction between a republican judge and a royalist general', nevertheless it is hard to believe that the German Communist Party was truly wholly indifferent to the fate of the Republic. Their action would appear to have been dictated principly by their continued animosity towards the SPD, and, as such, was tactically unsound.

At the election, held on 26 April, Hindenburg won by a small majority of 904,151 votes over Marx (after the first ballot it was not necessary to obtain an overall majority). The voting figures were as follows:

	votes to nearest 1,000	percentage of total votes
Hindenburg	14,656,000	48
Marx	13,752,000	45
Thälmann	1,931,000	6

It was only too painfully clear that if the Communists had not run a third candidate, or if the BVP had sunk its differences with the Centre, Hindenburg would have been beaten by Marx. In fact Hindenburg had attracted two million votes more than the combined vote of his forerunners in the first ballot, Jarres, Held and Ludendorff, while Marx had polled only three hundred thousand more votes than the total secured earlier by Braun, Hallpach and himself. Thälmann's share of the poll barely increased. What were the factors which assured the right-wing success? The Hindenburg Myth seems to have played a decisive part. The increase in the poll, two and a half million votes, cast probably by the apolitical, went straight to Hindenburg, the victor of Tannenberg, the embodiment of the good old days, the symbol of the departed monarchy and of Germany undefeated in the field and the author of the stab-in-the-back legend. That he had relatively little to do with the Tannenberg victory, that he had brought Germany to the verge of military and economic destruction in 1918, that he had advised the Kaiser to seek refuge in Holland and that he had forced Germany's politicians to sue for peace from a most unfavourable bargaining position, were facts of which the populace were either ignorant or which they chose to disregard. Here at last was the chance to have a leader who looked the part: not a jumped-up artisan in a morning suit, but a militarist with the splendour of his uniform and decorations, a true Ersatz-monarch, who might even make way at some future date for a restoration of the Hohenzollern dynasty.

The election demonstrated again, if further evidence is necessary, that republicans in Weimar Germany were in the minority. Hindenburg's election was greeted with wild enthusiasm from the right wing who proclaimed the advent of a monarchist, militarist, authoritarian millenium. The republican parties feared the extinction of the Republic under the supervision of the new President, a fear shared by foreign observers and exploited, particularly in France, by the sensational newspapers. Hindenburg's arrival in Berlin on 11 May did nothing to allay this apprehension. The right-wing para-military *Stahlhelm* turned out in force to welcome the aged officer, together with thousands of German citizens. Flags were flown from every building. Imperial black, white and red flags conspicuously out-numbered the republican tricolour. On the following day Hindenburg was sworn in at a ceremony in the Reichstag building. The oath, while omitting specific reference to the republican form of government, nevertheless contained an undertaking to preserve the Constitution and laws of the country. Hindenburg delivered a speech which was remarkably conciliatory in tenor: he reiterated his determination to carry out the obligations imposed on him by his oath, and to work for the welfare of the whole population in a spirit of cooperation.

His assurances proved to be more than mere lip-service. For the five years between 1925 and 1930 he conscientiously protected the Constitution, and the worst fears of liberal Germans were not fulfilled. While undoubtedly still an authoritarian and a monarchist, he accorded traditional Prussian respect to his oath. Even after 1930 he delayed the advent of Hitler as long as he could – though his motives were not always altruistic. His relations with Stresemann were little more than formal – in contrast to the warm mutual understanding and sympathy that had existed between Stresemann and Ebert – but his presence in the government lent respectability within Germany to the new foreign policy, which had previously encountered nothing but hostility from the right. Hans Luther described Hindenburg's intellectual qualities to Felix Hirsch, Stresemann's biographer: 'He combined a lack of specialist knowledge with common-sense'. The combination was unreliable for though his common-sense proved adequate while the Republic flourished, in the crisis of 1930–33 his inability to cope with complicated political issues precipitated the Republic's overthrow.

Franco-German *Rapprochement*

The major achievement of Luther's government was in foreign affairs. Stresemann's Verständigungspolitik produced its second success with the signing of the Treaty of Locarno in 1925. As early as 1922 the Cuno government had suggested the conclusion of a treaty with France which would guarantee the Franco-German frontier and renounce the use of force to determine international disputes. This suggestion which attempted to allay French fears of German revanchism was greeted unenthusiastically in Paris. Further initiatives made by Stresemann in 1924 were again cold-shouldered. The acceptance of the Dawes Plan and the consequent French withdrawal from the Ruhr had improved Franco-German relations sufficiently for Stresemann to repeat his offer on 20 January 1925, the day after Luther's government had taken up office. This initiative had been strongly encouraged by Lord d'Abernon, British Ambassador to Germany, with whom Stresemann enjoyed cordial relations, and whose sustained support for Germany's interests, motivated by a desire to prevent French hegemony in western Europe, was acknowledged with gratitude by the German government.

On 5 January 1925 the Allies announced the postponement of the evacuation of the Cologne Zone of Occupation, which, according to the terms of Versailles, was due to take place on 10 January, on the pretext that Germany had failed to implement the disarmament clauses of the peace treaty: the Inter-Allied Control Commission reported finding several illegal arms caches. Stresemann detected the real cause of this decision: French preoccupation with security. Accordingly Stresemann renewed the proposal that Germany should formally ratify the Franco-German border. The proposal was motivated not by any newly-won feelings of friendship towards the suspicious French government but by Stresemann's intuitive conviction that a lessening of tension between the two countries – which a voluntary acceptance by Germany of the frontier would produce – would accelerate the evacuation of the occupation forces from the Rhineland.

To avoid the customary accusation of francophilia from the Nationalists and of anti-Soviet conspiracy from the Communists Stresemann communicated his proposals secretly to the Allied governments. He maintained that Germany desired reconciliation with France and recognized her wish for security and that, to this end, Germany was willing to conclude a Rhine treaty to guarantee the Franco-German frontier and the continued demilitarized status of the Rhineland. He hoped to present the Nationalists, as Turner argues, with a *fait accompli* which would effectively disarm their criticism. This, Turner maintains, explains Stresemann's eagerness to include the DNVP in the cabinet, which would force them into accepting joint responsibility for Franco-German *rapprochement* and thereby for his Verständigungspolitik. Nationalist collaboration would also, he believed, encourage Allied belief in Germany's good faith.

The Geneva Protocol

Stresemann's decision was reinforced by the prospect of a new pact between Britain, France and Belgium, the so-called Geneva Protocol, which was being discussed at the current session of the League of Nations. This agreement was intended to provide an international platform for settling international disputes by peaceful means. The signatories of the Protocol would also be obliged, however, to come to the aid, with military force if necessary, of any member-state which was threatened or attacked. Its main purpose appeared to be the maintenance of the territorial *status quo* of 1919, and thereby to satisfy France's desire for *sécurité*. While several powers agreed to the provisions, Britain was unwilling to accept such far-reaching commitments, and in March 1925 Austen Chamberlain, the British Foreign Minister, announced Britain's refusal to sign the Protocol. He was, however, determined at all costs to maintain good relations with the French government and, accordingly, declared Britain's support for the German proposal that discussions on a security pact limited geographically to the Rhineland should be held.

The French Foreign Minister, Herriot, harboured several misgivings. His colleagues feared, not without justification, that the regulation of the German western frontier might be regarded in Germany as an invitation to raise also the problem of the eastern frontier, which, by virtue of France's guarantees to Poland and Czechoslovakia, she was pledged to defend. It was not until April 1925 when a conciliatory French government was formed under the premiership of Paul Painlevé with Aristide Briand as Foreign Minister that Stresemann's proposal received favourable attention.

Germany's attitude to the question of her frontiers was, to say the least, ambiguous. Though bitterly opposed by the Nationalists, the voluntary renunciation of all claim to Alsace-Lorraine simply made a virtue out of necessity. These territories could be regained only by force and Germany was in no position to use military power against the West. Indeed, the vast majority of Germans would have been totally opposed to such measures. Eupen and Malmédy, now incorporated into Belgium, were hardly of great significance; the present plan would not exclude their possible subsequent return to Germany by negotiation. The eastern frontier was another matter, and one which aroused great emotional feeling. Few Germans could accept the permanent detachment from the Reich of Danzig and Upper Silesia, which they justifiably believed to constitute a flagrant breach of the principle of self-determination, and while the creation of the Polish Corridor was laid down in Wilson's Fourteen Points and in the Armistice agreement, its existence remained a permanent irritant to Germany's relations with her eastern neighbours. Germany was not alone in her refusal to accept the eastern frontier; British unwillingness to guarantee Poland's borders had led to Chamberlain's decision not to sign the Geneva Protocol. Stresemann, while indeed an ardent champion of those Germans living under foreign rule (including German-speaking Austrians prevented by treaty from joining the Reich), realized that in view of Allied disagreement their interests could best be served by holding negotiations with the powers concerned. Willingness to conclude treaties of arbitration and an undertaking not to resort to war in times of dispute were intended as part of his policy of understanding and constructive appeasement, which, it was hoped, would bear fruit later.

In June the French government sent a cautious reply to the German note – their right-wing opposition was no less recalcitrant than Germany's Nationalists. They agreed with the Belgian government to negotiate on the understanding that the status of the Rhineland, as prescribed by Versailles, would not come under discussion, and that Germany would join the League of Nations, which the German government had itself suggested in September 1924. Britain's agreement to the talks was already known. In September the Allies invited Germany to take part in a conference to be held during the following month in Locarno, on the shores of Lake Maggiore in Italian Switzerland.

On 5 October the delegates met for their opening session,

Stresemann and Luther represented Germany, the Allies and their associates were represented by Briand (France), Austen Chamberlain (Britain), Vandervelde (Belgium), Scialoia and Mussolini (Italy), Beneš (Czechoslovakia) and Skrzński (Poland). Their discussions were held in an atmosphere of unusual cordiality, with the Allied delegates seizing the opportunity of re-establishing friendly relations with their German colleagues. The many anecdotes about informality and cordiality which characterized the conference's confidential session aboard the steamer *Fiori d'Arancia* (*Orange Blossom*) on Lake Maggiore capture faithfully the spirit of collaboration and amicability present at Locarno.

Germany profited considerably from the prevailing mood of generosity, and succeeded in exacting two important concessions from the Allies. Briand promised an early evacuation of the Cologne Zone of Occupation. Secondly, a formula was drafted which exempted Germany from article 16 of the League Convention, which obliged member states to intervene in the defence of another signatory against aggression from a third power, a clause which could have involved Germany in a war with Poland against Russia. From this time a member state was required to impose sanctions only 'to an extent which is compatible with its military situation and takes its geographic position into account' – an effective limitation from the German point of view.

The main provisions of the treaty concerned Germany, France, Belgium, Britain and Italy; Czechoslovakia and Poland were represented only in the treaties of arbitration. The major powers agreed to 'guarantee . . . the maintenance of the territorial *status quo* resulting from the frontiers between Germany and Belgium and between Germany and France and the inviolability of the said frontiers as fixed by . . . the Treaty of Peace signed at Versailles . . . also the observance of the stipulations . . . concerning the demilitarized zone' (article 1). They further agreed not to 'attack or invade each other or resort to war against each other' (article 2). They agreed to renounce military force in favour of an undertaking 'to settle by peaceful means . . . all questions of every kind which may arise between them and which it may not be possible to settle by the normal methods of diplomacy' (article 3). These included submission to the decisions of the League if it were requested to arbitrate between two parties (article 4).

In addition to these major agreements, treaties of mutual guarantee were signed between France and Poland and France and Czechoslovakia. These were recognized by Germany, and while she did not undertake formally to guarantee the Czech and Polish frontiers, treaties of arbitration were concluded between Germany and Czechoslovakia and Germany and Poland, which were to operate in the case of disagreement between the two sides. As Stresemann had predicted, the British declared themselves wholly unwilling to guarantee the eastern frontier of Germany.

Which power gained most by the agreements of Locarno? France's desire for security had certainly been satisfied: by Germany's recognition of French sovereignty over Alsace-Lorraine, by the British guarantee of the Franco-German frontier, by the renunciation of the use of force, and by the arbitration treaties signed by Germany and France's protégés, Poland and Czechoslovakia. In fact these concessions cost Germany little for she was renouncing territory that was already lost, and her renunciation of the use of force was, in view of her military weakness, no more than realistic. In contrast, Germany's political gains were considerable: the Ruhr adventure would never be repeated, further revisions of the terms of Versailles were likely, including a reduction in the reparation debt, there were prospects of an increase in foreign loans, and, most important, Germany's political rehabilitation would allow her to resume an influential position in European affairs. Moreover, these concessions had been gained without Germany's being required to recognize the eastern frontier, a considerable achievement for Stresemann and Luther. The treaty was initialled on 16 October and was to come into force as soon as Germany had been accepted as a full member of the League of Nations, which, it was then believed, would take place at the earliest opportunity. The major significance of the treaty lay not in its various provisions, important as these were, but in the new spirit of international understanding to which it testified.

As usual, the subtleties of the treaty were lost on the mass of the German population. The Berlin police authorities had to conceal the time of arrival of the returning German delegation, not, as Hirsch remarks, to restrain an over-enthusiastic, welcoming public, but to prevent possible assassination attempts, a bitter comment indeed on Germany's political immaturity.

Parliamentary reaction to the draft agreement was surprisingly reassuring. Those Nationalists who had supported the Dawes legislation, appreciated the financial benefits which would follow ratification of Locarno and pledged their support to the government. The party backwoodsmen were, however, outraged and on 20 October they forced the resignation of their deputies from the coalition. Ironically their fixation about the good old days prevented them from recognizing the benefits to be gained from Locarno. With their habitual arrogance and obtuseness they demanded a total revision of Versailles – a policy of all or nothing, urged upon them by the hostile campaign against the treaty, labelled a 'third Versailles', which Hugenberg was sustaining in his newspapers. German entry into the League also met with severe criticism, though a permanent seat on the Council, which was a German condition of membership, would, since it carried with it the right of veto, considerably strengthen the country's position.

Though Hindenburg did not regard the terms of Locarno with great personal sympathy – it smacked to him of capitulation to the French – he lent the much-needed support of his office to the government, now reduced since the resignation of the Nationalists to a rump coalition comprising the People's Party, the Bavarian People's Party, the Centre and the Democrats. Stresemann was aware that the passage of the Locarno bill through the Reichstag would be anything but easy. A gesture of good faith was needed from the Allies to allay German fears of a sell-out to the French. Largely on account of d'Abernon's good offices, the Allies eventually showed sympathy for Stresemann's difficulties and announced that the Allied Military Control Commission in the Rhineland would be reduced in size, and the evacuation of the Cologne Zone would begin on 1 December, the date fixed for the formal ratification in London of the Locarno Treaty. The government could now argue from a position of greater strength and on 27 November the Reichstag, thanks to Socialist support, accepted the Locarno Treaty by 275 to 183 votes, and entry to the League of Nations by 300 to 174 votes. Opposition to the bills stemmed as ever from the extreme right and left: Nazis, the majority of the Nationalists and Communists. After receiving Hindenburg's signature to the bills, Luther and Stresemann left for London.

On their return to Berlin on 5 December, the cabinet tendered its resignation to the President. They had announced their intention of doing so in November during the Reichstag debate on Locarno when the prospect of a change of government had ensured the decisive support of the SPD for the treaty. It was to be left to a new cabinet to guide Germany into the League of Nations.

Hindenburg, faced with the task of choosing a new chancellor, pressed for a broadly-based coalition to succeed Luther's minority cabinet. There followed a six-week interregnum while Germany frantically searched for a viable government, a crisis which once again did little to enhance the standing of parliamentary democracy. In terms of domestic politics Locarno had been a failure for Stresemann since governmental responsibility had failed to tame the Nationalists (Turner). Clearly they could not be considered as possible members of a new government if Stresemann's foreign policy was to be continued. Without DNVP participation, however, the only possibility of forming a majority cabinet lay in including the Socialists. The SPD leadership promptly reiterated the conditions it had laid down in the previous January, a collection of social reforms including the reintroduction of the eight-hour day, a reduction in the proportion of taxation borne by the lower-paid, and the provision of unemployment benefit. These conditions proved too much for the DVP, representing the interests of industrialists, to accept, and Germany was prevented once more by inter-party disagreement from enjoying a government with a parliamentary majority. With the question of the country's entry into the League on the parliamentary agenda for the next session, a strong cabinet would have been especially welcome. Hindenburg had, however, little option but to coerce the parties into forming another minority coalition, and he asked Luther to form a second middle-class cabinet. It had the same political composition as the outgoing rump coalition though it included several ministerial changes. Together, the Democrats, the Centrists, Populists and Bavarian Populists controlled only one hundred and seventy-one mandates out of a total Reichstag representation of four hundred and ninety-three.

On 20 January Luther announced his government's programme. It included proposals for improved welfare legislation, in an attempt to appease the Socialists whose 'toleration' was needed although they remained outside the government. The Reichstag managed narrowly to pass the requested vote of confidence in the government thanks to the decision of the one hundred and thirty-one Socialists to abstain, for, while they remained unconvinced by the government's promises, they were equally unwilling to prolong the crisis by joining the extremist opposition. The new cabinet, created as a stop-gap, was unlikely from the outset to survive for long. In fact it remained in office for four months.

The Flag Controversy and the Luther Cabinet

A temporary economic reverse experienced early in 1926 aggravated the parliamentary difficulties of Luther's minority cabinet. The SPD, willing at first to endorse the cabinet's legislation, withdrew its support in May over a decision concerning Germany's national flag.

On 5 May a decree was issued, bearing Luther's and Hindenburg's signatures, instructing German consular and diplomatic missions in European ports and overseas to fly alongside the Republican tricolour the flag of the merchant navy, which had retained after 1918 the former Imperial colours black, white and red – albeit with the black, red and gold of the Republic included in the top inner corner. Luther justified the decree on the grounds that it was inconsistent to greet abroad ships of the merchant navy with the Republican flag alone. More likely, he was motivated by a desire to accommodate Hindenburg, and his right-wing supporters, who wished to restore to its rightful position the traditional symbol of Germany's glorious past. His agreement constituted in the eyes of the republican parties an unwarranted and unpardonable attack on the integrity of the Republic. He provoked a fierce parliamentary dispute and, after the Democrats, supported by the Socialists and Centrists, had successfully tabled a motion of censure against the government – in which the Nationalists unpredictably abstained – Luther and his cabinet were obliged to resign on 12 May, after less than four months in office.

Marx Forms a Cabinet

The search for a new chancellor encountered the now familiar obstacles. Attempts to form a Grand Coalition under the leadership of, among the many names canvassed, Konrad Adenauer, at that time Centrist Mayor of Cologne, foundered on the DVP's unwillingness to accommodate the social demands of the Socialists and the Nationalists' refusal to underwrite Stresemann's conciliatory foreign policy. At Stresemann's suggestion the Centrist leader, Wilhelm Marx, who had already led two cabinets, received and accepted a presidential request to form a government. The coalition formed on 17 May remained, with the exception of the Chancellor, unchanged from that of the outgoing cabinet, i.e. Democrats, Centrists, Bavarian Populists and Populists. Still without a parliamentary majority the cabinet had once more to invoke the support of the Socialists, who thus continued to enjoy considerable influence over the government without bearing any responsibility for its decisions.

Referendum on the Expropriation of the Princes

Luther's resignation, the punishment of a scapegoat, had defused the flag controversy, although the presidential order remained in force. Its place was taken by a further parliamentary imbroglio about the long-fermented question of the expropriation of Germany's ex-monarchs, whose property had been seized in 1918. Discussion was hampered by the legal uncertainty about whether the seized possessions belonged to the state or remained private property. The princes were undoubtedly constitutionally entitled to compensation for the loss of any private property and yet the Socialists felt unable on moral and political grounds to condone the allocation of large sums of public money to those whose conduct before 1918 had contributed largely to the country's post-war economic troubles. Together with the Communists the SPD called in March 1926 for a popular referendum to resolve the issue. Constitutional law demanded the submission of a petition containing the signatures of at least ten per cent of the electorate (which at that time numbered about forty million) before a referendum was held. Over twelve and a half million signatures were collected and the referendum was called for 26 June. Despite the massive support for the petition, the proposal calling for expropriation failed to attract fifty per cent of the electorate which was required constitutionally before a measure could become law. Nevertheless, over fifteen million electors had voted in favour of expropriation, less than five million short of the necessary twenty million, an indication of the strength of feeling aroused by the controversy and of the support the left wing could muster on such an issue. The major significance of the referendum was, as Heiber remarks, party-political. The SPD upheld their refusal to participate in successive coalitions not only on the grounds of economic and social differences with the middle-class parties but also on purely ideological grounds, preferring, to the detriment of the Republic, to remain in semi-opposition to the government.

Von Seeckt's Dismissal

Conflict between the government and the Socialists was further aggravated by the activities of the Reichswehr leader, von Seeckt. It was disclosed that Seeckt had invited the son of the Hohenzollern ex-Crown Prince, the pretender to the Prussian throne, to participate as a volunteer in the army's autumn manoeuvres without requiring him to swear the obligatory oath of allegiance to the Republic. Aware of the political implications of his decision, Seeckt had nevertheless – or perhaps deliberately – neglected to consult the Minister of Defence, Otto Gessler, who ultimately bore responsibility for the action. Gessler, who since Noske's dismissal had occupied one of the most difficult and thankless ministerial posts, at once demanded Seeckt's dismissal, a correct decision. He had long since tired of being treated as a puppet by Seeckt who disparagingly referred to him as a 'mere civilian'. Hindenburg gladly accepted the opportunity of ridding himself of Seeckt, whom he disliked as a man and whom he considered a threat to his titular position of Commander-in-Chief of the Reichswehr. On 26 October, with the support of all political parties except the Nationalists, Seeckt was dismissed from office. It was an ignominious end to the career of a man who, while arrogant and authoritarian by nature, possessed undeniable organizational ability and talent. He had transformed the Reichswehr into a supra-political 'state within a state' and had even professed a 'neutral' attitude at the time of the Kapp Putsch and Hitler Putch. He had supervised plans for illegal rearmament and the clandestine operations of the Reichswehr in Soviet Russia. Unwittingly he had created a small, highly efficient army, isolated from the Republic, which provided the Nazis with a ready-made military machine only too willing to collaborate. Seeckt's successor, General Wilhelm Heye, Commanding Officer in East Prussia, though conscientious in performing his military duties, was as unwilling as Seeckt to submit to parliamentary control and more easily manipulated by Hindenburg and his advisers.

The Socialists were not to be satisfied simply with the punishment of a scapegoat. They continued their investigations into the activities of the army and especially the illegal (by the terms of Versailles) clandestine Schwarze Reichswehr, uncovering its contacts with the extreme right wing at home and with the government of Soviet Russia. On 6 December the *Manchester Guardian* published the text of a document originating from Junkers, the aircraft company, which contained details of a projected German aircraft factory to be constructed in the U.S.S.R. under the auspices of the Reichswehr and the Red Army. The article, which was reprinted in the SPD's newspaper, *Vorwärts*, alleged that Reichstag deputies were aware of the project.

On 16 December the Socialist deputy, Philipp Scheidemann, tabled a motion of no confidence in Marx's government which, he maintained, had connived in the Reichswehr's illegal activities. He further demanded the resignation of Gessler, the Minister of Defence, who maintained his ignorance of the army's transactions. The motion was put to the vote and was passed by two hundred and forty-nine votes to one hundred and seventy-one with the combined vote of the Communists, the Socialists and, unexpectedly, the Nationalists, who recognized in the collapse of Marx's cabinet their opportunity to lead a new government.

Marx's cabinet had governed for eight months, the average life-span of the sixteen governments which held office between February 1919 and March 1930.

But however genuine Scheidemann's grounds for censuring Marx and his colleagues might have been, his decision to overthrow the government without considering who could take its place constituted an act of political irresponsibility all too typical of the immature behaviour of democratic and anti-democratic parties alike. Such an impetuous action, particularly one committed by the man who had proclaimed the Republic, contributed in no small measure to popular disaffection with the system.

Marx's Fourth Government

The sad farce of finding a chancellor and forming a new cabinet began once again. The Centre, determined to keep the chancellorship in its control, forced Hindenburg to ask Marx to form a fourth cabinet, if possible a Grand Coalition ranging from the DVP to the

SPD. He failed for several reasons: the middle-class parties objected once more to the Socialists' demands for social reforms and to their accusation of underhandedness in the government's dealings with the army. DVP demands that the Nationalists should be given representation in the cabinet led to the formation on 29 January 1927 of a Right Bourgeois Coalition comprising Centrists, Bavarian Populists, Populists and Nationalists. The Democrats refused to participate in a government which included Nationalist ministers and thus prevented the coalition from obtaining a parliamentary majority. Moreover the parliamentary toleration of the Socialists could similarly no longer be taken for granted. While unable to voice support for the Republic the Nationalists, participating for only the second time in democratic government, paid token homage to the Constitution and to the Locarno Treaty, the price required by Marx.

Stresemann's Foreign Policy after Locarno Negotiations with the League

Apart from the temporary but regrettable setback over Germany's entry to the League, international relations improved after Locarno and Stresemann's foreign policy flourished throughout the period from 1926 to 1928. Luther's government applied early in February 1926 for membership of the League despite vigorous Nationalist opposition. The Council and Assembly of the League met on 8 March to discuss and, it was generally assumed, to accept Germany's application. While no state opposed Germany's entry to the League, several objected to Germany's being granted a permanent seat on the Council. This inner body of the League, which possessed the right of veto, was composed of the four Allies, Britain, France, Italy and Japan, and six elected representatives of the other member nations. If the status of a great power was thus to be conferred on Germany, other states wished to share her position of privilege. There followed a period of intense international haggling which failed to resolve the problem. To the manifest delight of the Nationalists the question of Germany's entry finally had to be postponed until the next session of the League due to be held the following September. The Nationalists used the League's snub as another rod with which to beat Stresemann and tabled a motion of censure against the government for endorsing a policy which implied voluntary recognition of Germany's war guilt. The Socialists voted with the government parties and defeated the Nationalists' attempt to wreck Stresemann's policy of understanding.

The Treaty of Berlin

Germany's application to the League strengthened Russian suspicions, aroused by the Locarno agreement, that Stresemann was reorientating German foreign policy towards the formation of a capitalist front with the West. Their contention that Locarno contradicted the terms of Rapallo received support from right-wing circles in Germany, which saw in *rapprochement* with the Soviet Union a means of further undermining Versailles and Stresemann's policy of understanding. Seeckt and several Nationalists hoped for greater rewards: a twentieth-century partition of Poland which, they argued, would at once secure Germany's eastern frontier from attack and break the Petite Entente between France and the new Eastern European states. Stresemann had originally intended to approach the Soviet government after Germany's acceptance into the League and the consequent ratification of Locarno, but the setback suffered at Geneva had forced him reluctantly to amend his timetable. New impetus was given to the Russo-German discussions which had been conducted tentatively since the beginning of the year and on 24 April a treaty was signed by representatives of the two states in Berlin. The Treaty of Berlin confirmed the terms of Rapallo. Economic and political ties between the two countries were to be strengthened. More important, the two countries agreed to observe benevolent neutrality in the event of attack by a third power and to abstain in such circumstances from an economic boycott of the other. Germany stressed that, as a result of the compromise reached at Locarno, she had already been relieved of any obligation (i.e. under article 16 of the League Covenant) to grant Poland military assistance against the U.S.S.R. The Berlin agreement was in effect a reinsurance treaty: it added little to Rapallo and remained consistent with the terms of Locarno. Its significance lies in the confirmation of Stresemann's policy of understanding with both East and West in his attempt to restore Germany's political equality in Europe. The Reichstag ratified the treaty on 30 June with almost unique unanimity, only three votes being recorded against acceptance.

League Entry

Allied reaction to the treaty was predictably one of concern but Stresemann succeeded with diplomatic tact and skill to allay their fears – he had no wish to jeopardize his *rapprochement* with the West. On 8 September Germany's application was resubmitted to the League and was accepted. A compromise solution had been adopted by those nations which had demanded equality with Germany. On 10 September in a ceremony symbolizing the hope of the member nations for a future without war Germany was admitted to the League and granted a permanent seat on the Council. Simultaneously the Locarno Treaty was brought into force.

Germany's political rehabilitation, apart from the two admittedly large outstanding problems of the reparations and the occupied Rhineland, was now virtually complete. It was to these two remaining problems and to a further improvement of Franco-German relations that Stresemann devoted his energies during the last three years of his life. His policy of understanding had won considerable respect for him abroad. His reputation at home was equivocal: many Socialists, while they approved his conduct of foreign affairs, remembered with suspicion his war-time policies, while the Nationalists continued to condemn his policy of understanding towards the Allies. Some of the force had been removed from their argument by the evacuation of the first Rhineland zone, the area around Cologne, by British occupation troops on 1 February 1926, a real psychological advantage for Stresemann and the Luther government, but this did not deter the Nationalists from returning to the attack whenever they considered it advantageous to them politically.

Thoiry

On 17 September, a week after Germany's acceptance into the League, Stresemann and Briand met in a small French inn in Thoiry, a village a few miles from Geneva, to hold informal, private discussions on a wide range of topics of common interest to their two countries. These included plans for the immediate evacuation of the second and third Occupation Zones in the Rhineland and the reunion of the Saarland with Germany, in return for German financial support for the ailing French currency and the repurchase in cash of the Saar coal-fields. That a German politician could con-

template granting a loan to a foreign power at this time was an
indication of the rapid recovery which had resulted from currency
reform and the Dawes Plan. The Thoiry Plan failed, not, as has
been suggested, simply on account of the intransigence of the French
Premier, Poincaré, recalled to office in July to stabilize the franc,
or of the traditional francophobia of the German Nationalists, but,
as Herzfeld has indicated, because the American government was
unwilling to allow an arrangement which would in effect, if not
intentionally, couple reparations with France's war-time debts
to the U.S.A., something which the Americans had refused to
contemplate since 1919. It was made clear to Stresemann once more
that his freedom of movement in economic and financial affairs
depended ultimately on the attitude of the American government.
The Thoiry Plan, had it been implemented, would doubtless have
provided the underpinning which the Republic needed and have
stifled Nationalist opposition to Stresemann's policies. It was,
however, to remain a lost opportunity. Despite this setback
Stresemann was able to persuade Briand to withdraw the Inter-
Allied Military Control Commission from Germany on 31 January
1927 and to instigate the establishment by the League of a Prepara-
tory Disarmament Commission which was to investigate the possibility of multilateral European disarmament.

The efforts of Stresemann and Briand as well as those of Austen
Chamberlain and Charles Dawes for the cause of world peace were
recognized in December 1926 when the Norwegian Nobel Committee
decided to award the Peace Prize to them jointly. This was an
indication of the high esteem with which he was regarded abroad in
contrast to the virulent opposition he encountered within Germany
and within his own party.

Social Legislation

Marx's Right Bourgeois Coalition had given an undertaking to
the Socialists in return for their toleration to introduce a programme of social legislation. Even Hindenburg spoke – in a manner
which echoed Bismarck's unexpected social conscience of the 1870s
– of the need to protect the interests of the working population.
Since the introduction of the Dawes Plan Germany's economic
recovery had exceeded the hopes of the most optimistic, and even
many right-wing politicians were now prepared to accept the luxury

of social security. Industrialists, now firmly in control once more, were happy to dispense largesse to the workers. They remained implacably opposed, however, to any suggestion that the principle of industrial partnership between employer and employee should be revived.

The Centrist Heinrich Brauns, Minister of Labour since 1920, proposed a bill which entitled workers to unemployment benefit. It was to be provided by a fund financed by a contribution of three per cent of the normal wage, divided equally between employer and employee. Though a thoroughly progressive piece of legislation, it failed to foresee the impossible strains which heavy unemployment would impose on the fund, as in fact happened in 1930, when its resources proved to be hopelessly inadequate. As Eyck points out, the maximum number of unemployed envisaged by the scheme was a little over a million, a figure which had already been well exceeded only a year previously. On 7 July 1927 the Reichstag approved the bill by a large majority – opposed by only the most extreme, such as the future Nationalist leader, Hugenberg, who advocated the imposition of forced savings as an alternative to unemployment insurance! Brauns introduced further measures in 1927 which improved the workers' pay and conditions. The statutory right to a higher rate of pay for overtime work was established. Negotiating machinery was set up to provide for the settlement by discussion of disputes between employers and employees. A State Board of Arbitration was also established with the right to intervene where necessary between unions and employers to prevent the outbreak of industrial strikes and lock-outs which would endanger the country's economic recovery.

Gessler's Resignation and Groener's Appointment
The Reichswehr controversy which had temporarily subsided at the end of 1926 flared up with renewed vigour in 1927. The restrictions in size imposed on the armed forces by the terms of Versailles appeared to have been evaded on a large scale, to judge by the considerable increase between 1924 and 1927 in the declared defence budgets. These were, however, deliberate falsifications, at which the Ministry of Defence, the inter-party Reichstag Budgetary Committee and successive governments connived. Some officials in the Ministry of Defence decided – with the Minister's approval – to invest secretly

large amounts of public money into, among other undertakings, the Phöbus Film Company, which promised to yield high dividends. The company failed and during the bankruptcy proceedings the ministry's investment was disclosed. Gessler, unable to offer an explanation for an action which was patently unconstitutional, offered his resignation on 14 January 1928.

His conduct illustrates the quandary in which many republican politicians found themselves. They considered secret evasion of the military restrictions imposed by Versailles to be wholly consistent with their attempts to achieve a *rapprochement* with the Allies. The clandestine subvention of the army and navy was simply intended to provide adequate defence forces. When such illegal activities were uncovered, however, those responsible had no option but to resign, although their motives had been wholly 'patriotic'. What the majority of republican politicians failed to realize was that the establishment of an illicit defence force which maintained the imperial tradition would prove easy game for one such as Hitler. This was, however, the result of the failure in 1918–19 to create a truly pro-republican Reichswehr, a situation which despite several desultory attempts could hardly be remedied after Seeckt had so successfully created his impregnable 'state within a state'.

Hindenburg seized the opportunity to install an old comrade at the Ministry of Defence, General Wilhelm Groener. His political and military qualifications were considerable: he had succeeded Ludendorff as Commander-in-Chief of the Reichswehr in 1918, had collaborated with Ebert in the prevention of a Bolshevik revolution and had served in four cabinets between 1920 and 1923 as Minister of Transport. Affiliated to no party but liberal in outlook, Groener defended the Republic to the best of his ability. Less fortunate was the appointment in 1929 of General Kurt von Schleicher to the newly created, powerful ministerial office, *Ministeramt*, which acted as a liaison between the Ministry of Defence and the Reichswehr. More will be spoken of Schleicher and his activities later.

The Resignation of Marx's Fourth Cabinet

The early months of 1928 saw a rapid disintegration of the Marx cabinet. Stresemann's foreign policy again came under severe attack from his Nationalist coalition colleagues. It became increasingly clear to Marx that the coalition would have to be reformed if

Stresemann was to continue to enjoy the broadly-based parliamentary support which he considered necessary in his attempts to secure further concessions from the Allies. On the question of the Occupied Rhineland only the inclusion of the SPD would provide a sufficiently strong backing for the government. The Centre delegates were willing to collaborate with the SPD as was the majority of the DVP members, but the Nationalists remained, naturally, wholly opposed to participating in a 'red' coalition. The difficulty resolved itself when a conflict arose within the coalition which brought about its fall. New elections produced the desired realignment of political forces.

The Centrists, supported by the Nationalists and the Bavarian People's Party, wished to introduce a bill altering the Reich School System. Under article 146 of the Constitution common schools serving all denominations had been established throughout the country, and those parents who wished to send their children to a confessional school were allowed to opt out of the state system. The three parties supporting the claims of Catholicism and Lutheranism now wished to replace common schools with purely confessional establishments. This proposal met with immense opposition within the government from the DVP, a staunchly secular party, and outside from the Socialists and Democrats. A compromise solution, which would have provided for both denominational and secular schools, likewise met with widespread hostility. The coalition partners were unable to reach a satisfactory decision, and on 15 February the two Catholic parties withdrew their support from Marx's cabinet and brought about its downfall. At Hindenburg's instigation the cabinet agreed to remain temporarily in office in order to enact a programme of urgent legislation before the Reichstag was dissolved. New elections, due at the latest by the end of the year, would be held immediately afterwards. The opposition parties agreed to support the government's programme and the outstanding legislation was completed on 30 March. On the following day the government resigned and it was announced that new elections would be held on 20 May.

The Electoral Campaign

The issue which dominated the election campaign was not the controversy about the school law, which had not reached the statute book, but a row about a pocket battleship. Under the terms of Versailles, Germany had been allowed to retain six battleships, which it might replace when necessary with ships of up to ten thousand tons. The navy was now in a financial position to re-equip itself with pocket battleships, which, as a result of the advance in technical skills, would possess considerably more power than their predecessors, although still within the prescribed limit of ten thousand tons. The Minister of Defence and the President, impressed by the blueprint of the proposed ships, endorsed the navy's request for funds to build one pocket battleship immediately and possibly three more in the future.

Financial support for the project was requested by the Minister of Defence in the budget discussions in March. The SPD who professed a doctrinal opposition to rearmament also regarded the project as frivolous. They argued that increased expenditure on the social services would be more appropriate, and they doubted the strategic relevance of the ships. Their objection was out-voted in the Reichstag, but they managed by skilful political tactics to postpone work on the ship until September. They were then able to fight the election with the somewhat primitive but effective slogan 'food for children before battleships'. It proved extremely successful.

The result appeared to be a victory for the left and a defeat for the liberal and conservative parties alike. But this interpretation is misleading. True, the socialists increased their parliamentary representation considerably, the SPD making its best showing since 1919. The improvement in their popularity cannot, however, be attributed to any real desire for socialism in the electorate, it was rather an indication of their satisfaction with the now apparently prosperous republican régime. The liberal parties suffered badly. The decline of the Democrats, evident in every election since 1919, continued as a result of their lack of forceful political personalities and their ill-formulated policy. The Centre also lost some support, possibly as a result of its internal difficulties. This was true also of the DVP whose right wing maintained their opposition to Stresemann despite his increased popularity. The DNVP's reversal of fortune indicated dislike of their indecisive policies and of their participation in a republican government rather than a conversion to moderation of their former supporters. Their lack of success prompted the party to elect a new leader, the extremist Alfred Hugenberg. The

Nationalists' lost support – and that of the Nazis – was transferred to other right-wing parties, and in particular to the increasingly popular Economic Party, now renamed the 'National Party of the German Bourgeoisie', *Reichspartei des deutschen Mittelstandes,* which gained twenty-three seats. The title was well chosen: the party was pledged to support the *petite bourgeoisie* against the

THE ELECTION OF 20 MAY 1928

The results of the election were as follows:

		Votes cast (to nearest thousand)		Number of seats		Percentage of total vote	
		Dec. 1924	1928	Dec. 1924	1928	Dec. 1924	1928
KPD	Communist	2,712,000	3,265,000	45	54	9·0	10·6
SPD	Social Democratic	7,886,000	9,153,000	131	153	26·0	29·8
DDP	Democratic	1,921,000	1,506,000	32	25	6·3	4·9
Z	Centre	4,121,000	3,712,000	69	62	13·6	12·1
BVP	Bavarian People's	1,135,000	946,000	19	16	3·7	3·1
DVP	People's	3,051,000	2,680,000	51	45	10·1	8·7
DNVP	Nationalist	6,209,000	4,382,000	103	73	20·5	14·2
NSDAP	National Socialist	908,000	801,000	14	12	3·0	2·6
Others		2,208,000	4,126,000	29	51	4·2	13·9
Total (to nearest hundred thousand)		30,700,000	31,200,000	493	491		

75·6 per cent of the electorate voted compared with 78·8 per cent in December 1924.

power blocks of the trade unions and big business. They also indulged in a virulent brand of jingoistic nationalism. As Rosenberg points out, the electorate had not changed its spots: though dissatisfied with the traditional parties of the right, it remained anti-semitic, anti-liberal, anti-socialist and wholly hostile to the régime. What was heralded at home and abroad as a victory for democracy and international understanding was a hollow success, as the economic crisis which was soon to follow proved, providing the Nazis with the necessary conditions to rally the right-wing extremists to their cause.

Müller's Cabinet of Personalities

Hindenburg, bowing to the election results, invited Hermann Müller, chairman of the SPD, to lead a government. The task of forming a viable coalition proved, as ever, difficult. A majority government would have to be broadly based, despite the relatively powerful position of the SPD. As a return of the Weimar Coalition would fail narrowly to produce the required majority (two hundred and forty seats out of four hundred and ninety-one) the only remaining possibility was the formation of a Grand Coalition, including the People's Party and the Bavarian People's Party. Both the DVP and the Centre had misgivings about Müller's proposal and made their participation in the coalition dependent on conditions which Müller found unacceptable. Stresemann in a telegram from Bühlerhöhe, where he was convalescing from an attack of a chronic kidney disease, suggested that Müller should avoid the difficulty of trying to accommodate rival party interests by creating a non-party 'cabinet of personalities' drawn from the ranks of the Grand Coalition parties. This 'shot from the Bühlerhöhe', as Stresemann's telegram became known after its publication in the press, was a disguised attempt to force his party into entering a Grand Coalition. It failed, and Müller had to pursue Stresemann's suggestion at its face value, namely to create a non-party government. In stressing the personal responsibility of individual ministers, rather than party loyalty, Müller and Stresemann had unintentionally revived a long-neglected principle of the Constitution, which demanded that deputies should act according to the dictates of their conscience. Whether a government guided by such a principle was viable, only practice could decide.

The cabinet which took office on 28 June indeed included a host of well-known politicians. In addition to the Chancellor there were three Socialist members: Carl Severing as Minister of the Interior, Rudolf Wissell as Minister of Labour and Rudolf Hilferding as Finance Minister. Thus the SPD controlled four of the most influential offices. The Populist, Julius Curtius, continued as Minister of Economics and Stresemann remained Foreign Minister. Groener also retained his influential post of Defence Minister. The Democrats were given two ministries, the Centre and the Bavarian People's Party were each given one portfolio.

Müller announced his government's policy on 3 July. While

giving the traditional undertaking to improve the standard of living, the government, he asserted, had no formulated social policy (the political composition of the cabinet prevented the enactment of any major internal reforms). Müller undertook to pursue Stresemann's foreign policy with vigour. Priority was to be given to obtaining a revision of Germany's reparation obligations and to effecting an early evacuation of the Allied-occupied Rhineland. It was hoped that the 'victory' for democracy scored in the recent election would win considerable sympathy abroad for Germany's difficulties.

The Formation of a Grand Coalition

Deprived of reliable majority in the Reichstag, the cabinet was exposed to the constant danger of being defeated both by anti-republican, extremist opposition and by the moderate parties. This clearly imposed great strains on the cabinet, a condition which was exemplified by the reaction of the SPD to the renewed pocket battleship controversy. On 10 August the cabinet decided to authorize the construction of the first ship, a *quid pro quo* in return for toleration by the right-wing parties. The decision provoked parliamentary opposition which was all the more vigorous since Müller had pledged support for general disarmament in his policy statement in July. The SPD, bound by its election promise, introduced a motion in the Reichstag, which opposed the scheme. In so doing the party representatives were bowing to pressure from their rank and file, who demanded that all Socialist deputies should support the motion. A farce was enacted in the Reichstag on 16 November when the Chancellor and other Socialist ministers left the government benches to join their party colleagues and vote against a measure which had been approved and introduced by Müller's cabinet. The motion was decisively defeated by two hundred and fifty votes to two hundred and two (SPD and KPD), the government was saved, and Groener was able to withdraw his threatened resignation. The Socialist Parliamentary Party had no intention of toppling the government for they realized that any successive government would go ahead with the construction of the ships. They felt, however, that they could not ignore the party-political necessity of making a gesture of opposition to placate their members. The SPD's ambivalent attitude to armaments – a conflict between doctrinaire anti-militarism and an unfounded fear of attack from outside – severely damaged their popularity. More serious was the adverse effect produced on the electorate by the spectacle of cabinet ministers' opposing the policy of the government to which they belonged. Such charades could only discredit parliament.

Müller's cabinet managed with difficulty to survive the strain inevitably imposed by its lack of party allegiance. Further considerable tensions resulted also from the selfish attitude of the Centre and the People's Party who consistently placed party advantage before the welfare of the country. It was not until April 1929 that government stability was achieved. After the Centre had been granted ministerial representation the cabinet of personalities was replaced by a Grand Coalition with a reliable parliamentary majority, the composition of the government remained largely unaltered.

Foreign Policy: Reparations and the Rhineland

Stresemann's foreign policy during 1928 and 1929 was directed towards achieving the evacuation of the Allied occupation forces from the Rhineland; this was dependent on both sides reaching a mutually acceptable solution of the reparations question.

The Dawes Plan, which since its inception had been regarded as an interim agreement, had conferred considerable benefits on Germany: the huge capital loans granted after the plan had been ratified had allowed the reconstruction of German industry and guaranteed the stability of the currency. Germany had had nevertheless no option but to accept the plan, even though it avoided revising Germany's total financial obligations. Now Stresemann demanded to be told the total sum which the Allied goverments considered Germany ought to pay – legally the obligation stood at one hundred and thirty-two thousand million gold marks, a sum now regarded by all parties as wholly unrealistic. Stresemann's concern to achieve a reduction in Germany's debt was motivated not by purely political considerations. The fact that Germany had paid the annuities on the nail should not be taken as a reliable indication of her economic position. True, Germany's industry had revived after 1925: the investment of large sums of foreign capital had allowed Rathenau's policy of industrial rationalization to be fully implemented. On the other hand, without the inflow of U.S. loans she would not have been able to meet her obligations under the

Dawes Plan. Stresemann and his advisers were convinced that the national economy simply could not afford to pay the two thousand five hundred million gold marks due in 1928. Of the total twenty-five thousand million marks in loans received between 1924 and 1929 – largely from the U.S.A. – twelve thousand million were short-term, 'hot' funds which, as Stresemann and the Allied Commissioner for Reparations, Seymour Parker Gilbert, recognized, were liable to be withdrawn at short notice if the world economy lost its buoyancy. As much of the money had been spent by the Länder in a spree of public buildings and works, withdrawal of funds would create severe difficulties for the German economy. Warnings by Gilbert and Stresemann had been consistently ignored by successive governments lulled into complacency by their unaccustomed affluence.

Gilbert voiced his opinion in a report to the Allied governments, delivered in December 1927. He argued that a revision of the Dawes agreement and a decisive regulation of the whole problem of reparations would be advantageous to both sides. His suggestion – all the more forceful since it came from an economic expert who could hardly be accused of bias towards Germany – initiated further discussions.

Stresemann, while visiting Paris in August 1928 to sign the Kellogg-Briand Pact, took the opportunity of putting Germany's views on reparations and the status of the Rhineland to Poincaré. The French premier's reaction was not encouraging: a settlement of the reparation question and the evacuation of the Rhineland were, he maintained, dependent on a reduction of the inter-Allied war debt, the sum owed by France (and Great Britain) to the U.S.A. The Americans, for their part, were unwilling to reduce the debt still further, having already shown France what they considered to be sufficient generosity. The outlook for Germany was discouraging.

Stresemann's desire to accelerate the evacuation of the Rhineland was not produced simply by the wish to rid the country of foreign occupying troops. They were for the most part unobtrusive and the cost of their upkeep, while met by Germany, was deductible from the reparation payments. It was of no great importance whether the troops occupying the area around Aachen and Cologne remained until 1930 and those around Trier and Kaiserslautern until 1935, the dates of withdrawal laid down in Versailles. Discussions within Germany about the Rhineland had, however, long since been stripped of all rational consideration and the problem had been endowed with emotional significance. Hirsch quotes Stresemann as having told his physician in July 1929, 'As long as there is one foreign soldier remaining on German soil, no domestic policy can be pursued', a reference to the hostile propaganda of the right-wing parties. They attributed the continued occupation to a lack of patriotism and firmness of purpose of successive governments in which Stresemann had served as Foreign Minister. 'Liberation of the Rhineland' had become one of the more forceful political slogans of the day.

Negotiations about the Young Plan

Further representations were made by the German government in September 1928. At the annual session of the League of Nations in Geneva Müller, representing Stresemann who had suffered a mild stroke in August, demanded that reparations and the Rhineland question be discussed at the full session of the League. While the British favoured immediate evacuation and holding discussions on reparations, the French delegate, Foreign Minister Briand, under orders from his germanophobe premier, Poincaré, was obstructive. There were unfortunate, bitter exchanges between the French and German delegates. Compromise was reached on 16 September: negotiations on both issues were to be held concurrently. The negotiations were to be conducted by economic experts from the six interested powers, Belgium, France, Germany, Great Britain, Italy and Japan. At Germany's insistence a representative from the U.S.A. was invited. Moreover equality of status was granted to the German delegation, a welcome improvement in the Allies' attitude to negotiations with the former enemy.

The first meeting of the economic experts took place in Paris on 9 February 1929. The delegates representing Germany included the president of the Reichsbank, Hjalmar Schacht, who, despite his origins in the Democratic Party, was fast moving towards the Nationalist camp, and Albert Vögler, the industrial magnate and right-wing member of the People's Party, not, perhaps, the most fortunate choice of representatives. The U.S. delegation included Owen D. Young, the chairman of the huge American industrial concern, the General Electric Company. He was elected unanimously to chair the discussions.

The negotiations proved to be protracted and difficult and at one stage it appeared as if they would break down totally. The Allies' proposals were unacceptable to the Germans, and Schacht's plans were likewise rejected by the Allies. It is a credit to Young's diplomatic skills that he was able to formulate a compromise plan acceptable to both sides. By the terms of this proposal Germany was to pay an average of two thousand million gold marks annually until 1988. Immediate respite was to be provided by a reduction of the annuity to 1·7 thousand million in the first few years. This compared favourably with the average annuity of 2·5 thousand millions laid down in the Dawes Plan. The total payments over the fifty-eight years amounted to 112 thousand million marks, 20 thousand million less than the original demand of the Reparations Commission. Germany was to be master in her own house once more with the withdrawal of the Allied reparations agent, Gilbert, and also of the American controllers of the Reichsbank and the state railways. The transfer of funds from Germany to the Allies was no longer to be effected by an inter-Allied authority but through a Bank of International Settlements which was to be established in Basle. This proposal, ultimately adopted, was a mixed blessing for though it restored complete monetary sovereignty to Germany it also deprived her of the fiscal and financial protection which she enjoyed under the previous transfer arrangements. It is possible that Germany would have been spared the full force of the financial crisis in 1930 had the Allied supervisory body still existed.

Young's aims were clear: by removing the reparations question further from the sphere of international politics, he hoped to accelerate the restoration of normal relations between Germany and the Allies, initiated in 1924 by the Dawes agreement. Young's good intentions were largely misunderstood in Germany, however. The reduction of the total sum and the return of the railways and the Reichsbank to German control were regarded as ephemeral concessions by the vast majority of the population which was understandably more impressed by the obviously negative features of the plan. Annuities, as Herzfeld has pointed out, would still have had to be paid in 1988, years after the death of the majority of those who had experienced the war. Moreover, 112 thousand million marks, if only 40 thousand million in real terms (i.e. if earned as interest on 40 thousand million invested at five per cent), was nevertheless an enormous sum. It was clear that the country would have to recourse to further borrowing abroad in order to meet even these reduced commitments. The hazards involved in obtaining new credits became evident within a short time: in 1930 the whole structure of the reparations scheme was destroyed when, as a result of the Wall Street Crash, American loans were withdrawn from Germany.

Opposition in Germany to the Young Plan

Even before the conference of experts had taken place, widespread opposition to the proposed modification of Germany's reparations debt was voiced within Germany. The National Opposition, determined to derive as much political capital from the situation as they could, launched an attack on Stresemann and the Müller cabinet for agreeing to take part in a conference whose outcome would do nothing to alleviate Germany's financial and political enslavement. Stresemann rejected their wholly unrealistic policy of all-or-nothing, preferring to regain Germany's equality by continuing the already successful Verständigungspolitik. Nothing would be gained by making impossible claims. The truth of the situation was that the Nationalists did not, of course, expect their demands to be met in full, they merely wished to discredit the government. Although a motion of no confidence, tabled on 20 November by the Nazis, was soundly defeated by two hundred and nineteen votes to ninety-eight, the campaign against the forthcoming settlement and, ultimately, against the government and the Republic continued. It marked the beginning of Hitler's successful bid for power.

The campaign was resumed when the terms of Young's draft agreement were debated in parliament on 24 May. The Nationalists argued that, far from benefiting Germany, the new proposal extended Germany's liability to such an extent that their children's children would be bound in 1988 by an agreement made sixty years previously. The premise which had initiated discussions was, they maintained, false: the whole question of Germany's liability rested on the acceptance of Germany's War Guilt, an imputation which they refuted in the strongest terms. The 'War Guilt Lie', which henceforth became the slogan of the National Opposition, must be repudiated. Agreement to a plan which would commit Germany to continued financial obligations, constituted, they contended, voluntary acceptance of War Guilt.

Stresemann again attempted to counter the Nationalists' extremism with rational argument, pointing out that Germany had little option but to participate in negotiations. Any form of resistance, passive or otherwise, was impossible. Even though the War Guilt Clause was objectionable, Germany had indeed lost the war – an opinion not shared by the Nationalists – and was obliged to negotiate with the Allies.

The Young Plan Referendum

The Nationalists were not to be deflected from their policy of discrediting the government. On 9 July they formed a National Committee whose task it was to organize a plebiscite to demand the introduction of a parliamentary bill against the Young Plan and the 'War Guilt Lie'. The Committee represented all those whose avowed aim it was to sabotage the régime and included such personalities as Hugenberg, Hitler, Heinrich Class, leader of the Pan-German League, and Franz Seldte, commander of the Stahlhelm, the right-wing para-military organization associated with the DNVP. The inclusion of Hitler in the Committee, whose other members were socially and politically acceptable, conferred an aura of respectability on him and he could no longer be dismissed as simply a racialist curiosity from Bavaria.

On 29 September Hitler and Hugenberg issued the draft of the so-called 'Freedom Law', the 'Law against the Enslavement of the German People', which was to be submitted to the constitutional procedure for plebiscites. The bill contained four paragraphs: paragraph 1 called for governmental denunciation of the War Guilt Clause; paragraph 2 demanded the annulment by the Allies of both the War Guilt Clause and articles 429 and 430 of Versailles which concerned war criminals, together with the evacuation of Allied occupying troops; paragraph 3 stated that further payment of reparations – and especially any commitment under the Young Plan – should be rejected; paragraph 4, in true demagogic style, laid down that any minister or governmental representative who rendered Germany liable to further payment of reparations (e.g. under the Young Plan) would be held guilty of treason and punishable under the terms of the penal code (which provided for imprisonment with hard labour for a period of not less than two years). The obvious impracticability of the proposals was of little concern to their sponsors for there was from the outset little chance that the bill would become law. This was not, of course, the object of an exercise which was essentially propagandistic. In the second half of October signatures supporting the submission of the draft to the Reichstag were collected. Slightly over four million were obtained, barely more than the minimum ten per cent demanded by the Constitution; they had been collected largely from the agrarian backwoodsmen to the east of the river Elbe.

Their failure to attract a larger number of signatures was attributable to several causes, not the least to Hindenburg's publicly voiced opposition to paragraph 4, whose provisions he wholly rejected. Hindenburg had no wish to be thought party to a political strategem which was clearly hostile to the state of which he was the head. The government had produced a trump card: in August spokesmen from the six interested powers had met in The Hague to discuss the experts' proposals. At the end of the month Stresemann was able, after encountering considerable difficulty from the British delegation, to secure an assurance from the Allies that the Rhineland would be evacuated five years ahead of schedule: evacuation was to begin in September 1928 and to be completed at the latest by the end of June 1930. The evacuation remained dependent, of course, on acceptance of Young's draft plan by the German parliament.

Stresemann's appearance at the Hague Conference was his last act as Germany's Foreign Minister. He died from a heart attack on 3 October shortly after participating in a heated and protracted meeting of his parliamentary party to discuss the crisis in unemployment insurance – in which he was overruled. It symbolized, Heiber suggests, the death of the Republic. It certainly deprived Germany, at a time when she could least afford it, of her most able and internationally most respected stateman. His death like that of the Republic was due in no small measure to the persecution by such men as Hugenberg, whose newspapers had sustained a campaign of vilification against his policies and his person.

The next stage in the procedure, the presentation of the bill to the Reichstag, took place on 25 November. The government declared itself in agreement with the substance of the draft: the twin iniquities of War Guilt and reparations but insisted that paragraph 4 would inhibit all government action and, in its unprecedented hostility to democratic procedure, was wholly unacceptable. Rejection of the Young Plan would, they reminded its opponents, result in a refusal by the Allies to continue the evacuation of the Rhineland. The bill was rejected by a large majority: eighty votes were cast for paragraphs 1–3 while paragraph 4 received only sixty votes. The Nationalist cause had been strengthened considerably by Schacht's well-timed if not wholly unexpected decision to abandon the Democrats' progressive policies in favour of Hugenberg's extremism. In an open letter to the government he stated his objections to the Young Plan. Though he had been a signatory at the conference of experts in Paris he refused to be further involved in negotiations with the Allies, on the transparent pretext that the experts' draft had been amended after his signature. His resignation from the chairmanship of the Reichsbank in March 1930 confirmed his conversion to German Nationalism and his hostility to the Republic. Having seen the error of his ways in good time he commended himself to Hitler and later became the Nazis' financial advisor.

The progress of the draft bill continued: since it had been rejected by the Reichstag it had now, according to the procedure laid down in the Constitution, to be submitted to a plebiscite, in which it would have to obtain support from over fifty per cent of the whole electorate, i.e. over 20 million votes, if it were to succeed. The plebiscite was held on 22 December 1929 and produced a resounding defeat for the bill's proposers, despite Schacht's widely publicized denunciation of Young's proposals. Only 5·8 million votes in favour of the proposed bill were cast, largely by the supporters of the two National Opposition parties.

The Political Significance of the Referendum

The rejection of the 'Freedom Law' gave the lie to the National Opposition's contention that the Republic was politically bankrupt. Several prominent German Nationalists had voted against their party's policy and had been expelled by Hugenberg. The rebels, who included Gottfried Treviranus, a leading Nationalist deputy, Cuno von Westarp, former party leader, and Walter von Kendell, Minister of the Interior in Marx's last government, subsequently established an independent Conservative Party, *Konservative Volkspartei*, which, while maintaining right-wing policies, condemned the DNVP's flirtation with Hitler whose fanaticism and extremism they mistrusted, and declared their support for the Constitution and the Republic.

The result of the plebiscite proves that at the end of 1929, in spite of the many defects of the system – the legacy of Versailles, the political immaturity of the population, the weaknesses of the Constitution and the attempted disruption of the National Opposition – the Republic still enjoyed widespread popular support. The ultimate cause of the downfall of the Republic cannot, therefore, be ascribed solely to these conditions though they undoubtedly provided a climate in which extremism flourished.

The Reichstag was now free to ratify the agreement reached at The Hague. On 12 March 1930 two hundred and seventy votes were recorded in favour of the Young Plan with one hundred and ninety-two against. Despite a last-minute attempt by the DNVP to delay the passage of the bill, it was ratified the next day by President Hindenburg who was determined not to allow further political manoeuvring by the opponents to the régime. His decision was greeted by expressions of outrage and threats of revenge from the National Opposition parties. Ludendorff even demanded that Hindenburg should be stripped of his title of Field-Marshal for his 'treachery'. (Ludendorff had, of course, managed with considerable expertise to extricate himself from a similar accusation in 1918.) It was to Hindenburg's credit that he now upheld the Constitution, even if his action was motivated by practical considerations: by the wish to alleviate the country's financial difficulties rather than by faith in the existing system.

The International Economic Crisis

On 24 October 1929, just three weeks after Stresemann's death, the New York stock-market in Wall Street collapsed and panic selling of stocks and shares by nervous investors and speculators occasioned the greatest crisis of confidence ever experienced by the capitalist world. The dependence of the German economy on the state of the U.S. stock-market was such that the effects of the Wall Street Crash were inevitably felt almost immediately in the Reich. Investors who had eagerly deposited short-term funds in Germany in the years following the ratification of the Dawes Plan now hastily withdrew their money. German industry, deprived of its finance, immediately suffered severely: innumerable firms declared themselves bankrupt and production in many concerns was severely curtailed. The inevitable consequence was a massive increase in unemployment which had concerned Müller's government since the previous winter, when there had been over two and a half million out of work. The unemployment fund which provided financial benefit for those out of work proved to be inadequate. The cost in terms of human misery and loss of dignity could hardly be measured.

The political consequence of the slump was further popular disaffection with the régime. An attack by Schacht on the Socialist Minister of Finance, Rudolf Hilferding, alleging ministerial incompetence in dealing with the economic situation led to Hilferding's resignation on 21 December. It foreshadowed the collapse of the Müller coalition three months later. The economic depression provided the condition essential for Hitler's rise to power. He was now able to exploit to the utmost the precarious economic, political situation. The Golden Years had come to a sudden end and with them the future existence of the Republic.

6

The End of the Republic

The Period 1929–33

THE FOUR years between 1929 and 1933 witnessed the disintegration of the Republic. Its destruction resulted from the unwillingness of the republican parties to accept political responsibility and the fortuitous coincidence of several fateful events and hostile conditions which, in other circumstances, the Reich might have overcome but which in the absence of effective government proved overwhelming.

The occasion, rather than the cause, of the parliamentary crisis which preceded the end of the Republic was the outbreak in 1929 of the international economic depression whose effects on Germany were swift and severe. Unemployment rose rapidly as industry suffered from the reduction in world trade. The two major parties in Müller's coalition, SPD and DVP, representatives of the two sides of industry, were unable to reconcile their differences over the problem of unemployment pay and the government was forced to resign.

The resignation of the government was seen by Hindenburg's anti-republican political advisers – devious men who exerted considerable influence over the ageing President – as a suitable pretext to replace parliamentary rule with a presidential government, the solution to Germany's critical position in the opinion of General von Schleicher, the Reichswehr's grey eminence. He suggested Heinrich Brüning, an ex-soldier, as the next chancellor. Brüning declared his willingness to govern if necessary by presidential decree as laid down in article 48 of the Constitution.

For fear of provoking a worse fate – the possibility of a Nazi government was all too real – the republican parties acquiesced. Despite the deepening economic depression it appeared as if

Brüning's austerity measures would succeed. Schleicher, fearing that economic success would strengthen the parliamentary cause, decided to oust Brüning from power. He advised Hindenburg to appoint another ex-soldier, Franz von Papen, to replace Brüning. Hindenburg, mesmerized by Schleicher's personality, agreed.

Not content with his machiavellian tactics in toppling Brüning's cabinet, Schleicher flirted with the Nazis – he was fascinated by the game of politics but possessed little practical knowledge of its substance. He hoped to tame the Nazis by offering them government responsibility. He had misunderstood Hitler's aims: the Nazis intended to obtain full control of the government, not to participate in a coalition. They had won a considerable victory in the Reich election in 1930, attracting the votes of those disillusioned and impoverished by the economic crisis.

Papen discovered that government of the country was made intolerably difficult by the illegal activities of the SA, the Nazi para-military organization. He banned it and asked Hindenburg to introduce a radical reform of the Constitution which would deal effectively with political extremism. Schleicher objected: the Reichswehr, which was sympathetic towards the Nazis, would not support such an action. Papen was forced to resign and Hindenburg, outraged by Schleicher's duplicity but unable to find a substitute, appointed him Chancellor. On assuming office Schleicher encountered the same difficulties as Papen. He made a similar request to Hindenburg for constitutional reform but the President refused adamantly to grant to Schleicher what Schleicher had forced him to deny Papen.

Papen, to avenge Schleicher's treachery, negotiated secretly with the Nazis, finally persuading Hitler to head a government of *Nationale Konzentration*, composed of Nazis, Nationalists and himself. Hindenburg, suspicious of Hitler to the last, finally allowed himself to be persuaded. Once in power Hitler harassed the other parliamentary parties, with the exception of the SPD, into passing an enabling bill which granted him dictatorial powers. The Nazi dictatorship had begun.

The Fall of the Grand Coalition

On 27 March 1930 Müller's cabinet resigned, thereby unwittingly bringing an end to parliamentary democracy and opening the way for a presidential dictatorship. The causes of the government's unwillingness to continue in office were many and involved: a major cause was the structural weakness of the coalition. The immediate grounds for their decision were, however, unequivocal: the inter-party disagreement over the unemployment fund and the refusal of the coalition parties to compromise the political positions they had adopted.

Since the Wall Street Crash in October 1929, the industrial countries of Europe had suffered from severe economic depression. With the fall in demand for industrial goods and the withdrawal of American funds from Germany, unemployment increased throughout the country. The rise in unemployment in turn by further reducing demand at home produced an economic vicious circle, and by February 1930 there were already three and a half million unemployed workers in Germany. The cost to the state of supplementing the funds which provided unemployment benefit was enormous, as the employers' and employees' contributions (three and a half per cent of the worker's income shared equally between the two) had become wholly insufficient to cover payments and the government was faced with the alternatives either of reducing the benefits or of increasing contributions. The Socialists, conscious of the severe hardship which many of their supporters were suffering, advocated an increase in the combined employer–employee contribution to four per cent and the introduction of an unlimited state subsidy to balance the income and expenditure of the fund. The People's Party, representing the industrialists' interests, rejected the Socialists' plan and made counter-proposals of further austerity measures: a reduction in wages and unemployment benefit. The ensuing inter-party struggle bore all the signs of a revival of the divisive class war between employer and employee, between capital and labour, and moreover revealed a growing impatience on the part of employees and employers with the inability of their parliamentary representatives to govern efficiently.

Heinrich Brüning, leader of the Centre parliamentary party, drafted a compromise solution, which provided for the maintenance of the three and a half per cent contribution together with a limited state financial subsidy to the fund. If, however, this subsidy were to prove insufficient, either the contributions would have to be raised or the benefits would have to be reduced. The likelihood that unemployment pay would be reduced appeared too great to several Socialist ministers and they demanded that their original proposal should be accepted. The DVP and the Centre refused, however, to accede to the Socialists' demands, and although Müller and two of his Socialist colleagues would have been willing to accept the Brüning compromise in order to preserve the coalition, their colleagues in the cabinet and the party obliged them to withdraw from the government. The two wings of the Grand Coalition showed themselves unwilling to sink party differences in the interests of a stable government and the cabinet had to resign. Now more than ever Stresemann's absence was felt, for the formation of successive coalitions had since he first assumed office in 1923 been largely his responsibility. Whether he would have succeeded in preserving the Grand Coalition in 1930 is of course another matter.

The destruction of parliamentary democracy – for that was the direct if unforeseen result of coalition's action – had been occasioned by an inter-party disagreement whose gravity was wholly disproportionate to its fateful consequences. It furnished conclusive proof of the unwillingness felt by the majority of party politicians to recognize that the principle of compromise is a *conditio sine qua non* of the parliamentary process. Equally serious, it betrayed an alarming lack of faith in the parliamentary system among its supposed adherents, the moderate political parties, and an inability or unwillingness to recognize their political duty. The failure of parliament is only partially attributable to the Republic's structural defects and to the economic crisis. The immediate consequence of their failure was a return to authoritarian rule in the form of presidential government, a process which Brüning recorded at the time; 'The more ineffective parliament becomes and the less united parties become, the stronger the President's position automatically becomes.' (v. Informationen zur politischen Bildung, die Weimarer Republik II, p. 9.) If the democratic political parties abdicated responsibility for the government of the country then the establishment of an undemocratic régime was inevitable.

The Presidential Camarilla

The fortunes of the Republic in its last three years of existence were strongly influenced by certain high-ranking army officers who enjoyed the confidence of the President. Hindenburg's entourage, a motley collection of devious political advisers who included General Kurt von Schleicher, Otto Meissner and Oskar von Hindenburg, advocated the abandonment of the parliamentary system and the introduction of a government by presidential decree. The arch-intriguer in the last, critical years of the Republic, and the man who bears much responsibility for its downfall was Schleicher who since 1929 had been chief of the Ministeramt, the department in the Ministry of Defence which dealt with all political matters affecting the army, the navy and their commanders. He was highly thought of by Hindenburg, whom he handled with skill and charm. Politically, Schleicher was both anti-socialist and anti-democratic, strategically he favoured unobtrusive, behind-the-scenes scheming, avoiding wherever possible direct political responsibility. His tactical skill was not matched by political acumen of the same order: he did not possess the intellectual ability to formulate or to realize a detailed policy. His notoriously unscrupulous abandonment of friends and colleagues whenever it suited his opportunist schemes suggests that the game of politics and not its substance fascinated him.

Groener, Minister of Defence, was one of Schleicher's admirers. He relied on his advice in implementing his policies and called him his 'cardinal in politics' (Eschenburg), that is, his tactician. This allowed Schleicher, who officially possessed no ministerial, executive power, to influence government decisions. Schleicher characteristically made fullest use of this position of privilege, especially after Groener took over the crucial post of Minister of the Interior in the autumn of 1931.

Schleicher also enjoyed great friendship with Meissner, Hindenburg's personal Secretary of State, another intriguer in the presidential camarilla. Like Schleicher he preferred to operate behind the scenes in his machiavellian attempts to oust the Republic and to institute an authoritarian right-wing régime – this despite the fact that he had served in the same office under Ebert. The third member of the cabal was Hindenburg's son, Oskar, whose presence, to cite an ironic saying of the period, had not been foreseen by the drafters of the Constitution. He was Hindenburg's self-styled personal adjutant. He was far from intelligent and easy prey for Schleicher and Meissner who made great use of him as a channel through which they could pump information to the President. They could moreover rely on him to exert his influence over his father in their interests.

The major tactical failure of the camarilla lay in their under-estimation of Hitler's ability to outbid them. By doing all in their power to maintain the presidential government and to prevent a return to parliamentary democracy they simply facilitated Hitler's coming to power albeit against their will. However, their considerable influence over the chronology of events between 1930 and 1933 assures them of a historically significant rôle in the destruction of the Republic and the Nazis' coming to power.

Brüning Forms a Government

The collapse of Müller's government presented Schleicher with a long-awaited opportunity of instituting a right-wing authoritarian régime, above all one which would favour the interests of the Reichswehr. On 28 March at Schleicher's suggestion Hindenburg asked Brüning, whom he had previously met briefly and whom he considered sympathetic to the interests of the Reichswehr, to head a minority cabinet which would enjoy presidential backing. The new chancellor would face a national crisis not unlike, if less obviously immediate than, that which confronted Stresemann in 1923.

Heinrich Brüning, forty-five years of age, leader of the Centre parliamentary party and a former Christian trade unionist, was an ascetic, scholarly man. He was a competent, hard-working politician and an economic expert, but it was his outstanding war record as a volunteer which, predictably, commended him to Hindenburg. The President commissioned him with forming a cabinet without ministerial responsibility – an attempt to revive, as Mann has shown, a form of Bismarckian diarchy of Kaiser and Chancellor, a partnership which had, however, to rely not on the divine right of the monarch, but on the emergency powers provided in § 48 of the Constitution.

Brüning, though a convinced supporter of the parliamentary system in principle, was persuaded that an alliance with Hindenburg would ultimately prove to be in the country's best interest. His 'Cabinet of Front Soldiers' retained the members of the Democrats, the Centre, the Bavarian People's Party and the People's Party, who had held office in Müller's government. In addition, he chose members of the Economic Party and splinter parties who had broken with Hugenberg's DNVP. Schiele, former Nationalist, made his participation in the government as Minister of Food and Agriculture conditional on an assurance from Brüning that the East Prussian agricultural estates would receive a massive government subsidy – *Osthilfe*. The government could count on a clear parliamentary majority with two hundred and forty-nine seats but this was no longer of great relevance since it was Hindenburg's patronage and favour which would decide the effectiveness and longevity of the cabinet. His patronage was governed formally by his oath to the Constitution, but in fact his sense of tradition and the influence of the palace camarilla ultimately dictated his decisions, easily overcoming his skin-deep allegiance to democratic ideals.

Brüning's Economic Programme

In a speech to the Reichstag on 1 April 1930, Brüning outlined the policy of the new government. It intended to cure the country's economic ills at the earliest opportunity by imposing deflationary austerity measures: the reducing of state expenditure in wages and salaries and an increase in taxation. The theories of the British economist, John Maynard Keynes, which advocated a diametrically contrary course to combat recession, and which today are accepted without question, were, of course, unknown to Brüning who believed that the problem of unemployment could be tackled only if the budget were balanced. Keynes subsequently demonstrated that a degree of inflation, produced by higher wages, was acceptable, since the increased purchasing power would cure the ills of a recession. After 1923 inflation, let alone deliberate devaluation, could never be advocated by a German government for the alarm such a decision would have caused in the population could in turn have provoked an even graver crisis.

The Reichstag was urged to co-operate with the government, but was warned that any opposition to 'this last attempt to reach a solution with this parliament' (Brüning) would be countered by invoking article 48, a threat which wholly contradicted the intentions of the Constitution. Democracy had, in effect, given way to a form of constitutional monarchy with Hindenburg as the Ersatzmonarch. Nevertheless, it appeared preferable to right-wing dictatorship which many moderate politicians believed to be the sole alternative.

Deterioration of the Economic Situation

Not surprisingly, the economic situation deteriorated and Brüning felt obliged to table emergency legislation to deal with the deepening crisis: state expenditure was to be cut to the bone, income tax was to be raised and contributions to the unemployment fund were to be increased to four and a half per cent while benefits were to be reduced, as were the wages and salaries of civil servants. The bill received widespread opposition. The Socialists advocated cuts in military expenditure; with over three million unemployed, the government would have to rethink its priorities. The Nationalists concentrated their attack on the continuing high level of unemployment benefits. Brüning's bills were rejected by 256 (KPD, SPD, NSDAP, DNVP) votes to 193, but the views of the opposition were now of little interest. Hindenburg decided to make use of article 48 and on 16 July 1930 the bills were enacted under the presidential emergency powers. The combined opposition in the Reichstag – Communists, Socialists, Nazis and some Nationalists – demanded the rescinding of the emergency legislation, a right guaranteed by the Constitution, and on 18 July by 236 votes to 221 they declared the legislation invalid. Brüning, his policies constitutionally outlawed, found himself in an *impasse*. He decided with Hindenburg's support to take the extraordinary step of dissolving the Reichstag and calling for new elections on 14 September. Though the application of article 48 was in itself nothing unusual – several chancellors, notably Stresemann in 1923, had made use of it – to dissolve parliament simply because it had rejected a piece of emergency legislation was a course of action which if not strictly unconstitutional was certainly of doubtful legal propriety. It is admittedly doubtful whether Brüning would have been able to find the necessary additional support within the membership of the old Reichstag, but his decision to hold new elections was tactically unwise, for it presented the Nazis with precisely the opportunity to increase their support which they had so long desired. It can only be concluded that Brüning, despite all warnings to the contrary, deluded himself into thinking he would be able to increase his parliamentary following.

The behaviour of the Socialists is equally puzzling: they appeared once more to place party dogma, the maintenance of unemployment benefits, above the preservation of parliament. Objection to

Brüning's economic measures is understandable – though they had no alternative solution to offer – but collaborating with the extremist parties to bring about the fall of Brüning's cabinet can only be termed irresponsible.

The deepening economic crisis, the increase in the number of unemployed to four million, and the austerity measures introduced by Brüning at the end of July played into the hands of the extremist parties on the right and the left. The Nazis went out of their way to win over the victims of inflation and the depression: the unemployed workers, and the impoverished middle classes. Though many saw through their cheap demagogy, much of their attraction lay in their messianic creed, which, though deliberately vaguely formulated, appealed to the atavistic prejudices of much of the electorate: anti-republicanism, anti-semitism and a romantic affirmation of national pride. This programme found widespread support, not only with the middle classes but also with farmers whom the slump had hit severely and whom they won over by recalling the German myth of the nobility of the soil and its tillers.

The Communists, for their part, did little to oppose the Nazis, but concentrated their attack on their traditional rivals, the Socialists. They naïvely supposed that a period of Fascist rule would convince the population of the need for a Bolshevik revolution. They even unwittingly aided the right-wing extremists, for, as Halperin points out, many worthy bourgeois fled to the Nazis for fear of Communist success in the election.

It was indicative of Brüning's serious-mindedness that he abjured the cheap propaganda of the extremists. His attitude towards politics and the business of government was such, however, that it blinded him to the need of winning the sympathy of the masses. He lacked popular appeal on account of his reserve and austere demeanour. The liberal parties were only too aware of their perilous position. Renewed economic difficulties were certain to injure them more seriously than other parties. The Democrats tried to rescue the situation by assuming a new title, German State Party, *Deutsche Staatspartei* (DStP), and amalgamating with the moderately right-wing Young German Order, *Jungdeutscher Orden*, in an attempt to widen their electoral appeal. A sounder suggestion that they should merge with the DVP came to nothing.

Emotional appeal replaced reasoned political discussion and the campaign was characterized by open violence. Several incidents involving armed Communists and Nazis occurred in the streets of Berlin. The worst fears of moderate politicians were fulfilled when the results of the election were known.

THE ELECTION OF 14 SEPTEMBER 1930
The results of the election were as follows:

		Votes cast (to nearest thousand)		Number of seats		Percentage of total vote	
		1928	1930	1928	1930	1928	1930
KPD	Communist	3,265,000	4,950,000	54	77	10·6	13·1
SPD	Social Democratic	9,153,000	8,576,000	153	143	29·8	24·5
DDP (DStP	Democratic State)	1,506,000	1,322,000	25	20	4·9	3·8
Z	Centre	3,712,000	4,127,000	62	68	12·1	11·8
BVP	Bavarian People's	946,000	1,659,000	16	19	3·1	3·0
DVP	People's	2,680,000	1,577,000	45	30	8·7	4·5
DNVP	Nationalist	4,382,000	2,458,000	73	41	14·2	7·0
NSDAP	National Socialist	810,000	6,407,000	12	107	2·6	18·3
Others		4,126,000	4,842,000	51	72	13·9	14·0
Total (to nearest hundred thousand)		31,200,000	35,200,000	491	577		

81·9 per cent of the electorate voted compared with 75·6 per cent in 1928.

The election results were disastrous for the moderate parties: the Socialists, who were discredited in the eyes of the electorate for their inability to maintain the Müller cabinet, and the Democrats whose opening to the right decreased their vote by seven per cent. The People's Party, now deprived of Stresemann's dynamic leadership, also lost considerable support, its representation being reduced by one third. The 1930 election marks the beginning of the extinction of the two liberal parties: their former supporters had apparently transferred their allegiance to the Nazis, who emerged as the new champions of the middle classes. The slight improvement in the fortunes of the Centre Party and the Bavarian People's Party reflected increased Catholic support for Brüning. Victory in the election, though not total, had clearly been secured by the Nazis who increased their representation in the Reichstag tenfold, a success which they had not considered possible. At the other end of the spectrum, in second place in the results were the Communists who increased their number of seats by almost fifty per cent, a result which when compounded with the success of the Nazis shows a surprisingly widespread willingness in the electorate to embrace extremist views. The Nationalists lost thirty-two seats, mainly to the newly-formed right-wing splinter parties: the Conservative People's Party and the Christian Socialist People's Service (*Konservative Volkspartei*, and *Christlich-Sozialistischer Volksdienst*). As Bracher has pointed out, the increase in Nazi support cannot be attributed simply to the electorate's disaffection with the traditional political parties, for they managed to attract to the poll many who had previously not bothered to cast their votes. The total number of votes cast, 35 million, rose by 4,218,000 over the 1928 figure, a record turn-out of eighty-two per cent, while the Nazis increased their vote by 5,600,000. It is fair to assume that many of the extra four million votes were recorded as a result of the Nazis' deliberate policy of winning the support of the youth political elements in the Reichswehr and previously apolitical members of the middle class.

The results presented a grave governmental problem, for a majority coalition needed a minimum of two hundred and eighty-nine seats, a sum which could only be attained by resuscitating the ill-fated Grand Coalition, an unlikely possibility in view of the continuing mutual antipathy of the Socialists and the People's Party. A coalition with the Nationalists or the NSDAP was even less feasible. Brüning, willing to remain Chancellor, would have to rely even more on Hindenburg's authority and the application of article 48. His position in the Reichstag had become paradoxically less precarious, for although his cabinet commanded only a small minority of votes and whereas the bear-garden tactics of the extremist opposition constantly disrupted parliamentary business, the Socialists no longer maintained their out and out opposition to Brüning's cabinet. Though they heartily disliked his economic policies, they feared that opposition from them might send Brüning into the arms of the Nazis, a far more terrifying prospect. There was, moreover, the even greater danger that if parliament continued to reject bills passed under article 48, then Hindenburg would again call for new elections; and these could only be to the benefit of the Nazis. Thus the Constitution of the country underwent a non-legalized change and parliamentary democracy gave way to a virtual presidential dictatorship, sanctioned, albeit with misgivings, by parliament. It resembled, as Mann comments, the quasi-parliamentary system which operated under Bismarck in the 1860s in that the fortunes of the country depended increasingly on the president's willingness to subscribe to his chancellor's policies. The bureaucracy, never a source of staunch support for the Republic, now found itself in an increasingly powerful position, entrusted more and more with decisions concerning the day-to-day government of the country. The strain of personal responsibility became intolerable for the eighty-four-year-old Hindenburg and his ability to appreciate the complexities of political issues, never highly developed, diminished during the crisis years, leaving him prey to the schemes of his advisers.

Leipzig Reichswehr Trial: Political Extremism in the Army

The German Supreme Court, the *Reichsgericht*, in Leipzig was the scene in the autumn of 1930 of Hitler's pledge to obtain power only by legal methods, one which won him much support among disgruntled but nevertheless anti-revolutionary electors. It also demonstrated the ease with which the Reichswehr would subsequently be incorporated into the Nazi state-machine.

An artillery regiment, stationed in Ulm, contained a group of committed *national*, that is anti-republican, lieutenants, subscribers to Ehrhardt's counter-revolutionary mission. Early in 1929 the three men, Ludin, Scheringer and Wendt, distributed leaflets in several garrisons which advocated *national* revolution to overthrow the pacifism and leftism of the army command. Though their views were not specifically Nazi, the lieutena· ts were in contact with the Nazi headquarters in Munich.

News of their activities reached the Ministry of Defence. Groener, deeply suspicious of Nazi intentions, decided, since the army authorities had clearly failed to discipline the accused, to bring them to public trial, a decision which evoked severe criticism even from politically moderate officers, who disliked the army's dirty washing being shown in public. Groener argued that the armed forces must remain aloof from party politics, their sole function was to serve and protect the state, a view which unfortunately was not shared by the majority of officers.

The trial opened on 23 September 1930, a few days after the election in which Hitler had increased his parliamentary representation from thirteen to one hundred and seven seats. It lasted two weeks. The accused maintained that Groener and the army command sought to encourage leftist, anti-*national*, pacifist sentiment in Germany and repudiated the suggestion that the armed forces should remain above party politics and serve the existing state; the army was not a police force charged with the maintenance of law and order; it must be the aim of the Reichswehr to 'liberate' the nation. All three were convicted of treasonable action and given sentences of eighteen months, imprisonment.

The trial is historically of twofold significance. It indicated the severe internal crisis which the Reichswehr was suffering, the estrangement of troops and leadership, and the development of Seeckt's supra-party-political force into an anti-democratic threat. It was the logical outcome of Seeckt's principle. It also gave Hitler, who was called as witness for the defence, a public platform from which he could announce his political intentions. Fearful of the fiasco of 1923, when he had attempted to seize power by force, Hitler now intended to adhere to the letter if not the spirit of the Constitution. He proclaimed from the witness box his firm undertaking to come to power only by legal means. This assurance of legality succeeded in winning him much support among right-wing sympathizers, who previously had shunned the Nazis for their revolutionary tactics. What they failed to take into consideration was that a coming to power by constitutional means did not ensure the subsequent maintenance of legality and adherence to constitutional procedure.

Unemployment and Political Extremism

The winter of 1931 brought a marked deterioration in the employment market: six million men were without work and, on account of the meagre sums paid in unemployment benefit, they and their families were reduced to a pitifully low standard of living. Cases of suicide became more frequent as the economic depression deepened. It is not surprising that Hitler used the situation to his own advantage, nor is it much less surprising that his hollow promises of better times were readily believed by the millions who had lost all faith in the Republic. The workers, many of whom were committed Socialists and Communists, provided less support for Hitler, however, than the middle class, who, ruined by the inflation of the early twenties, faced the prospect of economic disaster for the second time in ten years, and the highly trained – in particular university graduates and teachers – who discovered that their hard-won qualifications were worthless. It is significant that the rise of the NSDAP to the status of a mass movement began only with the slump in 1929. Hugenberg's influential press did much to exacerbate their fears, generating as it did widespread hostility to and suspicion of Brüning's government, which intended, so Hugenberg maintained, to allow the number of unemployed to rise to ten millions in the following year.

The extreme left- and right-wing parties judged the situation ripe for encouraging further internal unrest. The economic difficulties of the country were inflamed by the frequent outbreaks of street fighting and thuggery and by the real prospect of civil war between the rival para-military factions: the Nazi SA, the Nationalist-supported Stahlhelm and the Communist *Roter Frontkämpferbund*. In one such clash between Communists and Nazis in February 1930 an SA leader, Horst Wessel, was shot dead. He became a party hero overnight. A marching song was composed to celebrate his deeds and honour his memory. The Horst Wessel Song soon became a standard feature of all Nazi rallies and meetings.

The Harzburg Front

The leaders of the two right-wing parties, Hitler and Hugenberg, met in October 1931 in Harzburg, a small spa in the Harz mountains where they decided to form a common front of the two parties and the Stahlhelm, to be called the Harzburg Front. They were joined by a host of sympathizers for the anti-parliamentary, anti-republican cause: army leaders, industrialists and financiers, notable among whom was Hjalmar Schacht, the former Democratic President of the Reichsbank. Their common goal was the destruction of the Republic, their immediate target the Brüning government. The scene was impressive. The followers of the anti-republican parties marched through the streets of the small town, parading Imperial black, white and red banners, to the boundless enthusiasm of the huge crowd of spectators who lined the route. For the first time the Nazis were to receive financial support from industry and finance in return for an assurance that the party would support capitalism. It was simultaneously pledged to oppose the stranglehold of interest but this contradiction appeared not to concern those who donated funds. Nationalist politicians and industrialists failed to appreciate that Hitler would break this marriage of convenience as soon as he came to power and that the Front, while bestowing an aura of respectability on Hitler and the Nazis and increasing their popularity in future elections, would not serve their own party's interests in the long term. The Nazis appropriated the Stahlhelm slogan 'seizure of power', *Machtergreifung*, and set their sights on establishing in the near future a dictatorship which would have no room for their present political allies. While Hitler was quick to appreciate the short-term advantages of the alliance his determination to become Führer, the sole ruler of the state, was reinforced. Politically less astute figures, Hugenburg, Schleicher and Papen, continued to delude themselves by believing that they had reached a lasting understanding with Hitler. Political lightweights themselves, they too easily ascribed their own limitations to others and consistently underestimated Hitler's determination and single-mindedness.

German-Austrian Customs Union and Banking Crisis

The blame for Brüning's lack of economic success cannot be laid wholly at the door of the three extremist parties. The Allied countries, in particular France, gave him little support and in the case of Germany's customs union with Austria, actively blocked one of Brüning's few progressive, expansionist policies. The customs union between the two states was set up in March 1931 by Germany's Foreign Minister, Curtius, and the Austrian Chancellor, Schober. It created a community of some eighty million people with complementary economies. It was the threat of political union, specifically forbidden by Versailles and St Germain, which angered the French government under Briand, even though both Germany and Austria were careful to stress that Austria's political independence would be preserved. The British and American governments viewed the union with sympathy. France, however, referred the matter to the International Court of Justice at The Hague, which in 1931 gave judgement in France's favour by eight votes to seven. The extremists were now able to attack Brüning with renewed vigour. They had witnessed the destruction of their *national* vision of political union of the German-speaking peoples which they believed would follow the customs union, just as the German Empire had developed from the *Zollunion* in 1871.

The prevention of the union had disastrous consequences for Austria, whose economy suffered severely from the collapse on 31 May of her financial system with the bankruptcy of the *Creditanstalt*, her major banking institution. The failure of leading banks was not uncommon in the early 1930s, and reflected the international currency crisis, which was a further symptom of the depression. On 13 July the leading German *Darmstädter und Nationalbank* declared itself bankrupt. Brüning was forced to guarantee its deposits and to impose further stringent financial restrictions to prevent a total collapse of the country's financial structure, for the threat of further bankruptcies had provoked panic withdrawal of foreign credit from Germany by investers already alarmed by the Nazis' electoral success in 1930. One grain of comfort was provided by the American President, Hoover, who on 20 June declared a year's moratorium for all international debts. British, French and American central banks lent the Reichsbank four hundred and twenty million marks to prevent further economic collapse in Germany. Twelve months later Germany's remaining reparations debt was written off.

The Re-Election of Hindenburg

In the spring of 1932 Hindenburg's period of office as president came to an end; the government, conscious of the need to maintain a semblance of stability in the country, attempted unsuccessfully to extend his tenure by one year which, since it involved a constitutional amendment, required a parliamentary majority of two thirds. The Nazis refused to co-operate unless Brüning were dismissed at once. Hindenburg commendably refused to submit to this act of blackmail, for fear less of assisting an anti-democratic group than of dirtying his hands in party politics.

There followed a campaign as heated as the 1930 general election. Recent Land elections had shown the enormous growth in the Nazis' popularity and it was clear that mass support for Hindenburg would be the only means of preventing the election of Hitler, the Nazi candidate, and thus of preserving democracy. Hindenburg accepted the candidature doubtfully; he resented not only the defection of his former DNVP following, but also the support of the republican parties, which ironically were forced to canvas support for the candidate whom they had opposed in 1925. This paradoxical situation indicates the extent of the crisis of democracy, for the SPD decided against nominating their own candidate since this would have split the moderate vote and handed victory to Hitler. There were two minor contestants: Colonel Theodor Duesterberg, the leader of the Stahlhelm, nominated by the Nationalists who felt unable to support Hitler's candidature, and Gustav Winter who represented the victims of inflation. Ernst Thälmann was nominated by the KPD, who blindly adhered to their theory that a brief period of Nazi rule was a precondition for a Communist *coup*. The election was held on 13 March 1932. Votes were cast as follows:

	Number of votes cast	Percentage of total votes cast
Hitler	11,339,000	30·1
Duesterberg	2,558,000	6·8
von Hindenburg	18,662,000	49·6
Thälmann	4,982,000	13·2
Winter	111,000	0·3
Total	37,652,000	

Since Hindenburg had failed by 150,000 votes (0·4 per cent) to obtain the necessary majority, a second ballot had to be held. As the election proved that the popularity of the Nazis had increased considerably, Hindenburg was obliged to remain a candidate. His sense of honour forced him to oppose the Nazi upstart. The two candidates with the lowest share of the votes cast on 13 March were excluded from the second ballot held on 10 April. The result was as follows:

	Number of votes cast	Percentage of total votes cast
Hitler	13,420,000	36·8
von Hindenburg	19,360,000	53·0
Thälmann	3,710,000	10·2
Total	36,490,000	

Under the banner 'Only Hindenburg can save us from Hitler', the retiring president was re-elected. It was essentially a Pyrrhic victory for the moderate parties. Although over sixty per cent of the electorate had opposed Hitler, only a bare majority had come out in support of the only candidate pledged to uphold the Constitution. More than a third of the electors, thirteen million, had voted for Hitler, two million more than in March. Hindenburg had in fact been elected on a negative vote, i.e. not because he possessed the necessary qualities but because the electorate feared the alternative. Hindenburg was a symbol of the helplessness of the moderates (Mann). Moreover, as events were soon to show, Hindenburg was by no means the democratic saviour or the embodiment of integrity and selflessness which the self-deluding moderate parties had believed him to be, subject as he was to the pressure of his right-wing military entourage.

The result dissatisfied Hindenburg: although he had been re-elected by more than half the electorate, he had been supported by the 'wrong' people. His former comrades, notably Seeckt, and even the ex-Crown Prince, had publicly declared their support for Hitler. He did not relish the knowledge that his success was due for the greatest part to the Socialists, the Democrats and the Catholics, all of whom he instinctively despised. Would he, perhaps, be accused of having betrayed the right wing to the Socialists and Catholic Centrists?

Hindenburg's displeasure was focused onto the obvious scape-goat, Brüning, whose unflagging electioneering throughout the country had done much to rally support for Hindenburg who had remained aloof from the activities of the campaign. Had not his re-election, or the extension of his period of office, been complicated by the demands of the right-wing parties for Brüning's dismissal, a demand which had forced him, for the sake of honour, to submit himself to the indignity of the election campaign? Schleicher and the other members of the camarilla capitalized on Hindenburg's dislike of his chancellor, and advocated his dismissal.

The Dismissal of Groener

Brüning was not the first victim of the Schleicher clique. Groener, who had been Minister of Defence since the beginning of 1928, and who since October 1931 had also been Minister of the Interior, was the first to be ousted by the intriguers. Three days after Hindenburg's re-election, on 13 April, Groener finally decided to ban the two Nazi para-military organizations, the SA and the SS, thus incurring the implacable opposition of Schleicher, whose attitude to the Nazis had changed. The decision, not discussed with Brüning, but accepted by him, met with opposition from Hindenburg whose signature to the order was obtained only with the utmost difficulty. The ban, long overdue, had been advocated by many local authorities for some time; in particular, the Bavarian and Prussian Land governments had each threatened to act unilaterally if the Reich did not intervene. The action, praised by those who had the sense to realize the obvious and potential dangers of condoning the existence of a private army within the state, met with vociferous opposition from the right wing, not only Nazis but also Nationalists. They maintained that the two organizations fulfilled a responsible function in the maintenance of order in the country. On the other hand, if Nazi organizations were to be banned then similar left-wing groups such as the Reichsbanner – a democratic organization – should also be proscribed. The extremists, supported by the right-wing press, worked unabated for Groener's downfall, organizing disruption in the Reichstag when the ban was debated, a task made easier by Groener's well-known inarticulate manner when speaking in public. Schleicher, who for purely tactical reasons had originally supported his colleague's action, on seeing the reaction of the right wing, performed a volte-face and, in a highly unprofessional manner, abetted those who demanded the resignation of his immediate superior. Hindenburg was easily persuaded by the attitude of his son, Oskar, who supported his father's original misgivings, to join those who opposed Groener's action. It was through Oskar that Schleicher was able to gauge Hindenburg's true feelings. The Chief of Army Command, General von Hammerstein, who had succeeded Heye in 1930, likewise voiced his concern to Hindenburg at a discussion arranged, so Eschenburg suspects, by Oskar, and one in which Hammerstein seriously overstepped his authority and competence in presuming to attempt to influence a purely political decision. Groener was no match for the political intrigue of his former counsellor, now enemy, Schleicher. He made little attempt to persuade Hindenburg of the irregularity of Schleicher's behaviour. Both victims of personal inhibition – so Eschenburg relates –

neither Brüning nor Groener was emotionally adequate to overrule Schleicher's influence on Hindenburg. Groener's private life further alienated Hindenburg. At the end of 1930, Groener had married for a second time and his wife had given birth to a child shortly after the wedding, circumstances which in Hindenburg's eyes tarnished the honour of the army. On 10 May Groener announced his resignation from the Ministry of Defence (while remaining Minister of the Interior). Ironically, it had been Groener who, some thirteen years previously, had preserved Hindenburg's reputation in the confusion surrounding the transfer of power in November 1918.

Schleicher's behaviour in the affair smacked of treason, for he had usurped the function of government ministers and severely transgressed the terms of reference of his own office, the Ministeramt, whose duties were to advise and inform government ministers and to act as liaison between the Ministry of Defence and the Reichswehr. Schleicher's rôle developed into that of personal adviser to the President, bypassing the constitutionally responsible government. He maintained direct contact with Hindenburg through the constant intercession of Oskar, who, conscious of his dependence on his father for his position of privilege, was eager to assist those who, after his father's death, could be of service to him. The Presidential Palace kept in daily contact with the Ministeramt to receive Schleicher's advise on matters of policy. In Schleicher's plan to replace parliamentary democracy by presidential government the president would choose his chancellor and vest him with full executive powers, thereby circumventing the tedious procedure of parliamentary debate and sanction. His success in provoking Groener's resignation, which severely weakened Brüning's cabinet, prepared the way for the establishment of such a presidential government.

The Fall of Brüning's Cabinet

For some time Schleicher, whose personal relations with Brüning were now strained, had been growing increasingly uneasy about Brüning's chancellorship. Overtly Schleicher complained that Brüning had succeeded neither in restoring the economy nor in taming the Nazis. In fact, it is probable that Schleicher was more deeply worried by the real prospect that Brüning's economic policies would soon begin to show positive results and that he would conclude international agreements about reparations and armaments which would be favourable to Germany. Despite an increase in the number of unemployed from two million three hundred thousand men in March 1930 to six million in March 1932, Brüning's economic policies had not been wholly unsuccessful in that prices had been pegged, and rents and interest rates lowered to compensate for the reduction of ten per cent in salaries and wages enforced on 8 December 1931. Any marked success which Brüning achieved would hinder Schleicher's anti-democratic campaign, for Brüning would be acknowledged as Germany's political leader of the future and the Republic would survive stronger than before. Neither Schleicher nor his right-wing accomplices could countenance the prospect. His attitude to the Nazis, moreover, had become ambivalent: he had not yet fully renounced his former opposition to the party but hoped still to 'tame' Hitler and his colleagues by offering them posts of responsibility in the government. Alternatively he sought to provoke a split in the party, and had already begun negotiations with Frick and Strasser. These plans were unlikely to be acceptable to Brüning, and accordingly, he set about discrediting Brüning at the earliest opportunity. He did not have to wait long for a pretext: in May Brüning announced a government plan to settle unemployed city dwellers on the East-Elbian agrarian estates, an act which the Social Democrats had deliberately avoided in 1918–19. The proposal was sound: only those estates which had proved no longer economically viable were to be compulsorily purchased. Farmers had already discovered the difficulty of selling their over-priced produce – especially rye – to an impoverished population. Efficiently managed estates experiencing financial difficulties were already receiving generous government subsidies under the Eastern Relief Plan, Osthilfe. Moreover, the decision to attack the problem of unemployment by providing work rather than dole money had much to commend it on humanitarian grounds. The powerful Junker lobby, which included Elard von Oldenburg-Januschau, one of Hindenburg's neighbours and a personal friend, naturally opposed land reform. In this they were sure of Hindenburg's support, for, since they had presented him with the Neudeck estate, he had a vested interest in blocking the plan and, moreover, he was unlikely to risk permanently alienating their respect for him. With little encouragement from Schleicher, Hindenburg, who was visiting Neudeck during the Whitsuntide holiday, was convinced that Brüning, who had been denied access to the President, should be dismissed before his 'Bolshevik' agrarian policy could be introduced.

Brüning had always mishandled his relations with Hindenburg and, as Eschenburg points out, instead of trying to gain his confidence, he tried to convince him with rational arguments whose subtlety befogged the ageing President. He was the converse of Schleicher: a good politician but a bad tactician. Hindenburg demanded at Schleicher's suggestion that Brüning should open discussions with the Nazis and Nationalists, with a view to forming a new coalition and that new elections should be held. Aware of the danger to the Republic inherent in these demands, Brüning refused.

On 31 May 1932, less than two months after helping Hindenburg back into the presidency, Brüning was asked to resign from the chancellorship, without being granted the opportunity of defending his policies. He complied with the 'request' the following day, although, as Mann has observed, constitutionally he was entitled to remain in power if, by widening the coalition, he could assure himself of sufficient parliamentary support. That he did not consider this solution indicates his attitude to his position in the government: he was willing to head the cabinet only if he enjoyed presidential patronage, and since Hindenburg's support had been withdrawn he was not prepared to consider returning to parliamentary rule. Ironically, on the morning of 30 May, the day on which Brüning submitted the resignation of his cabinet to Hindenburg, he learned that agreement in principle had been reached in Lausanne by the Conference on Reparations to absolve Germany's reparation debt with a final payment of less than five thousand million marks. He had been dismissed 'a hundred metres from his goal', as he described his situation a few days earlier. This, as Eschenburg remarks, was the true reason for Schleicher's decision to ditch Brüning who, even if his policy had been extremely unpopular, had led the government efficiently and had devoted himself exclusively to his task. Such men of integrity were rare in the last years of the Republic.

The success of Schleicher's *coup* which brought down Brüning's cabinet on 30 May 1932 finally marked the end of parliamentary democracy and the end of the Republic in Germany. Despite his frequent recourse to emergency legislation, it had been Brüning's aim to defend the Republic from the Nazis, and in this he had been moderately successful. From now on, any attempt to uphold democracy was purely illusory. His successors in the chancellery failed to contain the right-wing threat, either from lack of imagination or from outright sympathy with Hitler's aim.

The 'Papen Intermezzo'

During the following eight months, a period of political turmoil, Hindenburg desperately sought to establish a viable government, hindered at every turn by the Nazis who tried with renewed vigour to manoeuvre Hitler into the chancellorship. The NSDAP, the Reichswehr and the President were the only forces of importance in the state. It was clear that in the long run the Nazis would emerge dominant. Hindenburg's attitude to Hitler and the party was becoming increasingly ambivalent: while he valued their anti-Marxist sentiments, he deplored their terrorist activities. Hitler remained a thorn in his flesh for personal reasons: he disliked the ambitious, upstart 'Bohemian corporal', as he nicknamed him, and repeatedly refused to nominate him Chancellor. His aim was not to outlaw the Nazis but to follow Schleicher's plan of taming them by allowing them to participate in the government, an attempt to have the best of both worlds, which, as Mann shows, was destined to fail from the outset.

Schleicher, having successfully provoked Brüning's fall, once more used his considerable influence with Hindenburg to propose a successor. He advocated Franz von Papen, a former Centrist member of the Prussian Land parliament, but not of the Reichstag. Schleicher had initiated negotiations with Papen as early as 26 May, the responsibility constitutionally of the president. He was well-connected: a member of a minor aristocratic Westphalian family, he had served as a major in the cavalry, possessed considerable industrial property, was a member of the reactionary *Herrenklub* in Berlin, and as a Catholic nobleman enjoyed good relations with the clergy. He was a vain man, limited in intellect and extremely superficial, though articulate and socially adept, 'a well-bred buffoon' (Mann). Politically he stood at the anti-democratic extreme right wing of the Centre Party and held strong nationalistic and monarchistic views, which he propounded in the conservative Centrist newspaper, *Germania*, in which he held a large number of shares. Schleicher and he had first met in the Officer Training Corps many years previously. His military, noble background commended him to Hindenburg who accepted Schleicher's suggestion. Schleicher believed his old comrade would be a 'pliable henchman' (Halperin), a puppet chancellor who could be trusted to implement his schemes. He had after all no experience as a diplomat, an administrator or a leading politician. Without discussing the matter with any party leaders, Hindenburg agreed to appoint Papen.

Papen's Government Takes Office

Schleicher presented Papen with a ready-made list of ministers, which Papen willingly accepted. The cabinet, only nominally non-party, was composed of representatives of several right-wing groups: agrarians, industrialists and army leaders, all members of the DNVP. Schleicher was obliged to assume the office of Minister of Defence, which conferred considerable power on him but also forced him into the political limelight out of the safety behind the scenes in the Ministeramt.

Papen's government, popularly called the Cabinet of Barons, took office on 1 June 1932. It contained no representatives from the bourgeois or left-wing parties, and for the first time in the history of the Republic the Centre Party – ironically Papen's own party – was not included in the government. It received a hostile popular reception. (Papen, for his part in the intrigue which led to Brüning's resignation and his own nomination, was ejected from the party.) The government commanded considerably less support in the Reichstag than its predecessor, for even the DNVP, from whose ranks his entire cabinet was drawn, could not be relied upon to underwrite the government's policies, and support from the Centre or the Socialists was ruled out by their disgust at Brüning's dismissal and their suspicion of Papen's intentions. Only Hindenburg and the army command stood behind them. Schleicher and Papen looked elsewhere for the much-needed support: they concluded a secret agreement with Hitler, which, if tactically accomplished, nevertheless betrays their lack of political insight. In return for a promise from Papen to lift the ban on the SA, to dissolve the Reichstag (the Nazis believed they would emerge with a majority at the next election) to turn a blind eye to any Nazi excesses perpetrated during the ensuing electoral campaign and to eliminate the last stronghold of the Socialists and of the Republic, the Prussian Land parliament of Braun and Severing, Hitler agreed to tolerate the new government. Papen's policy of appeasement was dangerous, for Hitler had no intention of keeping his side of the bargain unless it was to his advantage. Papen underestimated Hitler's duplicity, convinced, as his self-congratulatory memoirs betray, of his own superior political ability, a wholly unjustifiable conviction. He too was following a devious plan: though he could not formulate a coherent policy, he intended to reduce the appeal of the Nazis by achieving quick successes in domestic and foreign affairs. In the former, he hoped to bring about a Hohenzollern restoration and to establish a constitutional monarchy, a wholly unrealistic plan but one to which he clung throughout his period of office. In foreign affairs he was fortunate to inherit Brüning's not inconsiderable legacy – it was a sad feature of the Weimar Republic that less competent chancellors frequently enjoyed successes which were in fact due to the policy of their more astute predecessors. Agreement was finally reached at the Reparations Conference in Lausanne in July, only two weeks after Papen had taken office. The Young Plan was formally annulled; Germany was granted a further moratorium on payments of three years, when she would be due to make a final payment of three thousand million marks. Internally the economy showed encouraging signs of recovery: unemployment began to decline and industrial production increased. Though this was due to the recovery of international trading and not, of course, to any new policy introduced by the 'Barons', Papen happily took credit for the improvement and was able to alleviate slightly the deflationary policies of the previous government.

True to the terms of the agreement with the Nazis, Papen persuaded Hindenburg to dissolve the Reichstag on 4 July and on 16 July to remove the ban on the SA. The election campaign which followed in the weeks before the general election on 31 July was characterized by daily acts of terror in the streets of Germany's large towns, in particular in the capital, Berlin, whose police force was almost exclusively loyal to the Prussian Land and to the Republic. Thuggery, largely instigated by the Nazis but also returned by the Communists, the butt of their terrorism, occurred with daily regularity. It was such an act of political terrorism which provided Papen with an excuse to eliminate the Prussian parliament, a political rape in the name of law and order.

The Rape of Prussia

Prussia, always a problem by virtue of its predominance in the Reich both in geographic extent and population, was an irritant to Papen as the sole remainder of moderate republican government in Germany, and impossible to overlook since it controlled Berlin. He intended to transform Germany's semi-federal, democratic Constitution into that of a unitary, authoritarian state, a system of government which corresponded to his limited political outlook. To accomplish this constitutional change he clearly needed to incorporate Prussia politically and administratively into the Reich, an action which anticipated with remarkable accuracy Hitler's policy of co-ordination (*Gleichschaltung*).

On 19 May 1932 the Braun – Severing minority coalition of Socialists and Centrists in Prussia resigned, finally worn down by the continuous harassment of their opponents, the Nazis and Communists. As the two extremist parties were clearly unable to provide an alternative coalition, Braun and Severing agreed to continue as a caretaker government, placing themselves in an even more vulnerable position. Papen prepared for his attack on Prussia: he obtained Hindenburg's signature to an emergency decree under the powers granted by article 48 of the Constitution, which would replace the Prussian parliament by a Reich Commissioner in order to 'defend Prussia against the threat of a Communist takeover which the Land government ignored'. There was, of course, no real threat nor any danger that, as Papen hinted, the Socialists would form a coalition with the KPD, and the application of article 48 was therefore illegal.

A suitable pretext for the *coup d'état* presented itself on 17 July. As part of their rabble-rousing election campaign, the Nazis organized a deliberately provocative street demonstration in Altona, a Prussian town contiguous with Hamburg, whose population was almost exclusively working-class. Communist snipers fired on the Nazis, killing fifteen of the demonstrators. On 20 July Severing and Braun were informed in the Reich Chancellery that, as their government was clearly no longer maintaining law and order within Prussia, a state of emergency had been declared; they were to be removed from office and replaced by Papen as Reich Commissioner.

Though the action was clearly unconstitutional, it was difficult to see how the Prussian government could retaliate, for the effective power of democratic forces had been almost wholly eroded. Active opposition hardly commended itself – conditions were not as in 1920, the time of the Kapp Putsch. A general strike was unlikely to succeed as unemployment had understandably weakened the solidarity of the workers and the unemployed could clearly not participate in a strike. Though the Prussian police force could have been relied upon to assist the Reichsbanner, the Social Democrats' armed force, they would be no match for the Reichswehr and Stahlhelm, which Papen would doubtless have deployed against them; moreover Braun and Severing, moderate men, wished at all costs to avoid civil war. Thus they sought legal redress at the Constitutional Court at Leipzig. The Court procrastinated in passing judgement in a case where immediate action was clearly essential. On 25 October, nearly fourteen weeks after the *coup*, it announced its findings, couched in ambiguous terms. It concluded that although the action was unconstitutional and the former Prussian government was entitled to continue in power, it refused to rescind the presidential decree which had ordered the illegal action, a formula intended to allow Papen and Hindenburg to save face. Thus the rape of Prussia had been formally approved without anyone's coming to its aid, and the Constitution, as Papen openly stated, was meaningless in such a situation. Papen's action was by no means wholly favourable to his cause, for Germany and Papen could ill afford the loss of the last repository of moderate, progressive government. Having won supreme control of Prussia, Papen swiftly eliminated all possible centres of dissent within the Land. He purged the civil administration and the police force of all officials who professed republican sympathies, replacing them with right-wingers, a purge which, as Herzfeld points out, exceeded by far the attempts of the Weimar leaders to rid the civil service of Imperial sympathisers in the first years of the Republic.

The rape of Prussia was intended by Papen and Schleicher as a further step in replacing parliamentary democracy by presidential rule. In fact, as Carsten indicates, it helped Hitler to seize power six months later, for all potential republican opposition to the Nazis had already been eliminated in the largest and most heavily populated Land. If, however, Papen and Schleicher hoped that their *coup* would entice the Nazis into their government they had miscalculated badly, for it had merely whetted their appetites and encouraged them to raise their demands, especially after scoring their electoral success ten days later. It had also set the tone for the election campaign: the government's engagement in an illegal act legitimized the electoral activities of the extremists. The terrorist campaign continued throughout the month, forcing Papen after the election to issue an emergency decree which introduced special courts empowered to punish terrorism with the death penalty.

THE ELECTION OF 31 JULY 1932

The results of the election were as follows:

		Votes cast (to nearest thousand)		Number of seats		Percentage of total vote	
		1930	July 1932	1930	July 1932	1930	July 1932
KPD	Communist	4,590,000	5,370,000	77	89	13·1	14·3
SPD	Social-Democratic	8,576,000	7,960,000	143	133	24·5	21·6
DDP (DStP	Democratic State)	1,322,000	373,000	20	4	3·8	1·0
Z	Centre	4,127,000	4,589,000	68	75	11·8	12·4
BVP	Bavarian People's	1,059,000	1,203,000	19	22	3·0	3·2
DVP	People's	1,577,000	436,000	30	7	4·5	1·2
DNVP	Nationalist	2,458,000	2,187,000	41	40	7·0	5·9
NSDAP	National Socialist	6,407,000	13,779,000	107	230	18·3	37·3
Others		3,485,000	985,000	72	11	14·0	2·6
Total (to nearest hundred thousand)		35,000,000	37,200,000	577	609		

84·0 per cent of the electorate voted compared with 81·9 per cent in 1930.

The results show that, despite the success at the Lausanne Conference, the government suffered a colossal defeat; the Nationalists' representation was reduced to 37 seats. Apart from the Centre and Bavarian People's Party which maintained their position, the other bourgeois parties, whose support had formerly come largely from north German constituencies, the People's Party, *Landvolk*, Economic Party, State Party (formerly Democratic Party) and Christian Socialist Party retained only 22 seats out of 122 gained in 1928. The Socialists lost only 3 of their seats, a remarkably good performance, which reflects perhaps public antipathy to the Prussian *coup*, and also the fidelity of the bulk of German workers. The election was above all, of course, a success for Hitler. The Nazis had managed to double their representation in the Reichstag from 110 to 230 seats, a tribute to their successful aggressive campaign. Aeroplanes were used –for the first time in an election campaign – to ferry Hitler from mass meeting to mass meeting and to disseminate propaganda material. Their victory was also a reflection of popular dismay at the continuing deterioration in unemployment which had increased by thirty-three per cent during the past year and which the trade unions apparently could not combat, and a recognition of Hitler's ability to please a broad spectrum of the electorate with his promises of something for everyone. Despite the Nazis' success, Hitler had not managed to stem the growth of the Communists,who increased their representation by 11 seats to 89. Thus the two extremist parties now held a majority of 319 out of 608 seats, though any possibility of their forming a coalition was unthinkable. The result allowed Hitler to strengthen his legitimate demand for control of the government, claiming for his men the posts of Chancellor, Prussian Prime Minister, Minister of the Interior in the Reich and in Prussia, Minister of Justice, and three further portfolios. Hindenburg maintained his opposition to a government under Nazi control and repeated his offer of participation in a coalition, advocating once more the restoration of the monarchy. Hitler refused the offer and at the same time withdrew his toleration of Papen's government, with the result that Papen could count on the support of only one-tenth of the Reichstag, the 42 votes of the DVP and the DNVP. It was, as Herzfeld states, the biggest defeat suffered by a government in office since 1871.

Even after the election, Papen was still confident he could cajole the Nazis into compromise on his terms. On practical grounds his attempt was understandable – with only ten per cent of the Reichstag committed to supporting his government the future without Nazi backing was indeed bleak: the alternative was to rely once again on rule by presidential decree and to dissolve the Reichstag as soon as it showed signs of rejecting the president's emergency decrees. As Hitler maintained his claim for the chancellorship and the office of Minister of the Interior in Prussia as his minimum terms for compliance in a coalition, Papen and Hindenburg were obliged to pursue their defeatist alternative, which amounted to a total suspension of the Constitution.

On 13 August, Hitler decided to try his own fortune and initiated in a series of discussions with Schleicher, Papen and Hindenburg. Though supported by Schleicher, he received a sharp rebuff from the President who resented the claims of a parvenu to political power. A press communiqué which was issued at Papen's instigation and which threw an extremely doubtful light on this clandestine attempt to come to power irreparably soured relations between the Nazis and Papen's administration. Henceforth the Nazis intensified their vitriolic attacks on the government both by propaganda and by encouraging further civil unrest and disorder. Papen was provoked into issuing an emergency decree which provided for the death penalty for those convicted of acts of political terrorism.

The Nazis were, nevertheless, obliged to exercise a certain caution, for their party funds remained depleted after the last electoral campaign and if their opposition to Papen's régime were too violent he might well be provoked into calling for new elections which would possibly make the party bankrupt. Moreover, it was by no means certain that they would repeat their overwhelming success of July, for some of the party rank and file, especially the left-wing under the leadership of Gregor Strasser, were showing signs of disaffection with official party policy and threatened to break away from the main party.

The Dissolution of the New Reichstag

They were, however, unable to influence events in the Reichstag despite Göring's success in obtaining the post of speaker, an influential position. Faced with the likelihood of a vote of no confidence being recorded against his government as soon as the Reichstag reconvened, Papen took the precaution of obtaining Hindenburg's signature to a further order of dissolution to be used in case of difficulty from the opposition. His prediction proved accurate, for on 12 September, when the new parliament was opened, the Communists tabled the expected motion of no confidence in the government. There followed a bizarre spectacle. Papen tried to catch Göring's eye in order to be able to table the presidential dissolution order before the motion was passed. Göring, of course, was intent on deriving maximum gain from the spectacle of the self-destruction of democracy and refused to acknowledge Papen's attempt to speak. The Chancellor was forced to slap the order on the Speaker's table, but not before a resounding vote of no confidence was recorded against him: there were five hundred and twelve supporters of the motion and only forty-two Conservative opponents. Both sides testified to the paralysis of the Weimar system: many of those who supported the motion had the sole aim of rendering the government impotent, while the Conservatives who backed Papen endorsed his desire to exclude parliament from the workings of government (it was, of course, a fundamental breach of the Constitution to deny the Reichstag the opportunity of rescinding the former presidential decrees).

Papen chose the latest possible date for the holding of new elections, 6 November 1932, which, he hoped, would allow him sufficient time to be able to enact several important economic measures including the alleviation of unemployment now that the international economic situation was slowly improving. Moreover, he hoped to force the Nazis into co-operating with him for he reasoned another electoral campaign was bound to impose severe strain on their already depleted party funds. If another election was held he would have to gamble on the likelihood of the Nazis' losing several seats to the Nationalists. That the campaign, the fifth in the space of sixteen months, would also further damage the system of government in the eyes of the electorate and of foreign observers, was a consideration to which Papen paid little heed. Short-term gains took precedence over more fundamental considerations.

The main feature of the election campaign, in the opinion of the majority of electors a dreary, negative exercise, was the Potempa affair, an indication of the excesses which the Nazis were prepared to commit in order to achieve their ends. At the beginning of August five Stormtroopers bestially murdered a Communist opponent in the Upper Silesian village, Potempa, and were condemned to death by a state court under the terms of the recent emergency decree. Hitler reacted to this verdict by praising these heroes who 'lived and died for Germany,' an open endorsement of the SA's thuggery and one which was to cost the Nazis considerable support among those who realized the significance of his remarks. A further tactical mistake was the Nazis' support for the Communist-inspired transport strike in Berlin in November 1932 during which acts of violence and sabotage were carried out by the military organizations of both parties. The two extremes had found a common cause in their determination to overthrow the existing order but as an attempt to win over the working-man's vote it failed. It also produced a bourgeois backlash against the Nazis who became regarded as new supporters of the Bolshevik proletariat, a reaction with which the Nazi leaders had clearly not reckoned.

The strike had, incidentally, harmed the Communists' standing as well, for their willingness to collaborate with the Nazis was seen as an indication of their political blindness. They continued to act on Moscow's orders, believing that, contrary to all evidence, their political enemies were not the Nazis but the Social Democrats, or as they labelled them, Social Fascists. This, they held, justified their collaboration with the Nazis in attempting to overthrow the Republic, the creation of the SPD.

Indicative of the collapse of the parliamentary system was the choice of party which faced electors in Berlin. Their ballot paper listed as well as the seven major parties thirty-one minor and splinter parties. Their titles betray the preoccupation of the electorate with the economic crisis; they include the Radical Middle-Class Party, the Party for a Crisis-proof Economy, the Party for Pensioners, Sufferers from Inflation and Pre-war Wealthy, the Party of Unemployed for Work and Bread, the Militant League of Sufferers from Reduced Wages and Salaries and the Party of the Dispossessed Middle Class.

The significance of the results, though they record a considerable set-back for the Nazis, is not as straightforward as this reverse of fortune might suggest. Admittedly, the Nazis suffered a real defeat, two million votes and 34 seats – they were now regarded by many former supporters as 'brown' Bolsheviks – but their losses brought little succour to the republican parties. The Socialists' representation declined further by 12 seats to 121, the lowest number since 1924, and the Centre and Democratic Party (German State Party) also declined in power. The other extremist parties on the other hand, improved their position: the DNVP by 14 seats and the KPD by 11 seats. The decrease in support for the Nazis was thus counterbalanced by a return of the Bolshevik spectre. The increase in the Nationalists' fortunes was of small comfort to Papen, for he still could rely for support on only a handful of Reichstag deputies, and the prospects of his government remained poor.

THE ELECTION OF 6 NOVEMBER 1932

The results of the election were as follows:

		Votes cast (*to nearest thousand*)		Number of seats		Percentage of total vote	
		1932		1932		1932	
		July	Nov.	July	Nov.	July	Nov.
KPD	Communist	5,370,000	5,980,000	89	100	14·3	16·9
SPD	Social Democratic	7,960,000	7,251,000	133	121	21·6	20·4
DDP (DStP	Democratic State)	373,000	339,000	4	2	1·0	1·0
Z	Centre	4,589,000	4,230,000	75	70	12·4	11·9
BVP	Bavarian People's	1,203,000	1,097,000	22	20	3·2	3·1
DVP	People's	436,000	661,000	7	11	1·2	1·9
DNVP	Nationalist	2,187,000	3,131,000	40	51	5·9	8·8
NSDAP	National Socialist	13,779,000	11,737,000	230	196	37·3	33·1
Others		985,000	1,003,000	11	12	2·6	2·9
Total (to nearest hundred thousand)		37,200,000	35,700,000	608	584		

80·6 per cent of the electorate voted compared with 84·0 per cent in July 1932

What were Papen and Hindenburg now to do? They appeared to be faced with equally unpalatable alternatives: either of trying to muddle through with government by presidential decree (the combined votes of the Nazis and Communists, 296 out of 583, ruled out any prospect of a return to parliamentary government) or of attempting once more to reach agreement with the Nazis. Papen decided to adopt a third solution: he would continue in power by amending the Constitution. With Hindenburg's assistance, he intended to create a 'New State', even though this would involve Hindenburg's violating his presidential oath. The essential features of the 'New State' were an authoritarian president, the end of universal franchise, the banning of extremist political parties and their military organizations (i.e. above all the NSDAP, the SA and the SS) and the dissolution of trade unions and commercial organizations – a mixture of 'unrealistic day-dreaming and political ideology'

(Bracher) which was intended to transform the country into a dictatorship. Papen had, of course, wholly misjudged the situation, the inevitable result of his lack of political awareness. Realization of the plan would require the support of the Reichswehr, the sole remaining force in the state which possessed any real power. Papen had, however, failed to reckon with the attitude of his benefactor, Schleicher, whose backing as Minister of Defence was clearly essential if the support of the armed forces was to be enlisted for this 'second revolution from above' (Bracher). Schleicher rejected the proposal out of hand: Germany's small army of one hundred thousand men could not, he maintained, cope with a civil war on two fronts (i.e. Communist and Nazi) which Papen's constitutional amendments would surely provoke; he maintained, moreover, that it was unlikely that the Reichswehr would agree to oppose the Nazis with force. In reality Schleicher's attitude appears to have been dictated less by a fear that the army was too weak than by his desire not to be seen to accommodate the wishes of an unpopular chancellor, and by his growing conviction that the only solution to Germany's governmental crisis was after all to bring Hitler into the executive. He still accepted the false premise that governmental responsibility would tame the Nazis and contacted them in the middle of November, offering them posts in a new cabinet which he himself would head. Hitler, however, refused once again. As Papen still wholly opposed any concessions to the Nazis, Schleicher decided to organize opposition to the Chancellor both inside and outside the cabinet. Schleicher's ministerial colleagues accepted his views unquestioningly and when faced with their combined opposition Papen had no option but to resign. Hindenburg, persuaded by Schleicher's prediction of civil war if Papen remained in power, reluctantly accepted his resignation.

Schleicher's Chancellorship

Hindenburg contacted Hitler to discuss Nazi participation in a new government. Hitler remained intransigent as ever, insisting once more on full control of the government in a 'cabinet of national concentration', that is, one which would allow him to establish a National Socialist dictatorship. Hindenburg held out against Hitler's demands for he still remained deeply suspicious of him, albeit for snobbish rather than political reasons. Moreover, to offer the cabinet to the Nazis would be to surrender the country to the programme of one political party and since 1930 Hindenburg had doggedly adhered to the cause of supra-party government. Having rejected Hitler's candidature for the chancellorship, Hindenburg was forced *faute de mieux* to ask Schleicher, as spokesman of the army, the only alternative force in the country, to take over the mess for which he was largely responsible. Schleicher predictably was reluctant to accept the chancellorship. His rôle had always been that of the clandestine intriguer and he had no wish to step out of the sanctuary of the Ministry of Defence into what was without doubt the most unenviable political post in the history of the Republic. Schleicher's machiavellian tactics had finally ensnared him and on 3 December 1932 against his better judgement he became the thirteenth chancellor of the Republic. No more able than Papen to rely on parliamentary support, Schleicher would be forced to rule by presidential decree but since Hindenburg had lost faith in his former adviser, Schleicher's days as Chancellor were clearly to be few.

The composition of Schleicher's cabinet was with two exceptions the same as that of Papen's government. He attempted to grapple with the immense problems of government he faced with an ambitious supra-party, supra-class programme which, he hoped, would lead to the formation of a united front. The self-styled 'social general' wished to introduce a number of economic reforms, including increased unemployment benefit, increased Osthilfe and a renewed attempt to resettle the agrarian lands east of the Elbe with unemployed city dwellers. He further planned to reduce the number of those out of work by introducing military conscription, thereby increasing the strength of the army threefold. Though no-one disagreed with the need for economic reform, few agreed with Schleicher's proposed measures. The right-wingers, especially the landowners of eastern Germany, whose vested interests were at stake, launched a violent attack on the new proposals for agrarian reform. They had eased Brüning out of the chancellorship on this very issue and were now faced with what they considered to be an even more obnoxious form of 'agrarian Bolshevism'. Schleicher soon discovered the distinction between organizing cabals behind the scenes and having to shoulder responsibility for the government without friends. He still hoped to be able to govern without relying solely on the support of the armed forces. His overtures to the non-socialist trade unions were rebuffed, for none of them was convinced by his sudden conversion to social welfare. He even tried, unsuccessfully, to gain the confidence of the SPD and the socialist unions. Attempts to reach a compromise with the Nazis likewise met with failure. Having been unsuccessful in persuading Hitler to collaborate in the government, he unwisely tried to woo the left-wing of the NSDAP led by the veteran party member, Gregor Strasser, to whom he offered the post of vice-Chancellor and Minister of Labour in his government. Hitler, already uneasy about his position in the party since its reverse in the November election, swiftly thwarted this threat of internal dissent by summarily dismissing Strasser.

Eighteen months later, on 30 July 1934, both Strasser and Schleicher paid the penalty for their attempted collaboration when, during the Night of the Long Knives, they, together with many opponents of the Nazis and personal enemies of Hitler, were assassinated by SS troops.

In December, largely at the insistence of the Nazis, the Reichstag adjourned until the end of January. It was not that they wished to alleviate Schleicher's burden by removing the threat of parliamentary sanction, but rather that they could not afford the expense of a further general election which would result if a vote of no confidence in his government were passed. This did not imply, of course, that the Nazis were reconciled to Schleicher's tenure of office and they eagerly added their voice to those of the Socialists and right-wing extremists who demanded his resignation. Having failed to split the NSDAP, Schleicher found himself at a loss for a policy and after only six weeks in power he was driven to the conclusion that the only course of action open to him was to dissolve the Reichstag and to create the very military dictatorship which he had refused Papen some two months earlier. By now, however, he had exhausted his personal credit with the President. Hindenburg was no longer willing to comply with Schleicher's plans, and maintaining once more his need to be protector of the Constitution, he rejected Schleicher's demand.

Hindenburg's decision to withdraw support from Schleicher was not, of course, entirely his own – he had been influenced as ever by the palace camarilla and particularly by Papen, whom he continued to admire. Papen exchanged rôles with Schleicher in the gruesome game of intrigue, and Hindenburg, now suffering from increasing senility, concurred. Having prevented Hitler from coming to power while he was Chancellor, Papen now gave him every assistance. His motives were mixed: certainly he was eager to avenge Schleicher's betrayal of him, but he was equally moved by his conviction that he now had an opportunity to regain his lost position of influence. He still naïvely believed that he could control Hitler within a government.

Accordingly Papen set about restoring Hitler's political standing. At the annual banquet of the Herrenklub on 16 December 1932 he delivered a speech on Hitler's behalf. He succeeded in enlisting renewed and increased political and financial support of industrialists, many of whom were growing increasingly impatient with conditions under successive impotent cabinets, and in exploiting their desire for a 'strong man' at the head of the government. Great importance was attached by a number of industrialists and financiers to the revival of Nazi popularity in the recent Land election held in Lippe, where, reversing the trend of the previous general election, the NSDAP obtained a decisive victory with over forty per cent of the vote. They desired a non-Socialist chancellor who would command the respect of the masses and resolve the economic crisis which they simplistically regarded as a manifestation of class conflict. The only possibility was Hitler. On 4 January 1933, unknown to Schleicher, a meeting of the Nazi and Nationalist leaders and Papen was held at the home of a prominent Cologne banker, Kurt Freiherr von Schröder, where Hugenberg and Hitler agreed to revive the Harzburg Front and to form a coalition headed jointly by Hitler and Papen. Such an alliance would, it was believed, curb the excesses of the Nazis; the conviction that power would tame and not absolutely corrupt Hitler was still held.

Schleicher, since he had irretrievably lost Hindenburg's support, could no longer have recourse to the ultimate deterrent of threatening a dissolution of parliament. Hindenburg refused to grant Schleicher his request: proclamation of a state of emergency (which, ironically, Schleicher had prevented Papen from obtaining). Presented with the choice of retaining Schleicher at the head of a military dictatorship which wholly excluded parliament and adopting the constitutionally permissible alternative of a broad coalition which included Hitler, Hindenburg decided to take the 'legal' course. Deprived of the period of grace in which he had hoped to realize his policies, Schleicher was obliged on 28 January 1933 to tender his resignation.

Hitler Becomes Chancellor

Hindenburg, obliged once again to find a new chancellor, favoured Papen. For a few hours he continued to reject Hitler's candidature, intuitively adhering to his mistrust of the parvenu Nazi leader, whom he accurately suspected of intending to establish a party dictatorship. His entourage, after they had met Hitler, Hugenberg and Papen at Ribbentrop's house in Berlin on 22 January, argued differently. Meissner, Oskar and Papen, speaking for large sections of industry and agriculture, pressed Hitler's claim. He was not after all, they argued, intent on complete control of the government, having demanded only the offices of Chancellor for himself, Minister of the Interior and State Commissioner for Prussia (i.e. Chief of Police) for Göring. The other nine members of the cabinet were to be drawn from the Nationalists, partners with the Nazis in the Harzburg Front. This would assure a large DNVP majority within the government and prevent any possible attempt by the Nazis to gain the upper hand. This compromise succeeded in misleading not only the political intriguers in the presidential palace and in Hugenberg's party but also a broad spectrum of German politicians including, surprisingly, the Socialists. In reality the new coalition would serve Hitler purely as a stepping stone to absolute power. Hindenburg's misgivings were finally outweighed by the pressure from his advisers and, after years of scheming and agitating, Hitler managed to attain the leadership of the government by constitutional means with his much vaunted adherence to legality, albeit quasi-legality, intact. His political stature thereby increased and the fears of many former opponents, who now naïvely believed that Nazi terrorist activities would cease, were, temporarily, allayed.

On 29 January 1933, Hindenburg appointed Hitler Reich Chancellor and Papen Vice-Chancellor. The Vice-Chancellorship was a post of little influence, a fact which Papen in his political naïveté did not appreciate. Papen and Hindenburg confidently expected to keep a tight rein on Hitler and to continue to determine governmental policy. They had, however, sorely underestimated the situation, for neither the failing, aged President nor his mediocre vice-Chancellor – nor for that matter the broad mass of the German people – was a match for Hitler's political astuteness.

Hitler's Cabinet Takes Office

The cabinet of 'National Concentration' which took office on 30 January 1933 had come to power by a technically legal procedure. Its composition – three Nazis and nine non-Nazis – was considered by most politicians an adequate guarantee to prevent Hitler from establishing a National Socialist dictatorship, especially since it was believed that the Reichswehr stood firmly behind the DNVP. Indeed at first sight the Nationalists and their supporters appeared to hold the upper hand: they controlled the Vice-Chancellorship (von Papen), the Foreign Ministry (von Neurath), the Ministries of Defence (General von Blomberg), of Justice (Gürtner), of Finance (Count von Schwerin-Krosigk), of Labour (Seldte), of Post and Transport (von Eltz-Rübenach) and the Ministry of Economics (Hugenberg). The relative strength of the parties did not, of course, depend necessarily on the number of ministries they controlled. The three portfolios held by the Nazis granted them a position of considerable power and influence: apart from Hitler who headed the cabinet, Dr Wilhelm Frick, the Party Chairman, was made Minister of the Interior and Hermann Göring, Speaker of the Reichstag, became Minister without Portfolio and Prussian Minister of the Interior and, as such, was placed in control of the Prussian police, the force which was responsible for maintaining law in two thirds of the Reich.

On 1 February Hitler addressed the Reichstag, declaring that the fourteen years of democratic misrule had come to an end and that a national awakening, *nationale Erhebung*, would take place which would transform the fortunes of the country. It was clear from the outset that Hitler intended to eliminate parliament from the machinery of government. Papen had finally persuaded Hindenburg to accept Hitler as Chancellor so that a strong coalition could be formed: with support from the bourgeois parties the Reich government would, for the first time in three years, enjoy a parliamentary majority. Hitler, however, insisted on governing by presidential decree, thus rendering Papen's whole exercise futile. As early as 1 February he had already insisted that new elections be held 'to achieve a broad majority' in parliament; this convenient pretext would allow him to claim that an overwhelming popular vote – for the Nazis were certain to receive increased support – had endorsed his decision to seize power. Papen, still underestimating Hitler's cunning, persuaded Hindenburg to agree to the demand and elections were arranged for the first practicable date, 5 March 1933. The German Nationalists, who, torn with internal strife, could hardly hope to profit from further elections, withdrew their original objection when Hitler gave Hugenberg an assurance that the results would not effect the composition of the government, i.e. the Nationalists would retain their ministries.

The Beginning of the Nazi Revolution

The Nazis had five weeks in which to implement the first stage of their revolution, to ensure that the election results would enable them to assume complete control of the Reich. Wherever possible, i.e. in those Länder which already had Nazi governments, Party members replaced central and local government officials who remained loyal to the Republic. Göring replaced the Chiefs of Police in several Prussian cities with Nazis and encouraged close co-operation between the Prussian Police Force and the SS, the SA and the Stahlhelm. Legal immunity was guaranteed to any policeman who used fire-arms against Communist agitators.

On 4 February an emergency decree was issued by the government 'for the protection of the German People'. While purporting to prevent a violent electoral campaign it in fact granted the government widespread powers to restrict the freedom of the press and of public assembly. This allowed the police effectively to ban the election campaign of the opposition parties. The Nazi Revolution had begun in earnest.

The Reichstag Fire

On the evening of 27 February the Reichstag building went up in flames; the events surrounding its destruction have been the subject of conflicting historical interpretation for the past thirty-five years. Latest evidence, published in 1969 by the 'European Committee for the Scientific Investigation of the Reasons for and Consequences of the Second World War', suggests that the fire was planned by the Nazis who used a tunnel connecting the Reichstag with the house of the Speaker, Göring, to introduce incendiary materials into the building. Marinus van der Lubbe, a young simple-minded Dutchman and a self-confessed Communist, appears to have been lured by bogus advertisements placed by the Nazis in the Dutch Communist press into volunteering to set fire to the Reichstag single-handed.

Van der Lubbe was brought to trial at the High Court in Leipzig together with three leading Communists with whom he allegedly conspired. The court to its credit refused to submit to political pressure and acquitted the Communists while it found van der Lubbe guilty of arson. A retrospective law was introduced by the government which allowed them to order van der Lubbe's execution – he was beheaded with an axe.

Whether the Nazis organized the fire, or the Communists, as Hitler maintained, or van der Lubbe alone, remains a mystery. The main historical significance of the fire was that it allowed the Nazis to intensify their monomanic campaign against the Communist Party, which, they warned, clearly intended to stage a *coup d'état*. There is no evidence to suggest that the KPD envisaged revolution at this time for they still clung to their conviction that a period of Nazi rule was now a precondition for any left-wing Putsch.

The Nazis imprisoned thousands of Communists on the night of the fire to prevent a 'Bolshevik revolution' and used the event as a justification to introduce the next day a further emergency presidential decree 'for the protection of the people and the state'. The Nazis could now offer themselves as champions of law and order, in the defence of which the majority of civil and personal liberties, guaranteed by the Constitution, were suspended. These included the secrecy of the post, the inviolability of the home and personal property, free speech, freedom of assembly and the right to trial on summary arrest. The powers of the police were also extended, an opportunity which Göring used to establish the secret state police force, *Gestapo*. Worse, the public was deprived of any legal means with which to challenge misuse of the law. The destruction of the KPD continued: many supporters not arrested were beaten up by Nazi thugs. The Party was not outlawed, however, lest, as Jarman suggests, the Socialists benefited at the polls; an electoral victory of the SPD would have been disastrous for Hitler's plans.

The Election of 5 March 1933

It is perhaps surprising that the results of the election showed that there was still a large reserve of support for the Left; despite the imprisonment of the Communist candidates, and the banning of party newspapers, the representation of the KPD and SPD was only slightly reduced. The Nazis, moreover, had enjoyed a monopoly of radio propaganda and had had at their disposal an election fund of some three million marks, donated by the Ruhr industrialist, Krupp, and his associates, who saw this as an election to end elections. Nazi propaganda, under the supervision of Dr Josef Goebbels, a man of considerable talents, presented the electorate with the alternative of a return to the chaos of parliamentary democracy with the spectre of a Bolshevik revolution, the now traditional Red Scare, and a National Revolution which the Nazis would organize.

The increase in the Nazi's vote, now forty-four per cent of the total poll, seems to have come from disillusioned Communists, the new young voters and those who, previously apolitical, were

THE ELECTION OF 5 MARCH 1933

The results of the election were as follows:

		Votes cast (*to nearest thousand*)		Number of seats		Percentage of total vote	
		Nov. 1932	1933	Nov. 1932	1933	Nov. 1932	1933
KPD	Communist	5,980,000	4,749,000	100	81	16·9	12·2
SPD	Social Democratic	7,251,000	7,104,000	121	120	20·4	18·2
DDP (DStP	Democratic State)	339,000	332,000	2	6	1·0	0·9
Z	Centre	4,230,000	4,298,000	70	73	11·9	11·0
BVP	Bavarian People's	1,097,000	1,206,000	20	19	3·1	3·1
DVP	People's	661,000	430,000	11	4	1·9	1·1
DNVP	Nationalist	3,131,000	3,139,000	52	52	8·8	8·0
NSDAP	National Socialist	11,737,000	17,266,000	196	288	33·1	43·9
Others		1,003,000	379,000	12	4	2·9	1·0
Total (to nearest hundred thousand)		35,700,000	39,300,000	584	647		

88·5 per cent of the electorate voted compared with 80·6 per cent in November 1932.

willing to vote in an election which promised to be the last for some time. The Centre and the Bavarian Peoples' Party managed to increase their representation – exceptionally, Bavaria had become the temporary haven of democracy in a sea of unrest.

Preparations for a Seizure of Power

The coalition now commanded a majority in parliament of three hundred and forty out of six hundred and forty-seven seats. This was now of purely academic interest, for the Nazis were determined not to rule constitutionally but to assume dictatorial powers. The three Nazi ministers decided at once to introduce an enabling bill, *Ermächtigungsgesetz*, into parliament, which would transfer full legislative and executive power to the party. This would need a majority of two-thirds to enter the statute book since it involved a constitutional amendment. They would have, therefore, to persuade the bourgeois parties to support their bill, if the semblance of legality by which they laid great store were to be preserved. Meanwhile further preparations for dictatorial rule were carried out: the 'Nazification' on 6 March of the police forces in those Länder with democratic governments and the replacement of Länder parliaments by Nazi administrators, *Reichskommissare*, on the model of Papen's rape of Prussia.

The Day of National Awakening

At the suggestion of Dr Goebbels, who on 13 March was officially created Minister for Propaganda and Popular Enlightenment, Hitler announced that the new parliament would be opened on 21 March, the 'Day of National Awakening'. The opening ceremony was staged in the Garrison Church at Potsdam, the burial place of the Hohenzollern monarchs. Inside the church the ex-Crown Prince stood behind the empty Kaiser's throne, a reminder of Germany's past glory. Hitler made a deliberately emotional speech: he contrasted the shame and confusion of 1918 with the rebirth now of Germany's national honour, made a warm tribute to Hindenburg who had appeared in his uniform of Commander-in-Chief of the army, and shook him solemnly by the hand. The symbol of Germany's past, the aged field-marshal, was now seen in this theatrical ceremony to be reconciled with the representative of the New Germany, Adolf Hitler, the lance-corporal. Hindenburg then descended alone into the crypt to pay homage at the tomb of Frederick the Great as if to invoke his blessing for the new régime. After the ritual, troops of the SA and Stahlhelm staged a ceremonial march past. The fear of revolution, Nazi or Communist, was forgotten, the future appeared rosy in the eyes of those intoxicated by the 'Spirit of Potsdam'. Germany's Day of National Awakening had been a great popular event and a supreme example of a demagogic propaganda stunt.

The Enabling Bill

Two days later the Nazis showed their teeth and the true nature of the 'Spirit of Potsdam'. Under the pretext of destroying Marxism they introduced into parliament, now forced to meet in the Kroll Opera House, a 'decree to alleviate the distress of the people and the Reich', the enabling bill. It granted the government the right for four years to enact legislation – even that which ran contrary to the Constitution – without obtaining the agreement of parliament; the laws would come into force immediately they received the Chancellor's signature. The decree guaranteed the integrity of the Länder and the church and purported not to affect the rights of the President, though since his signature to legislation was no longer required, this assurance was of little value. Since all the Communist deputies and a dozen Socialists had been jailed, the government could rely on three hundred and sixty votes out of about five hundred and fifty-five, but only if they received full support from the Nationalist deputies, which seemed unlikely. Hitler therefore, needed the agreement of the bourgeois parties to obtain the necessary two-thirds majority. He approached the chairman of the Centre Party, Monsignor Kaas, and assured him that the constitutional clauses suspended in February would be restored after a period of transition; a letter to guarantee this would be delivered to Kaas. The Centrists argued that by refusing to agree to the law they would have little real effect on the political situation and that Hitler might be driven to use the powers he already possessed, dissolve the opposition parties including themselves and pass the enabling law without further reference to parliament. The Centre Party, which had collaborated in nearly every cabinet since the inception of the Republic, had shown itself amenable to the end. The promised letter did not arrive.

On 23 March Hitler introduced the bill into parliament. The Kroll Opera House was surrounded by SS troops and occupied by SA men, the walls were festooned with swastikas. Speaking against a chant from those outside who demanded 'the law or murder', Otto Wels, leader of the SPD, voiced the only opposition to the bill, an act which demanded considerable personal courage. He said, 'No one can demand or expect the Social Democratic Party, after the persecution which it has suffered in recent weeks, to vote in favour of the tabled enabling law. . . . No enabling law gives you the power to destroy ideals which are eternal and indestructible.' Hitler replied vituperatively and contemptuously that he did not need their support. The bill was passed by four hundred and forty-four votes to the ninety-four votes of the Socialists. Its acceptance was greeted by the Horst Wessel Song.

The Nazis' success was widely acclaimed, not only by their supporters or by those who liked to be on the winning side, but by many for practical reasons: to safeguard their economic security and their physical safety. The gullible, and there were many, refused to believe that the Führer condoned political terrorism. They swallowed the myth of a Bolshevik Plot and ascribed, because they wanted to, civil unrest to Communist provocation.

The Completion of the Nazi Revolution

The completion of the Nazi Revolution was achieved in a short time now that dictatorial power was in the hands of the party. Under the slogan of co-ordination, *Gleichschaltung*, all public bodies and organizations were incorporated into the Nazi state. On 11 May Goebbels organized a rally of Berlin students 'Against the Ungerman Spirit' at which twenty thousand politically and morally offensive books were ceremoniously burned on huge pyres at midnight. The books destroyed included the works of Marx, Kästner, Freud, Thomas Mann, Remarque, Tucholsky and many others.

The political parties, with the exception of course of the NSDAP, were dissolved, the SPD and KPD by government decree on 23 June 1933, the DDP, DVP and Centre voluntarily on 28 June, 4 July and 5 July, respectively; even the Nazis' coalition partner, the DNVP, was forced to dissolve itself. On 14 July the government enacted legislation which proclaimed Germany to be a one-party state and on 1 December the union of state and party was proclaimed.

The Länder were formerly stripped of their sovereignty on 30 January 1934 and the Reichsrat was dissolved on 14 February. All formal parliamentary and bureaucratic opposition to the central party authority in Berlin had been destroyed.

On 2 May 1933 the trade unions were abolished. They were replaced in October 1934 by the party-dominated Workers' Front, *Deutsche Arbeitsfront*, which purported to resurrect the former partnership between workers and employers. In fact, it simply subordinated both to direct party rule. Similarly all non-party youth organizations were proscribed and their membership assimilated into the Hitler Youth, *Hitlerjugend*, HJ, and the League of German Women, *Bund deutscher Mädel*, BDM. The civil service, the police, the judiciary and the professions were purged of non-party sympathizers – though not wholly – and on 30 June 1934, the 'Night of the Long Knives', *Röhmputsch*, the threat of internal and external opposition to the party and to Hitler was eliminated when members of the SS and the Gestapo carried out wholesale assassination. Their victims included Röhm, Strasser, Schleicher, and hundreds of SA members and left-wing Nazis. Other dissidents, political and racial, were incarcerated in concentration camps, at first subjected to hard labour, later often transferred to extermination camps where several million human beings were gassed in the name of Nazi civilization.

On 2 August 1934 President Hindenburg died. Within an hour of his death Hitler announced that the offices of chancellor and president (and, automatically, that of Commander-in-Chief of the Reichswehr) were to be combined and that he was the new head of state. Hitler's adolescent dream of becoming Führer of the German people had been realized.

7

Conclusions

TWO INTERDEPENDENT considerations dominate the study of the Weimar Republic: the failure of parliamentary democracy and the success of Adolf Hitler and the National Socialist Party. The reasons for the failure of the Republic to establish itself as an acceptable form of government are many, and their relative importance remains a source of constant debate. The collapse of parliamentary democracy in Germany resulted partly from the inability of her leaders to resolve the enormous economic and social tensions which dominated politics and partly from their inability to deal effectively with the immense difficulties, political, economic and financial, which were imposed on Germany by foreign states. The fundamental reason for their failure, however, was their faltering faith in the régime which they had created, and an equally serious lack of self-confidence.

The birth of the Republic was, to say the least, inauspicious: parliamentary democracy was forced onto the German people without their having demanded its introduction and without their understanding its nature or its aims. Its imposition was an attempt on the part of the military to appease the Allies and to exonerate themselves from the responsibility of losing the war; subsequently, the former military command was able to accuse civilian politicians, who had been obliged to conduct armistice and peace negotiations with the enemy, of having stabbed Germany and the German army in the back.

The outbreak of the popular revolution in November 1918 aggravated the divisions between the rival groups of the Left. Their aims ranged from a desire for cautious evolution to a determination to establish a dictatorship of the proletariat, and mutual suspicion of the Social Democratic factions effectively determined the failure of the revolution: Ebert's fears that the left-wing Independent Socialists and the Spartacists intended to stage a Bolshevik putsch obliged him to seek support from the army leadership, an action which compromised his party and precluded the introduction of much-needed democratic reforms. Pressing short-term needs, the restoration of law and order, the alleviation of food shortages and the provision of work for the unemployed, were given precedence over long-term socialist aims, while the workers' councils, the initial source of revolutionary spirit, willingly threw in their lot with the conservatism of the Majority Socialists, agreeing with employers on a *modus vivendi* which secured the future of capitalism in Germany.

From the outset the attitude of the Allies undermined the standing of the Republic. They forced the newly-elected German government into accepting a dictated peace treaty whose terms were severe and which contradicted on several counts the spirit of Woodrow Wilson's peace programme. Their contention that Germany was guilty for the outbreak of the war was regarded by all in Germany as a groundless and gratuitously offensive assertion, while the demand for huge war reparations was seen as a deliberate attempt to cripple the German economy. Right-wing opponents of the new régime were thus handed powerful weapons with which they could attack the government, moderate Socialists and Centrists, and, through them, the Republic. To the uncritical the accusation that Germany had been stabbed in the back appeared to have been proved.

The elected National Assembly, charged with drawing up a Constitution, produced a document which, though a model of liberal ideals, failed totally to appreciate the needs and difficulties of a modern industrial society. It was of course essential that the electorate should agree to uphold the principles of democratic government if it was to function, and that anti-democratic activities should be firmly discouraged, but, while confirming the introduction of government by parliamentary democracy, the delegates failed to take into account the necessity of convincing the majority of the population that the new, parliamentary system was preferable to the authoritarian régime of the monarchy. The Constitution allowed extremists unlimited freedom to undermine the parliamentary system, and vicious opposition to the régime – as opposed to parliamentary opposition, vital to democratic government – flourished, stemming both from the Communists on the extreme left and the Nationalists and National Socialists on the extreme right. The governing republican parties were presented with the daunting task of promoting the cause of moderation in the face of foreign hostility and overwhelming domestic opposition, as large sections of the electorate became disaffected with the régime and found refuge in extremism, but successive cabinets proved unable to deal with the enormous problems which assailed them. Political education of the population was not considered; official bodies and organizations were not purged of their anti-democratic elements: the educational system remained wholly authoritarian in outlook, the established civil service and the judiciary were left intact, and the army was allowed to develop into a state within a state whose unqualified support for the legally elected government could by no means be taken for granted.

The decision of the National Assembly to provide the president with wide emergency powers proved to be a severe error of judgement, for, while such powers suited a man of Ebert's political attitudes, they allowed his successor, Hindenburg, to exert an authority over government which was wholly disproportionate to his competence. While the National Assembly could not, of course, foresee the election in 1925 of a monarchist field-marshal to the presidency, effective safeguards against the misuse of presidential powers, which became common between 1930 and 1933, should have been included in the Constitution.

The Constitution created further difficulties, in particular in its cumbersome electoral procedure, for proportional representation produced an unworkably large number of political parties and prevented the formation of viable, one-party governments. Multiparty coalition cabinets had to be formed which were, in their nature, prone to instability. Moreover, the SPD, the major political party, aggravated the situation by displaying an ambivalent attitude towards participation in government. Though the Republic was largely their creation they fought shy of accepting continuous governmental responsibility, preferring to resume their traditional rôle of opposition party. The negative attitude of the SPD, together with a widespread over-concern with party doctrine further undermined – by default – the parliamentary system. Germany appeared to be a republic deprived of republicans with a parliament bereft of parliamentarians.

The consolidation of the Republic after the revolution of 1918–19 was hampered in the early years of its existence by a series of hostile acts both at home and abroad. Left- and right-wing *coups d'état* were staged against the régime: in 1919 in Munich a Communist putsch which the army brutally put down, and in 1920 the Kapp Putsch in Berlin which was thwarted by a general strike. In 1923 Munich was also the scene of the Hitler-Ludendorff Putsch, a further attempt to overthrow the Republic, which, though unsuccessful, once more demonstrated the vulnerability of the régime and its dependence for survival on the co-operation of the army command.

Successive governments in the early twenties pursued a policy of fulfilment towards the terms of Versailles, hoping thereby to appease the Allies, to restore good international relations and to demonstrate Germany's economic plight. Erfüllungspolitik was, however, misunderstood at home – in many cases deliberately – and cynically rejected abroad, in particular by France and Belgium. Early in 1923, acting on a flimsy pretext that Germany had failed to fulfil her reparation obligations, French and Belgian troops invaded the Ruhr to extort a 'productive pledge'. In the ensuing chaos the Republic all but disintegrated. The government's policy of passive resistance towards foreign occupation aggravated the country's economic difficulties and accelerated the depreciation of the currency. Galloping inflation in turn resulted in disastrous economic and social consequences: an enormous proletariat of impoverished workers, *déclassé* bourgeois and intelligentsia, was created, many of whom became irrevocably alienated from the régime and, in their nostalgia for an authoritarian form of government, turned for solace to the extremist parties.

The Verständigungspolitik of Gustav Stresemann might possibly have secured the future of the Republic had its aims and results been more widely appreciated in Germany and had he not met with an untimely death in 1929. After 1924 Germany was reaccepted as an equal in international politics and her economic recovery, which did much to reassure the population, was apparently complete. Germany's economic revival and the consequent popular acceptance of the Republic depended, however, wholly on the presence in the country of foreign loans. When following the Wall Street Crash in

1929 these were suddenly withdrawn, the underlying instability of the régime was once more exposed. The economic depression, which affected Germany particularly severely, provoked a crisis in the ruling coalition between the SPD, representative of the growing number of unemployed workers, and the DVP, spokesman for the employers. For reasons of party-political doctrine they were unable – or unwilling – to reach a compromise and brought about the collapse of what was to be the Republic's last parliamentary government. Thus the depression acted as a catalyst, exposing again the fundamental weaknesses of the régime: governmental instability and the doctrinaire inflexibility of the political parties, which had been temporarily concealed behind a façade of sham prosperity. In refusing to discharge their mandate to govern the country the popularly elected deputies opened the way for an authoritarian régime. It was one which large numbers of the electorate welcomed, for, what, they argued, was the value of parliamentary democracy if political parties rendered it impotent?

Heinrich Brüning who headed the first presidential government could, given longer in office, possibly have rescued and revived the parliamentary system, but his success as Chancellor in curing the economic crisis was completely dependent on Hindenburg's support. The aged President was already prey to the political influence of his palace camarilla, a band of inept, devious advisers. They were, however, no match for the machinations of Hitler, who, exploiting the economic and political crisis to the utmost, promised all things to all men. The Nazis' programme of authoritarian government and economic miracles offered an attractive alternative to the chaos of parliamentary government and the misery of the economic depression. It is a measure of the depth of public despair that electors in their millions unquestioningly accepted the Nazis' manifesto and transferred their allegiance in successive elections to the party.

While the events of the last three years of the Republic were dominated by the political intrigue of Hindenburg's entourage, it is wrong to suggest that they engineered Hitler's coming to power; in fact, they tried to prevent his assuming sole control of the country. They simply acted as pawns in a game which, given the failure of parliament, the voluntary abdication of the political parties and popular disaffection for the Republic, was logically bound to end with the establishment of undemocratic government. It is one of the fateful coincidences of history that at that very time there existed a demagogue who possessed the personality and the political ability of Adolf Hitler. While the chronology of the events leading to Hitler's accession depended to a considerable degree on the manoeuvrings of the presidential camarilla which thought to tame Hitler by offering him government responsibility and to use him in their anti-parliamentary schemes, and while the occasion of his coming to power was provided by the economic crisis, the fundamental cause was the failure of parliamentary democracy.

The depressing conclusion to be drawn is that, given the reluctance of the electors and politicians of the Weimar Republic to come to terms with the realities of parliamentary democracy, the Republic merely provided a democratic interlude between the authoritarian Empire and the dictatorial Third Reich.

Abbreviations of Political Parties

BVP *Bayrische Volkspartei*, Bavarian People's Party
DDP *Deutsche Demokratische Partei*, German Democratic Party
DNVP *Deutschnationale Volkspartei*, German National People's Party
DVP *Deutsche Volkspartei*, German People's Party
KPD *Kommunistische Partei Deutschlands*, Communist Party of Germany
MSPD *Mehrheitssozialdemokratische Partei Deutschlands*, Majority Social Democratic Party of Germany
NSDAP *Nationalsozialistische Deutsche Arbeiterpartei*, National Socialist German Workers' Party
SPD *Sozialdemokratische Partei Deutschlands*, Social Democratic Party of Germany
USPD *Unabhängige Sozialdemokratische Partei Deutschlands*, Independent Social Democratic Party of Germany
Z *Zentrumspartei*, Centre Party

Bibliography

Below is a list of works quoted. Those particularly recommended for further reading are marked with an asterisk.

(A) *In English*

  (i) *General Studies*

   Eyck, Erich, *A History of the Weimar Republic*, London, 1962, 2 vols.

   *Halperin, S. William, *Germany Tried Democracy – A Political History of the Reich from 1918 to 1933*, New York, 1965.

   Jarman, T. L., *The Rise and Fall of Nazi Germany*, New York, 1961.

   *Mann, Golo, *A History of Germany since 1789*, London, 1968.

   *Nicholls, A. J., *Weimar and the Rise of Hitler*, London, 1968.

   Rosenberg, Arthur, *A History of the German Republic*, London, 1936.

   Taylor, A. J. P., *The Course of German History*, London, 1966.

   Vermeil, Edmond, *The German Scene, Social, Political and Cultural, 1890 to the Present Day*, London, 1956.

  (ii) *Specialized Works*

   *Allan, William Sheridan, *The Nazi Seizure of Power, the Experience of a Single German Town 1930–1933*, London, 1966.

   *Bullock, Alan, *Hitler, a Study in Tyranny*, London, 1962.

   Carsten, F. L., *The Reichswehr and Politics 1918–1933*, London, 1966.

*Gay, Peter, *Weimar Culture, the Insider as Outsider*, London, 1968.

Goodspeed, D. J., *Ludendorff, Soldier, Dictator, Revolutionary*, London, 1966.

*Hitler, Adolf, *Mein Kampf*, translated by Ralph Mannheim, introduction by D. C. Watt, London, 1969.

Nicholson, Harold, *Peacemaking 1919*, London, 1964.

Nolte, Ernst, *Three Faces of Fascism*, London, 1965.

The Road to Dictatorship, Germany 1918–1933, ten contributions by Th. Eschenburg, E. Fraenkel, K. Sontheimer, E. Matthias, O. K. Flechtheim, K. D. Bracher, H. Krausnik, H. Rotfels, E. Kogon, London, 1964.

Ryder, A. J., *The German Revolution 1918–1919, a Study of German Socialism in War and Revolt*, Cambridge, 1967.

Stolper, Gustav, Häuser, Karl and Borchardt, Knut, *The German Economy*, London, 1967.

Turner, Henry Ashby, *Stresemann and the Politics of the Weimar Republic*, Princeton, 1965.

(B) *In German*
  (i) *General Studies*

Buchheim, Karl, *Die Weimarer Republik, Grundlagen und politische Entwicklung*, Munich, 1961.

*Eschenburg, Theodor, *Die improvisierte Demokratie, gesammelte Aufsätze zur Weimarer Republik*, Munich, 1963.

*Heiber, Helmut, *Die Republik von Weimar. Dtv-Weltgeschichte des 20 Jahrhunderts* vol. 3, Munich, 1966.

*Hermann, Hans H., *Bestandsaufnahme einer Republik*, Reinbeck, 1969.

Herzfeld, Hans, *Die Weimarer Republik, Deutsche Ereignisse und Probleme*, Frankfurt am Main, 1966.

Informationen zur politischen Bildung: Die Weimar Rerepublik, 2 vols., Bundeszentrale für politische Bildung, Bonn, 1964.

Pross, Harry (ed.), *Die Zerstörung der deutschen Politik, Dokumente 1871–1933*, Frankfurt am Main, 1959.

  (ii) *Specialized Works*

Besson, Waldemar, *Friedrich Ebert, Verdienst und Grenze, Persönlichkeit und Geschichte* vol. 30, Göttingen, 1963.

Bracher, Karl Dietrich, *Die Auflösung der Weimarer Republik, eine Studie zum Problem des Machtverfalls in der Demokratie*, Villingen, 1964.

Hirsch, Felix, *Stresemann, Patriot und Europäer, Persönlichkeit und Geschichte* vol. 36, Göttingen, 1964.

Anschläge. Deutsche Plakate als Dokumente der Zeit 1900–1960, edited by Friedrich Arnold, Munich, 1963.

Selective Index

Adenauer, Konrad 182
Allied Reparation Commission 60, 103–6
Arco-Valley, Count Anton von 54
Armistice 18 f., 22 f., 29, 31–3, 56, 107, 122, 177, 253
Auer, Erhard 54

Baldwin, Stanley 144, 160
Banking crisis 222
Barth, Emil 21, 27 f., 30 f., 40
Barthou, Louis 114
Bauer, Gustav 53, 68, 85 f., 88
Bauer, Max 89
Bavarian People's Party 49, 54, 99 f., 108, 133 f., 137, 154, 158–66, 165 f., 171–3, 180 f., 183, 186, 192, 194 f., 212, 216, 234, 239, 248 f.
Bavarian Revolt (1923), 144–9
Bavarian Soviet Régime 46, 54 f., 123, 256
Bell, Hans 69
Beneš, Eduard 178
Berlin, Treaty of 187
Bethmann Hollweg, Theobald von 8–10, 14
Bismarck, Otto von 1–3, 6, 48, 50, 72, 189, 218
Blomberg, Werner von 245
Braun, Otto 171, 231–3
Brauns, Heinrich 190
Brest-Litovsk, Treaty of 15 f., 67
Briand, Aristide 111, 136, 176, 178, 188 f., 199, 221
Brockdorff-Rantzau, Ulrich von 53, 58 f., 67 f.

Brüning, Heinrich 78, 207–9, 212–17, 220–2, 224–31, 241, 257

Cannes Conference 111 f., 132
Centre Party 5, 13, 15, 20, 46, 48 f., 50, 52 f., 68 f., 81, 87, 89, 98–101, 105 f., 116, 137, 143, 148, 153 f., 158 f., 163, 165 f., 171–3, 180 f., 183, 186, 192–5, 197, 209–10, 212, 216, 224, 229 f., 232, 234, 238 f., 248–51, 254
Chamberlain, Austen 176 f., 189
Chicherin, Georgy 114 f.
Christian Socialist People's Party 217, 234
Class, Heinrich 202
Clemenceau, Georges 57–9, 61
Communist Party 41, 85, 89, 99, 102 f., 106, 112, 133, 137, 143, 147, 155, 157–9, 161, 163, 165 f., 170–3, 175, 180, 183, 185, 194, 196, 214–17, 219 f., 223, 231 f., 234–6, 238–40, 247 f., 250 f., 255
Community of Labour 36 f., 83, 87, 190, 254
Conservative Party 5, 13–15, 20, 48
Conservative People's Party 204, 217, 237
Constitution, the 71–84, 101, 103, 116, 133, 143, 145, 149, 152, 167 f., 170, 174, 183, 186, 195, 203–5, 207, 211–14, 217–19, 224, 232 f., 236 f., 239 f., 242, 244, 247, 250, 254 f.
Coolidge, Calvin 144
Councils, Soldiers', Sailors' and Workers' 26 f., 30 f., 35, 37 f., 43 f., 51, 54 f., 85, 87, 254
Cuno, Wilhelm 137–9, 141 f., 175

Currency reform 150 f., 155, 157
Curtius, Julius 195, 221

d'Abernon, Edgar Vincent 175, 180
Dawes, Charles G. 156 f., 189
Dawes Plan, the 144, 153, 156 f., 159–62, 164 f., 167, 175, 189, 197 f., 200, 205
Depression, the, *see* Wall Street Crash
Dithmann, Wilhelm 30 f., 40, 43
Drexler, Anton 123, 127–9
Duesterberg, Theodor 223

Ebert-Groener Pact 25, 34 f., 39 f., 254
Ebert, Friedrich 7, 11, 16, 25, 28, 29 f., 34–40, 43 f., 51 f., 68, 71, 77 f., 92, 96, 100, 110, 113, 136 f., 140, 142, 145 f., 149, 152, 154 f., 159–61, 166, 168–70, 174, 191, 211, 254 f.
Economic Party 194, 212, 234
Ehrhardt, Hermann 88 f., 91, 107, 127, 133, 147, 218
Eichhorn, Emil 42
Eisner, Kurt 54, 116, 123
Elections
  to National Assembly, 19.1.1919, 50 f.;
  presidential, 1919 (by National Assembly), 51 f.; 1925 77, 255; 1932 222–5, 228
  to Reichstag, 6.6.1920 97–100; 4.5.1924 155 f., 158 f., 164; 7.12.1924 165 f.; 20.5.1928 192–4; 14.9.1930 208, 214–16; 219, 222; 31.7.1932 231, 234–6; 6.11.1932 237–40, 242; 5.3.1933 245–9
Empire, German 1–6
Eltz-Rübenach, Paul von 245
Enabling Bill, Nazi 249–51
Erfüllungspolitik 97, 107, 112 f., 132, 135 f., 157, 256
Erzberger, Matthias 13, 31, 33, 49, 53, 68 f., 79, 86 f., 105–7, 110, 116, 132
Expropriation of Princes, Referendum on 183 f.

Falkenhayn, Erich von 8
Fatherland Patriotic Party 49, 159
Feder, Gottfried 128 f.
Fehrenbach, Konstantin 101, 105 f.
Flag controversy 182
Fleet, Revolt of the 25–7
Foch, Ferdinand 18, 31 f.

Fourteen Points, The 17, 19, 22, 51, 56–9, 62–6, 177, 254
Frederick the Great (King of Prussia) 250
Freikorps 40 f., 43, 55, 83, 88, 117, 123, 145
Freud, Sigmund 251
Frick, Wilhelm 227, 245

Gansser, Emil 168 f.
Gareis, Karl 108
Geddes, Sir Eric 57
Geneva Protocol 176 f.
Genoa Conference 113–15
German–Austrian customs union 221 f.
German Democratic Party (German State Party) 46–8, 50, 52 f., 55, 68 f., 81, 88 f., 98–101, 106, 110, 137, 143, 148, 151, 154, 158 f., 163–7, 171 f., 180–3, 186, 192–4, 198, 212, 215 f., 220, 224, 234, 238 f., 248, 251
German National People's Party 48, 50, 69 f., 72, 85 f., 90, 98 f., 103, 105–8, 112, 133–7, 139, 143, 146, 150, 152 f., 157–9, 161, 163–7, 170, 172, 175–7, 180–9, 192–4, 198, 201 f., 204 f., 208, 213 f., 216 f., 220 f., 223, 225, 228, 230, 234 f., 237–9, 242–4
German People's Party 47, 50, 69, 72, 86, 90, 98–103, 106, 136 f., 142 f., 146, 148, 154, 158 f., 164–6, 170, 172, 180–3, 185 f., 192–5, 199, 207, 209–10, 212, 215–17, 234, 239, 248, 251, 257
German Workers' Front 252
Gessler, Otto von 92 f., 95, 110, 145 f., 148, 167, 170, 172, 184 f., 190 f.
Gestapo 247, 252
Gilbert, Seymour Parker 198, 200
Gleichschaltung 232, 251 f.
Goebbels, Josef 248 f., 252
Goethe, Johann Wolfgang von 51
Göring, Hermann 236 f., 244–7
Groener, Wilhelm 24 f., 34 f., 38–40, 190 f., 196, 211, 218 f., 224–6
Gürtner, Franz 245

Haase, Hugo 7, 11, 30 f., 40
Hague Conference 203, 205
Haig, Douglas 18
Hammerstein, Kurt von 225
Harding, Warren G. 104
Harzburg Front 220 f., 243 f.

Haverstein, Rudolf 140, 151, 157
Heinze, Rudolf 147
Held, Heinrich 171, 173
Helfferich, Karl 71, 86 f., 132 f., 151, 157, 159 f.
Hellpach, Willy 171
Herriot, Edouard 160 f., 176
Hertling, Count Georg von 15, 17, 20
Heye, Wilhelm 184
Hilferding, Rudolf 195, 206
Hindenburg, Oskar von 211 f., 225 f., 244
Hindenburg, Paul von 8–10, 14–16, 19, 22–4, 31, 33, 35, 38, 69–71, 77 f., 148, 154, 163, 170–4, 180–2, 184 f., 189, 192, 195, 203, 205, 207 f., 210–18, 222–9, 130–3, 235 f., 239–46, 249, 252, 255, 257
Hintze, Paul von 19
Hitler, Adolf 49, 61, 71, 98, 117–19, 145, 149 f., 174, 191, 201 f., 204, 206, 208, 212, 218–23, 227, 229–33, 235–7, 240–7, 249–53, 257 f.
Hitler, Alois 117
Hitler–Ludendorff Putsch 98, 132, 148 f., 156, 184, 256
Hitler Youth (HJ) 252
Hoffmann, Johannes 55
Hoover, Herbert 222
Hugenberg, Alfred 164, 166, 180, 190, 193, 202–4, 220 f., 243–6

Independent Social Democratic Party 11 f., 15 f., 21 f., 25, 27, 29–31, 36, 38, 40–2, 50, 54, 67, 72, 85, 89, 91, 98–100, 102 f., 254
Inflation 65, 97, 110 f., 133 f., 136, 138, 140–3, 150 f., 156, 166, 213, 223, 256

Jarres, Karl 170–3

Kaas, Ludwig 250
Kahr, Gustav von 49, 107 f., 116, 132, 134, 145–50, 155
Kampfbund 145
Kapp Putsch 71, 88–93, 103, 107 f., 110, 184, 233, 256
Kapp Wolfgang 89–92, 159
Kästner, Erich 251
Kellogg–Briand Pact 198
Keudell, Walter von 204
Keynes, John Maynard 104, 213

Knilling, Eugen von 108, 134, 145
Korfanty, Wojciech 109
Krupp, Gustav 95, 248
Kühlmann, Richard von 18
Kun, Béla 55, 57

Landauer, Gustav 55
Landsberg, Otto 30, 53
Landvolk 234
Lausanne Conference 228, 231
Law, Andrew Bonar 138
League of German Women (BDM) 252
League of Nations 57, 66 f., 108 f., 154, 167, 176, 178–81, 186–8
Leipzig Reichswehr Trial 218 f.
Lenin, Vladimir I. 15, 41, 102, 113
Lequis, Arnold von 39
Lerchenfeld-Köfering, Count Hugo von 108, 133 f.
Levien, Max 55, 123
Leviné, Eugen 55, 123
Liebknecht, Karl 12, 28 f., 37, 41–3, 49
Liebknecht, Wilhelm 12, 32
Lloyd George, David 57 f., 111, 114 f., 138
Locarno, Treaty of 61, 154, 175–80, 186–8
London Ultimatum 97, 105, 111
Lossow, Otto von 132, 145 f., 148–50
Ludendorff, Erich 8–10, 14–26, 47, 70 f., 80, 145, 148–50, 171, 173, 191, 205
Ludwig III (King of Bavaria) 29, 54
Lueger, Karl, 119 f., 130
Luther, Hugo 151, 166 f., 174 f., 178–82, 188
Lüttwitz, Walther von 88–91
Luxemburg, Rosa 12, 37, 41–3, 49

Macdonald, J. Ramsay 160 f.
Majority Social Democratic Party 11, 15 f., 20–2, 25, 27–31, 34 f., 37 f., 40, 42, 44, 46, 50, 52 f., 55 f., 68 f., 81–3, 85 f., 88 f., 91 f., 98–103, 254
Maltzan, Adolf von 113–15
Mann, Thomas 251
Marx, Karl 251
Marx, Wilhelm 81, 154 f., 159–61, 164, 166, 171–3, 182 f., 185 f., 189, 191 f.
Max, Prince of Baden 17, 20, 22–5, 27 f., 51
Mein Kampf 71, 117–21, 125 f., 128
Meissner, Otto 211, 244

Michaelis, Georg 14 f.
Müller, Hermann 68 f., 96, 100, 142, 153, 195–7, 199, 201, 206–8, 210, 212, 216
Mussolini, Benito 126 f., 145, 178

National Liberal Party 5, 13–15, 20 f., 46, 48, 54, 158
National Socialist German Workers' Party 56, 64, 68, 85, 96, 98, 121, 123 f., 126–31, 146, 149 f., 155, 157 f., 161, 163, 165 f., 168, 171 f., 180, 194, 201, 204, 207 f., 214–23, 225–53, 255, 257
NSDAP party programme 128–31, 215, 257
Naumann, Friedrich 46
Nazi Revolution 246–52
Neurath, Konstantin von 245
Nicholson, Harold 57, 67
Night of the Long Knives (Röhmputsch) 122, 242, 252
Noske, Gustav 26, 40, 43, 53, 55, 83, 88 f., 91 f., 95, 184

Obleute 16, 21, 27 f., 40, 42, 102
Oldenburg-Januschau, Elard von 227
Organization Consul 107, 127, 133
Orlando, Vittorio Emanuele 57
Osthilfe 213, 227 f., 241

Painlevé, Paul 176
Pan-German League 202
Papen, Franz von 208, 221, 229–37, 239–46, 249
Parliamentary Democracy, Introduction of 14, 19–22, 24, 31, 253
Passive Resistance 97, 138 f., 141–4, 156, 256
Peace Resolution 13 f., 86, 107
Pieck, Wilhelm 41
Pöhner, Ernst 116
Poincaré, Raymond 111 f., 135 f., 138 f., 142, 144, 156 f., 160, 188, 198 f.
Pötsch, Leopold 117
Preuss, Hugo 46, 49, 53, 68, 71–3, 84
Progressive Party (Left-liberal) 3, 5, 13, 20, 46, 53
Prussia, Rape of 230–3, 235, 249

Rapallo, Treaty of 97, 115 f., 132, 187
Racialist Party 149, 157 f., 168 f.

Rathenau, Walther 47, 97, 106 f., 110–16, 132–5, 140, 197
Rearmament, Illegal 95 f., 113, 184 f., 190 f.
Reichsbanner 163 f., 225, 233
Reichstag fire 246 f.
Reinhardt, Walther 89, 92, 95
Remarque, Erich Maria 251
Reparations 58, 60 f., 111, 134, 136–8, 144, 156 f., 179, 197 f., 222, 226 f., 254, see also Allied Reparation Commission, London Ultimatum, Cannes Conference, Genoa Conference, Dawes Plan, Young Plan and Lausanne Conference
Rhineland, Occupation of the 61, 168, 175, 178, 180, 188, 192, 196–9, 202–4
Ribbentrop, Joachim von 244
Röhm, Ernst 127, 131, 252
Röhmputsch 122, 242, 252
Roter Frontkämpferbund 163, 220
Ruhr, occupation of the 97, 105, 126, 138–44, 150, 156 f., 160–2, 171, 179, 256
Russian Revolution 15 f.
Russo-German Commercial Treaty 113

S A (Sturmabteilung), The 163, 202, 208, 220, 225, 230 f., 237, 239, 246, 250–2
Sailors' Revolt 38 f., 253
St Germain, Treaty of 128, 221
Schacht, Hjalmar 46, 151, 156, 199 f., 204, 206, 220
Scheer, Reinhard 25 f.
Scheidemann, Philipp 28–30, 38, 52, 55, 67, 92, 133, 185
Schiele, Martin 167, 213
Schiffer, Eugen 91 f.
Schleicher, Kurt von 191, 207 f., 210, 212, 221, 224–30, 236, 240–4, 252
Schober, Johannes 221
Schönerer, Georg von 119
Schröder, Kurt von 243
Schwerin-Krosigk, Count Lutz von 245
Scialola, Vittorio 178
Schiller, Friedrich 51
Seeckt, Kurt von 89, 92–6, 113, 140, 145 f., 148–50, 155, 184, 187, 219, 224
Seisser, Hans von 149
Seldte, Franz 202, 245
Separatism 29, 49, 54, 116, 130 f., 147 f.

Severing, Carl 231–3
Siemens, Carl von 47
Simons, Walter 113
Skrzñyski, Alexander 178
Social Democratic Party 2 f., 4–7, 10–13, 34, 44, 46, 75, 77, 97, 103, 105 f., 112, 116, 136 f., 142 f., 145–8, 152–5, 158–61, 161–72, 181–9, 192–6, 214–17, 219, 223 f., 227, 230, 232–5, 238 f., 242, 244, 247 f., 250 f., 254 f., 257
Spartacist League 12, 16, 18, 21 f., 25, 35, 37 f., 41–4, 254
Spartacist Putsch 41–3
S S (Schutzstaffel), The 225, 239, 242, 246, 251 f.
stab-in-the-back legend 34, 45, 70 f., 105, 173, 253 f.
Stahlhelm 163, 174, 220 f., 223, 246, 250
Stinnes, Hugo 47, 95, 141
Strasser, Gregor 227, 236, 242, 252
Stresemann, Gustav 47, 96, 98, 116, 142–8, 150–4, 157, 159, 161, 164, 166 f., 170–2, 174–6, 178–81, 183, 186–9, 191 f., 195–9, 201–3, 210, 212, 216, 256

Thälmann, Ernst 171–3, 223
Thoiry 188 f.
Thyssen, Fritz 47
Tirpitz, Alfred von 4, 159, 172
Toller, Ernst 55
Trade Unions 36 f., 53, 84, 87, 242, 252
Treviranus, Gottfried 204
Trotsky, Leo 15
Tucholsky, Kurt 251

Unemployment 162, 190, 207, 209 f., 213–15, 219 f., 231, 237, 241, 254, 257

Upper Silesian Plebiscite 64, 108–11, 132, 177

Van der Lubbe, Marius 247
Vandervelde, Émile 178
Väterländische Verbände 117, 132
Versailles, Treaty of 56–70, 104, 106, 108–10, 113–15, 128, 132, 134 f., 140, 168, 177–80, 185, 187, 191, 193, 198, 202, 205, 221, 254, 256
Verständigungspolitik 98, 144, 153, 157, 165, 174, 176, 201, 256
Vögler, Albert 199

Wall Street Crash and Depression 83, 154, 201, 205 f., 209, 214 f., 221 f., 227, 256–8
Weber, Max 46
Wels, Otto 35, 39, 251
Wessel, Horst 121, 220, 251
Westarp, Cuno von 204
Wilhelm I (German Kaiser) 1, 3
Wilhelm II (German Kaiser) 3, 6–10, 13 f., 20–8, 59 f., 70, 105, 173
Wilhelm (German Crown Prince) 163, 184, 224, 249
Wilson, Woodrow 9, 17, 19, 22–4, 31, 51, 57, 62–6, 104, 128, 254
Winter, Gustav 223
Wirth, Joseph 96 f., 105–8, 110, 112–14, 133, 135–8
Wissell, Rudolf 195
Wolff, Theodor 46

Young German Order 215
Young, Owen D. 199 f.
Young Plan 199–205, 231; referendum on 202–5

Zeigner, Erich 147